THE HISTORY AND PHILOSOPHY OF ISLAMIC SCIENCE

THE HISTORY AND PHILOSOPHY OF ISLAMIC SCIENCE

OSMAN BAKAR

ISLAMIC TEXTS SOCIETY

This edition published 1999 by
Islamic Texts Society
22a Brooklands Avenue, Cambridge CB2 2DQ, UK

ISBN 0 946621 83 7 paper

First published 1991 as *Tawhid and Science*
by Secretariat for Islamic Philosophy and Science
& Nurin Enterprise, Malaysia

British Library Cataloguing in Publication Data
A catalogue record for this book is available from
the British Library.

Cover Illustration: *Taqwīm al-Ṣiḥḥah* of Ibn Buṭlān
By permission of the British Library
© British Library Or.1347, folio 3r.

Printed in Malta by Interprint Limited

Contents

In the Name of God, Most Merciful, Most Compassionate

Preface

The essays presented in this book deal with various facets of the history and philosophy of Islamic science. By 'Islamic science' we mean the totality of the mathematical and natural sciences, including psychology and cognitive science, cultivated in Islamic culture and civilization for more than a millennium beginning from the third century of the Islamic era (the ninth century of the Christian era).

These sciences are Islamic not just because they have been produced by Muslims. As a matter of fact, many non-Muslims made important contributions to the growth and development of Islamic science. Rather, these sciences deserve the name 'Islamic science' because they are, conceptually speaking, organically related to the fundamental teachings of Islam, the most important of which is the principle of *tawḥīd.* This book seeks to reveal different dimensions of the organic link that exists between *tawḥīd* and science as seen through Muslim scientific eyes.

The essays cover four major themes, namely, (1) the epistemological foundation of Islamic science, (2) Man, Nature, and God in Islamic science, (3) Islamic science and the West, and (4) Islam and modern science. Through these essays, we seek to convey the important message that Islamic science, the most immediate predecessor of modern science, shares with the latter many outstanding features such as the rational and logical nature of its language, the adoption of scientific and experimental methods of inquiry, and the international character of its scientific practice and organization.

However, we strongly feel that it is incumbent on us to highlight the fact that there are also important differences between the two sciences. Islamic science is at the same time of a religious nature in the sense that it is consciously based upon the metaphysical, cosmological, epistemological, and ethical and moral principles of Islam. In the light of its spiritual and moral conception of nature, Islamic science adopts goals and methodological principles that are different in several respects from those of modern science. In Islamic culture, the place of science in relation to other branches of knowledge such as the religious and social sciences is also somewhat different from the one we see in modern Western culture.

A salient feature of our essays is their interdisciplinary character. We have also adopted a blend of historical and philosophical approaches to the study of Islamic science. We hope this book is of value for all who are concerned with the problem of knowledge in all its dimensions, whatever their discipline.

Except for chapters one, five, ten and eleven, all the essays have previously appeared in learned journals or as chapters of books published outside Malaysia. They are reprinted here with only minor changes:

"The Question of Methodology in Islamic Science," *Muslim Education Quarterly*, 2:1 (Autumn 1984), pp. 16-30; also published in *Quest for New Science: Selected Papers of A Seminar*, Centre for Studies on Science, Aligarh (India), pp. 91-109.

"The Meaning and Significance of Doubt in al-Ghazzālī's Philosophy," *The Islamic Quarterly*, 30:1 (1986), pp. 20-31; also in *Iqbal Review*, April - June 1985, pp. 29-48.

"The Unity of Science and Spiritual Knowledge: The Islamic Experience," in R. Ravindra (ed.), *Science and Spirit* (International Cultural Foundation: New York, 1990), pp. 87 - 101.

"The Philosophy of Islamic Medicine and Its Relevance to the Modern world," *MAAS Journal of Islamic Science*, 6:1 (Jan - June 1990), pp. 39-58.

"Umar Khayyām's Criticism of Euclid's Theory of Parallel Lines," *MAAS Journal of Islamic Science*, 1:2 (July 1985), pp. 9-18.

"Islam and Bioethics," *Greek Orthodox Theological Review*, 31:2 (1986), pp. 157-179.

"Designing a Sound Syllabus for Courses on Philosophy of Applied and Engineering Sciences in a 21st Century Islamic University," *Muslim Education Quarterly*, 7:3 (Spring 1990), pp. 19-25.

The essays brought together here have been written over a period of about seven years, the earliest being published in 1984. Entitled "The Question of Methodology in Islamic Science," the essay was originally presented as a seminar paper at an international seminar on *The Quest for New Science* held at Aligarh University, India in April 1984 and organized by the Center for Studies on Science, Aligarh. Other essays originally written for international seminars/conferences are chapter four (presented at the *Unity of the Sciences Conference* in Los Angeles), chapter six (presented at *International Seminar on Islamic Philosophy and Science* in Penang), chapter nine (presented at a conference on *Muslim-Orthodox Christian Relations* in Boston), and chapter eleven (presented at the *International Conference on Islamic Civilization* in Kuala Lumpur).

In bringing together a collection of essays written over a long period of time and covering so many topics and issues, even if these are one's own, there is always the problem of thematic unity which one must address. That there is a thematic unity in our essays presented here we are quite satisfied. In fact, we can claim that the said problem has never arisen at all in our case, primarily because the essential intellectual framework of our philosophy of science has remained unchanged ever since we first embraced it in 1971 when we were a postgraduate student in mathematics (specializing in *group theory*) at Bedford College, University of London.

We are grateful to Dato' Hj. Musa Mohamad, the Chairman of the Board of Advisors, the Secretariat for Islamic Philosophy and Science, the Science University of Penang, and also the Vice

Chancellor of the University, for being kind enough to publish this work. We also wish to thank Nurin Enterprise for having agreed to be a co-publisher.

It also affords me great pleasure to record my sincere thanks to the University of Malaya. Most of the essays brought together here were written during our doctoral studies in Islamic philosophy at the Department of Religion, Temple University, Philadelphia. Our postgraduate studies (1981 - 1986) were financially supported by the University of Malaya.

Osman Bakar
Dean's Office,
Faculty of Science
University of Malaya
Kuala lumpur
May 1991

CHAPTER 1

Religious Consciousness and the Scientific Spirit in Islamic Tradition

As an integral religious tradition encompassing all aspects of human life, Islam deals not only with what man must and must not do, but also with what he needs to know. In other words, Islam is both a way of acting and doing things and a way of knowing. Of the two ways, the aspect of knowing is the more important. This is because Islam is essentially a religion of knowledge. Islam looks upon knowledge as the central means to salvation of the soul and to the attainment of human happiness and prosperity in this life as well as in the hereafter.

The first part of the testimony of faith in Islam, *Lā ilāha illa' Llāh* ("There is no god but God"), is a statement of knowledge concerning Reality. Muslims look upon the various sciences, natural, social, and others as so many different bodies of evidences which point to the truth of this most fundamental statement in Islam. This statement is what is popularly known in Islam as the principle of *tawḥīd* or Divine Unity.

Tawḥīd: The Source of Scientific Spirit

Muslim religious consciousness is essentially the consciousness of the Unity of God. The scientific spirit is not opposed to this religious consciousness, since it is an integral part of the latter. To possess a consciousness of Divine Unity is to affirm the truth that God is One in His Essence, in His Attributes and Qualities, and in His Works. One important consequence of affirming this central truth is that one has to accept the objective reality of cosmic unity. As a source of knowledge, religion is emphatic in maintaining that all things in the universe are interrelated in a web of cosmic unity through the cosmic laws governing them. The cosmos is made up of many levels of reality, not just the physical. But it constitutes a unity because it must manifest the oneness of its metaphysical source and origin religiously called God. In fact, the Quran strongly argues that cosmic unity is a clear proof of Divine Unity.[1]

The scientific spirit of Muslim scientists and scholars flows, in fact, from their consciousness of *tawḥīd*. There is no doubt that, religiously and historically speaking, the origin and development of the scientific spirit in Islam differs from that in the West. Nothing better illustrates the religious origin of the scientific spirit in Islam than the fact that this spirit was first demonstrated in the religious sciences.

Muslims did not begin to cultivate the natural sciences in earnest until the third century of the Islamic era (the ninth century of the common era). But when they did so they were already in possession of a scientific attitude and a scientific frame of mind, which they had inherited from the religious sciences. The passion for truth and objectivity, the general respect for fully corroborated empirical evidence, and a mind skilled in the classification of things were some of the most outstanding features of early Muslim religious scholarship as can clearly be seen

1. "If there were, in the heavens and the earth, other gods besides God, there would have been confusion in both!" *The Quran*, Chapter XXI (The Prophets), Verse 22.

in their studies of jurisprudence and the prophetic traditions.

A love for definitions and conceptual or semantic analysis with great emphasis on logical clarity and precision was also very much evident in Muslim legal thought as well as in the sciences related to the study of various aspects of the Quran such as in the science of Quranic commentaries *('ilm al-tafsīr)*. In Islam, logic was never conceived as being opposed to religious faith. Even the grammarians, who initially opposed the introduction of Aristotelian logic *(manṭiq)* by philosophers like al-Fārābī,[2] did so on the belief that their Stoic-like juridical-theological logic, known as *ādāb al-jadal* (art of argumentation), was already sufficient to meet their logical needs.

Among Muslim philosophers and scientists, logic was always viewed as an indispensable tool of scientific thinking. They also considered logic a form of *ḥikmah* (wisdom), a form of knowledge which is extolled by the Quran. In their use of logic, they were as much concerned with clarity and consistency as with truth and certitude. They were too aware of the fact that logic is a double-edged instrument which can serve both truth and error.

Logic was developed by Muslim philosophers and scientists within the framework of a religious consciousness of the Transcendent. In their view, logic, when used correctly and by an intellect that is not corrupted by the lower passions, may lead one to the Transcendent itself.[3] An obvious function of logic in relation to religious truths is to help explain their rationality and clarify their overall consistency in the face of outward appearances of incoherence and contradiction.

Some philosopher-scientists, such as al-Fārābī, wrote works which sought to demonstrate that Aristotelian logic found strong

---

2. See M. Mahdi, "Language and Logic in Classical Islam," in G.E. von Grunebaum, ed., *Logic in Classical Islamic Culture* (Wiesbaden, 1970), pp. 51-83; see also Osman Bakar, *Al-Fārābī: Life, Works and Significance* (Kuala Lumpur: The Islamic Academy of Science, 1987), p. 18.
3. For a profound discussion of this role of logic in relation to the Transcendent, see F. Schuon, *Logic and Transcendence* (London: Perennial Books Ltd., 1975).

scriptural support in the Quran and the prophetic *ḥadīths.* When a religious scholar of the stature of al-Ghazzālī wrote a work with a similar purpose, and with full conviction embraced Aristotelian logic in its entirety, the last significant traces of opposition to that logic from the religious quarters disappeared. *Manṭiq* in its Islamic home became an important tool not only of the philosophical sciences but also of the religious sciences.

It is indeed significant that *al-burhān,* the term used in Muslim logic to denote the scientific method of demonstration or demonstrative proof, is derived from one of the names of the Quran.[4] According to al-Ghazzālī, the Quranic term *al-mīzān,* usually translated as the balance, refers among other things to logic. Logic is the balance with which man weighs ideas and opinions to arrive at the correct measurement or judgment.

The Spirit of Experimentation in Islamic Science

The extensive use of logic in Islam did not lead to the kind of rationalism and logicism one finds in the modern West precisely because the use of reason was never cut off from faith in divine revelation. Muslim scholars were imbued with a strong religious awareness of the Transcendent. They generally affirmed the idea of the superiority of divine revelation to human reason. Similarly, the importance attached to logical thinking did not stifle the spirit of experimentation among Muslim scientists.

Long before Roger Bacon introduced and popularized the experimental method into European science, empirical studies of nature, namely studies based on observation and experimentation, were already widespread in the Muslim world. Such kind of studies were certainly carried out by Muslims on a far more extensive scale than had ever been attempted in all the previous civilizations. Many contemporary historians of Islamic science were struck by what they call the characteristically modern spirit of Muslim empirical approach to the study of nature.

Famous Muslim scientists like al-Rāzī, Ibn Sīnā, al-Bīrūnī,

4. See *The Quran,* Chapter IV (Women), Verse 174.

Ibn al-Haytham, al-Zahrāwī, Nasīr al-Dīn al-Ṭūsī, Quṭb al-Dīn al-Shīrāzī, and Kamāl al-Dīn al-Fārsī, just to mention a few, were all noted for their observational powers and experimental tendencies as displayed in their wide ranging studies of the natural sciences, including medicine. Many works have been written on the achievements of these scientists in the experimental domain. Therefore, it is not necessary to repeat them here.[5] The primary consideration here is not to discuss Muslim achievement in experimentation in itself but in relation to their religious and spiritual consciousness.

Just as the extensive use of logic did not lead to secular rationalism which rebels against God and religion, so also the widespread practice of experimentation did not lead to an empiricism which regards sensual experience as the source of all knowledge. The traditional Islamic epistemology (theory of knowledge) provides all the necessary safeguards against such kinds of philosophical deviations. Islam is the religion of unity *(tawḥīd)* and equilibrium *(iʿtidāl)*. As such, it upholds the idea of the hierarchy and unity of knowledge and of modes of knowing. All possible avenues to knowledge are duly recognized, and each accorded a legitimate place and function within the total epistemological scheme of Islam.

Logical thinking, mathematical analysis, observation, experimentation, and even rational interpretation of sacred Books all have their legitimate roles to play in the scientific enterprise of early Muslim scientists. As long as Muslims were faithful to the true spirit of *tawḥīd*, implying a faithfulness to the idea of the hierarchy and unity of knowledge, they were spared of that unfortunate and intellectually precarious situation whereby one mode of knowing is affirmed at the expense of other modes, or the validity of some modes of knowing negated in the name of upholding the supremacy of some other modes.

In accordance with the principle of *tawḥīd*, Muslims affirm

5. See, for example, S. H. Nasr, *Islamic Science: An Illustrated Study* (London: World of Islam Festival Publishing Company Ltd., 1976); also his *Science and Civilization in Islam* (Kuala Lumpur: Dewan Pustaka Fajar, 1984).

that God alone is the Absolute and that everything else is relative. As the Absolute Truth *(al-Ḥaqq)*, God is the source of all other truths which, however, admit of a hierarchy or degrees of relativity. These levels of relative truths are known to man through a variety of ways. According to Islam, man has been equipped with all the necessary faculties of knowing which enable him to know all that he needs to know. Says the Quran:

> He (God) Who has made everything which He has created most good: He began the creation of man with (nothing more than) clay. And made his progeny from a quintessence of the nature of a fluid despised. But he fashioned him in due proportion, and breathed into him something of His Spirit. And He gave you (the faculties of) hearing and sight and feeling (and understanding): Little thanks do ye give![6]

Muslims are therefore reminded by the Quran that all the faculties of knowing, which man possesses – his five physical senses, his internal senses such as the faculties of memory and imagination, and his rational and spiritual faculties, namely the intellect and the heart – are God's precious gifts to him for which he must always be thankful. To be thankful to God is not merely to acknowledge the divine origin of all these faculties of knowing, but also to use each of them in a legitimate way that is proper to its nature and function. The legitimate use of each faculty demands that its proper domain of competence and its limitation be duly recognized. As clearly emphasized in the Quranic verse just cited, the different components of man have been fashioned by God "in due proportion." For this reason, there is quite a voluminous literature on this subject written by Muslim scholars over the centuries. Muslim philosopher-scientists treated this subject under the discipline of faculty psychology to which they contributed many original ideas and theories.[7]

---

6. *The Quran,* Chapter XXXII (Adoration), Verses 7-9.
7. See F. Rahman, *Avicenna's Psychology* (Westport, Connecticut: Hyperio Press, Inc., 1981 reprt.).

The importance of sensual experience as a source of empirical knowledge of the world was very much emphasized by Muslims. But they also emphasized the fact that the physical senses, as instruments of knowledge, have their limitations. Here comes the intervention of religious consciousness. The Muslim belief-system dictates that there are phenomena and realities which are beyond the ken of the physical senses even with the aid of the most powerful and sophisticated of telescopic and microscopic instruments.These non-physical phenomena and realities demand the use of appropriate non-physical faculties of knowing. Physical reality is only an aspect of the whole of reality. It is regarded by Muslims as the lowest of the many levels of reality, the highest being God.

Even at the level of physical reality, a Muslim's religious consciousness influences his intellectual attitude toward that reality and his scientific study of it. A Muslim knows that the physical world does not have an independent existence of its own. The physical world, like all other worlds, owes its existence to God. It is always linked to God. The moment it is cut off from God it ceases to exist. Deism is something alien to Islamic thought. Muslims had never entertained the idea of the universe as a clock and of God as the clockmaker who, having created the clock to its completion and perfection, left it to function on its own.

The spirit of Muslim observation and experimentation is shaped by this religious consciousness. It was not religious doubt and scepticism which inspired the success stories of Muslim experimental science. The spirit of Muslim experimentation was inspired rather by the certainty of God as the Absolute and as the source of all truths.

Muslims carry out observations and experimentations with the firm conviction that they are seeking to know an aspect of the reality of God. According to the twelfth-century Muslim philosopher, Suhrawardī, the world is none other than God's knowledge of the world. To know the world, therefore, means to know God's knowledge of the world. The Muslim conviction that whatever truths or knowledge they were to discover about nature could not be opposed to the teachings of their sacred Book comes from that book itself. The Quran exhorts believers to observe the signs of God manifested in the natural world, within the souls of men, and in the pages of human history and society.[8] It also calls upon them to verify all claims to truth and knowledge to ensure that justice prevails and that doubt gives way to certitude. Scientific experimentation is only one of the many forms of this verification process.

The Religious Significance of the Quest for Objectivity

Despite the claim made by many people today that modern science is the most objective knowledge of the natural world ever attained in the history of human civilizations, the truth of the matter is that modern science is no more objective than, say, Islamic science which is its most immediate predecessor. The quest for objectivity is not unique to modern civilization. In the Islamic perspective, the quest for objectivity in intellectual pursuits not only is legitimate and desirable, rooted as it were in man's inner nature, but also possesses a profound religious significance.

Objectivity is an essential element of the scientific spirit. Without objectivity, knowledge as a collective human enterprise would not be possible. The primary meaning of objectivity is related to two principal ideas. One is the idea of impartiality and a "disinterested" perspective as opposed to bias, prejudice and an "interested" point of view. The other idea, which is related to the first, refers to the principle of collective or public verification. Objective knowledge is that knowledge which is open to public

---

8. "We shall show them Our signs on the horizon and within themselves until it will be manifest unto them that it is the Truth". *The Quran*, Chapter XLI (Abbreviated Letters), Verse 53.

In another place, the Quran says: "Have they not journeyed through the land and beheld the end of those before them who were more numerous than they and mightier in strength, and who left a greater mark upon the earth? Yet all that of which they possessed themselves availed them not." Chapter XL (The Believer), Verse 82.

verification. Not surprisingly, in the modern world, empirical knowledge is deemed the only objective form of knowledge, since it is this type of knowledge which is accessible to and verifiable by most people. The Islamic point of view, however, as I will explain shortly, is quite different. A piece of knowledge is not considered any more objective than another simply because it is verifiable by a greater number of people than is possible in the latter case.

Impartiality, disinterestedness and justice in knowledge, as in other domains of human life, are noble human qualities and as such they are universally esteemed. These qualities serve as ideals for all men to emulate whatever the difficulties may be when it comes to their actual realization. Islamic scholarship has been very much concerned with the cultivation and acquisition of these qualities. Islamic civilization can take pride on the fact that, compared to many other civilizations, it has been quite successful in manifesting these qualities in the different domains of knowledge.

In the Islamic tradition, the sense of objectivity, understood as referring to the qualities of impartiality, disinterestedness, and justice in the domain of knowledge, is inseparable from the religious consciousness of *tawḥīd*. The situation in the modern world is different. Religion is regarded by many people today as the greatest impediment to the realization of impartiality and justice. To its many critics, religion breeds bias, prejudice and sectarian points of view. In other words, to many modern minds, religion would be the last thing that can deliver objectivity in scholarship. But secular, modern scholarship has yet to show that by discarding religion from its worldview, it can attain a higher standard of impartiality, universality, and justice than had been demonstrated in religiously based scholarship, especially traditional Islamic scholarship.

In the discipline of comparative religion, for example, the degree of scientific objectivity attained by medieval Muslim scholarship, as demonstrated, for example, in al-Bīrūnī's tenth-century study of the Indian religion,[9] is yet to be surpassed. Referring to the scientific nature of medieval Muslim works on natural science, Bernal, a contemporary Marxist historian of science, noted with some surprise how little difference there is between reading these medieval works and their modern counterparts.

According to Islam, man desires and needs objectivity because, being created in the image of God, he seeks to emulate the divine qualities. To be objective is, in a sense, to emulate God. Man is capable of objectivity because, in principle, he has been endowed with the qualities associated with this objectivity. Impartiality, disinterestedness, and justice are not just human qualities. Rather, they are divine qualities which are also manifested in man. Religion, more particularly its spiritual dimension, provides the doctrines and the practical means whereby these qualities can be made to blossom in the human individual. Therefore, there is an important conceptual relationship between scientific objectivity and religious consciousness. Objectivity in scholarship is not merely of scientific but also of religious significance in the sense that it presents itself to us as one of the many outward manifestations of man's unique position in relation to God, even if many people today have forgotten this truth.

Objectivity in modern scholarship is mainly confined to the empirical or experimental domain. Islamic intellectual tradition, however, speaks of objectivity on the higher planes of human consciousness as well. This position maintained by Islam is a logical outcome of its belief that there are many levels of objective truth. Physical, mathematical, and metaphysical truths are all objective in nature. Corresponding to each level of objective truth, there is a particular form of verification or proof involving the particular faculty of knowing through which that objective truth is cognized. Objectivity is also possible in the domain of non-empirical knowledge, such as in religious and spiritual

9. See al-Bīrūnī, *Alberuni's India*, trans., E. C. Sachau (London: Kegan Paul, Trench, Trubner & Co., Ltd., 1910).

knowledge or in philosophical and metaphysical knowledge, precisely because all men, in principle, possess the higher faculties of knowledge. Islam maintains that objectivity in its highest sense belongs to the intellectual order. This objectivity refers to the intellectual power of discernment which enables man to distinguish between the Absolute and the relative or between God and what is other than God.

Conclusion

In Islam, religious consciousness of *tawḥīd* is the source of the scientific spirit in all domains of knowledge. Consequently, Islamic intellectual tradition does not entertain the idea of the natural sciences alone as being scientific or as being more scientific than the other sciences. Similarly, the idea of objectivity which is so essential to the scientific enterprise is inseparable from religious consciousness and spirituality.

CHAPTER 2

The Question of Methodology in Islamic Science

In any attempt to revive the Islamic scientific tradition in the contemporary world, or to create a science of the natural world that is at once new and traditional[1], one of the central questions that call for our special attention and that need to be thoroughly treated and resolved is the question of *methodology*. Why is this question of central importance to us? It is because, in reality, there are fundamental differences between the conception of methodology of science in Islam, or for that matter in every other traditional civilization, such as the Chinese or Indian civilization, and the conception of methodology in modern science.

In our customary way of thinking, however, we have been entertaining ourselves to a very different idea altogether. For so long we have succumbed to the notion that modern science has been created by means of a single methodology only, the famous

---

1. Traditional science is that science which, while being organized and orderly knowledge of an objective order, is also of a religious character since it is based upon the application of the Divine Principle to the domain of study in question. On the meaning and significance of the traditional sciences in the contemporary world, see Nasr, "The Role of the Traditional Sciences in the Encounter of Religion and Science – An Oriental Perspective," *The Wiegand Lecture* delivered at the University of Toronto in October 1983, and published under the same title in *Religious Studies*, 20 (1984), 519-541.

so-called *Scientific Method*[2]. The idea of only one type of science of nature being possible, through the use of the *Scientific Method*, greatly influenced our whole way of looking at the pre-modern sciences, including Islamic science. The degree of application of the *Scientific Method* became the universal yardstick of the scholarly community in determining the degree of scientific creativity and 'purity' of pre-modern minds.

With very few exceptions[3], the usual Muslim response to the above modern assertion about scientific methodology has been to seek to demonstrate that Islamic civilization preceded the modern West in the application of the *Scientific Method*, and that it exerted a great influence upon the latter civilization in the domain of scientific thought. That the *Scientific Method* was widely practiced in Islamic science is now a well-established fact in the pages of the history of science, as we have already mentioned in the previous chapter. But we also know that this is by no means the only method employed by Muslim scientists even in their creation of that element of Islamic science, which best corresponds to the current meaning of the term 'science'.

One of the most important findings established by Professor Nasr's pioneering works on Islamic science, viewed as an independent scientific and intellectual tradition, is that there is no single method which is used in that science to the exclusion of other methods. On the contrary, Islamic science has always

2. A Nobel prize winner for Medicine writes, "Unfortunately, we in England have been brought up to believe that scientific discovery turns upon the use of a method analogous to and of the same logical stature as deduction, namely the method of *Induction* – a logically mechanised process of thought which, starting from simple declarations of fact arising out of the evidence of the senses, can lead us with certainty to the truth of general laws. This would be an intellectually disabling belief if anyone actually believed it . . .". See P. Medawar, *Pluto's Republic* (Oxford University Press, 1982), p. 33.
3. On this exceptional response, which seeks to present Islamic science as having a methodology of its own, see the various works of Professor Seyyed Hossein Nasr on Islamic science. In particular, see *Science and Civilization in Islam*; *An Introduction to Islamic Cosmological Doctrines* (Cambridge, MA: Harvard University Press, 1964) and (London: Thames & Hudson, 1978); *Islamic Science*; "Reflections on Methodology in the Islamic Sciences" in *Hamdard Islamicus*, 3:3 (1980), 3-13.

sought to apply different methods in accordance with the nature of the subject in question and modes of understanding that subject. Muslim scientists, in their cultivation and development of the various sciences, have relied upon every avenue of knowledge open to man, from ratiocination and interpretation of sacred Scriptures to observation and experimentation.

Even in modern science itself, the idea of a single methodology alone as being responsible for its creation has been demolished by numerous works on methodology of science, which have appeared over the last decade or so. Instead, the idea of a pluralistic methodology has now gained wide currency among contemporary historians and philosophers of science. Some of them have gone to the extent of even accepting sacred Scriptures as an integral component of this pluralistic methodology[4]. Similarly, a number of professional scientists, mostly physicists, from R. Oppenheimer and E. Schrödinger to Fritjof Capra, have turned to Oriental doctrines in the hope of finding solutions to certain dilemmas and problems encountered at the frontier of modern physics[5].

Viewed as a whole, it can be said that one of the most interesting and significant developments to have taken place in modern science is the realization that the creative process which has produced that science is far more complex than what has been popularized as the *Scientific Method.* But does this new awareness and acceptance of a pluralistic methodology in the creative process of modern science now mean that the fundamental differences between the Islamic conception of methodology of science and the modern one have disappeared? To this question, we say in the affirmative that fundamental differences remain.

Where do the differences lie? The methodology of science in Islam is based on an epistemology that is fundamentally different

---

4. See P. Feyerabend, *Against Method,* verso Edition (1982), p. 30.
5. See E. Schrödinger, *My View of the World* (Cambridge,1964); Fritjof Capra, *The Tao of Physics* (Boulder: Shambhala, 1975) and *The Turning Point: Science, Society and the Rising Culture* (Bantam edition, 1983), Chap. 9.

from the dominant epistemology of modern science, which so far has remained largely unaffected by this new intellectual development, although an increasing number of scientists, historians and philosophers of science have spoken of the need for a new epistemological paradigm that can provide a coherent view of the world revealed by modern science[6]. It is true to say that, as an empirical way of knowing things, the *scientific method* of modern science is hardly distinguishable from the *scientific method* of Islamic science. Philosophically speaking, however, it is not looked at in the same way in the two sciences in relation to their respective epistemologies. Similarly, the problem of the creative process is viewed differently in the two sciences. It can be said that it is one thing to admit the reality of a pluralistic methodology and to entertain its desirability; it is another to possess a unified vision of that pluralistic methodology.

It is because of the lack of a unified vision in contemporary philosophy of science that all the positive intellectual gains that can possibly accrue from the new realization of what the creative process in modern science is, or is not, appear to have been lost in all sorts of philosophical interpretations. In one such interpretation, a pluralistic methodology is construed as a kind of theoretical anarchism which nevertheless possesses a value of its own within the epistemological scheme and in the advancement of scientific progress[7]. Others deny altogether the possibility of us

6. For example, see Morris Berman, *The Reenchantment of the World* (Cornell University Press, 1981); Kurt Hubner, *Critique of Scientific Reason* (The University of Chicago Press, 1983). For those works which argue strongly for an epistemological paradigm that is rooted in the traditional worldview, see Huston Smith, *Beyond the Post-Modern mind* (New York: Crossroad, 1982) and an updated and revised edn. (Wheaton, Ill.: The Theosophical Publishing House, 1989); also his *Forgotten Truth: The Primordial Tradition* (Harper & Row, 1976); E.F. Schumacher, *A Guide for The Perplexed* (Harper & Row, 1977); Nasr, *Man and Nature: The Spiritual Crisis of Modern Man* (Kuala Lumpur: Foundation for Traditional Studies, 1989).
7. P. Feyerabend, *op. cit.* The whole book, as it itself says, is an anarchistic theory of knowledge. Its introduction summarizes the book's contents as follows: "Science is an essentially anarchistic enterprise: theoretical anarchism is more humanitarian and more likely to encourage progress than its law-and-order alternatives".

ever knowing the true nature and reality of man's intellectual creativity while at the same time acknowledging its special position in scientific methodology[8].

Also, the pluralistic methodology currently accepted by certain segments of the scientific community does not encompass the totality of methodologies of Islamic science. Modern science cannot at one and the same time retain its present epistemological foundation, and adopt revealed sacred Scriptures and intellectual intuition, as this term is traditionally understood, as part and parcel of its methodology, without falling into philosophical contradictions. How can it do so when its very epistemology was itself the product of a conscious rebellion against, and rejection of the idea of revelation and all that it implies. In truth, the acceptance of one necessarily implies the rejection of the other.

If certain contemporary philosophers of science speak of incorporating sacred Scriptures into the modern methodology of science, they do not mean to accord them the same epistemological status as given by the traditional sciences. Were modern science to do just precisely that, it would cease to be modern science as it is presently understood and cultivated. It would imply a spiritual transformation or rebirth of modern man[9]. This only goes to show that, in the traditional view, the question of methodology is conceptually inseparable from the ultimate purpose of human cognition, which has to do with the question of the spiritual destiny of man.

In the case of epistemological paradigm of Islamic science, based as it is upon the idea of Unity *(Tawḥīd)*, it does possess a unified and coherent vision of what the multiplicity of methodologies means. These methodologies, in fact, issue forth ultimately from the Quranic view of Reality and of man's place in that Reality. More generally, Professor Nasr has clearly shown that an organic relation exists between Islam and the Islamic sciences.

8. For a discussion on this topic, see, for example, P. Medawar, *op. cit.*, Chap. entitled *Introduction and Intuition in Scientific Thought.*
9. For a profound treatment of this theme, see Nasr, *Man and Nature.*

Specifically, this organic relation can clearly be seen in that aspect of Islamic science, which pertains to its methodology.

It is the aim of this chapter to discuss the principles underlying this relationship. In the light of these principles, it then becomes transparent why in Islamic science all of these different methods are considered as valid ways and means of knowing Nature within their respective domains of applicability. These methods are not contradictory, but rather complementary means of realizing the final goal of the Islamic sciences, namely, the Unicity of Nature, which is itself derived from the twin source of *Revelation and Intellectual intuition*[10]. Consequently, the different sciences based on these different methods of knowing are also seen to be in complete harmony with each other, and not as conflicting disciplines with rival claims to truth. If this organic relation between Islam and the methodology of Islamic science is always born in mind, then we may assert that no science developed by present-day Muslims can claim itself as being totally Islamic in form and character so long as the methodology employed remains embedded in the epistemological paradigm of modern science, even though all the different methods and techniques of study and research that are associated with that methodology are also accepted as important elements of the methodology of Islamic science.

In this discussion of the principles of methodology in Islamic science, we have drawn much of the material from Professor Nasr's numerous published works on various facets of Islamic science, which we strongly believe could provide the necessary point of departure for all current attempts by Muslim scientists at creating once again that science in the contemporary world. Admittedly, on the question of methodology alone, for example, there is so much that remains to be studied of Islamic science.

---

10. The Unicity of Nature, which is the goal as well as the basis of the Islamic sciences, is derived from the application of the principle of *al-Tawḥīd* (Unity) contained in the first Shahadah, *Lā ilāha illa' Llāh*, to the domain of Nature. It is understood to mean the interrelatedness of all things that exist. See Nasr, *Islamic Cosmological Doctrines*, pp. 4-5.

Such a study would of course be of great help to today's scientists to understand better the dynamics of the creative process that has produced Islamic science in the past. Still, what has been written so far on the subject has more than just provided a preparatory ground work for further research. It has also enabled us to have the first clear glimpse of traditional Muslim scientific minds at work and of the inner reality underlying their intellectual creativity, which is so central to our understanding of the conception of methodology in Islamic science.

Principles of Methodology in Islamic Science

To speak of methodology is to speak of ways or methods by means of which man can gain knowledge of Reality, either in its partial or total aspects. Therefore to speak of methodology is first of all to speak of man who is the subjective pole of knowledge, that is to say, the subject that knows. This pole consists of all the faculties and powers of knowing within man, which are hierarchic in nature. In other words, man is capable of having multiple levels of consciousness. Next, to speak of methodology is to speak of the Universe, which is the objective pole of knowledge, that is to say, the object that is knowable, and which is also hierarchical. In other words, the Universe has multiple levels of being or existence. Islamic methodology of knowledge *(al-'ilm)* deals precisely with the essential relationship between this hierarchy of man's faculties of knowing and the hierarchy of the Universe, and with principles governing that relationship.

From Islamic intellectual history, we inherit a vast amount of literature dealing with the question of methodology of knowledge. All the different intellectual schools in Islam, such as those of *kalām*, the *mashshā'ī* (Peripatetic), the *ishrāqī* (Illuminationist) and the *al-ḥikmat al-muta'āliyah* (transcendent theosophy) schools of Islamic philosophy, as well as those of *ma'rifah* (gnosis), which are mainly identified with the Sufis, have touched upon the same subject matter, but from different perspectives, and with different points of emphasis and ends in view, as well as with varying degrees of intellectual profundity, sophistication and rigor[11]. The terminologies employed and the detailed picture conceptualized of the dynamics of man's acts of knowing may vary from one school to the other, but all of them are categorical and united in their view in asserting the hierarchic nature of both man's faculties of knowledge and the Universe. In this chapter, we will make occasional references to the views of some of these intellectual schools on the specific points under discussion.

It is now the assertion of many present-day historians and philosophers of science that the set of phenomena chosen to be studied by a particular scientific collectivity is actually determined by a particular view of reality, which has been accepted *a priori* by that collectivity[12]. In the case of modern science, the reality with which it is solely concerned is the Cartesian reality that has become reduced to mind and matter, viewed as two totally distinct and separate substances[13], which for the mainstream of that science, and for modern western philosophy in general, became an accepted fact. In the case of Islamic science, the whole cosmos with which it is concerned displays a far great-

---

11. On these various intellectual schools, see Nasr, *Islamic Life and Thought* (Albany: SUNY Press, 1981); Majid Fakhry, *A History of Islamic Philosophy* (New York: Columbia University Press, 1983). As for the views of these schools on the question of the methodology of knowledge, see Nasr, "Intellect and Intuition: Their Relationship from the Islamic Perspective" in S. Azzam (ed.), *Islam and Contemporary Society* (Islamic Council of Europe, 1982), pp. 36-46.
12. See T. S. Kuhn, *The Structure of Scientific Revolutions* (University of Chicago Press, 1970); Michael Polanyi, "The Growth of Science in Society" in *Knowing and Being* (1969), pp. 73-86. K. Hubner writes in his *Critique of Scientific Reason*, "Factual assertions and fundamental principles are entirely to the contrary, merely parts of theories: they are given within the framework of a theory; they are chosen and valid within this framework; and subsequently they are dependent upon it. This holds for all empirical sciences – for the natural sciences as well as those pertaining to history", p. 106.
13. This Cartesian dualism is now being challenged by a number of physicists. See, for example, D. Bohm, *Wholeness and the Implicate Order* (Routledge & Kegan Paul, 1980), in which he develops a theory of quantum physics that treats the whole of existence, including matter and consciousness as an unbroken whole.

er qualitative richness of reality than the modern one despite the latter's pride in claiming itself as being an infinite universe.

The anatomy of this Islamic cosmos, in its multiple grades and states, is based on the data furnished by the Islamic Revelation itself. It is therefore the Islamic Revelation which defines the whole domain of study to which the Islamic sciences should be directed. The Muslim mind which accepts such a view of the cosmos has, prior to that, already accepted Revelation as the highest source of knowledge. The Muslims' conception of Revelation has important consequences for the methodology of science in Islam, as we shall see later.

The traditional cosmos, that is to say, the whole of God's created order consists of three fundamental states: the *material or corporeal* state; the *psychic* or *animistic* state; and, the *spiritual* or *angelic* state. In Sufi terminology, these three states are respectively called *nāsūt, malakūt* and *jabarūt*[14]. The material world, also called the *gross* world, is immediately enclosed and dominated by the psychic domain, also referred to as the subtle world. These two worlds together form the domain of 'nature'. And it is the angelic world which governs all natural laws in both the subtle and gross domains (See Fig. 1).

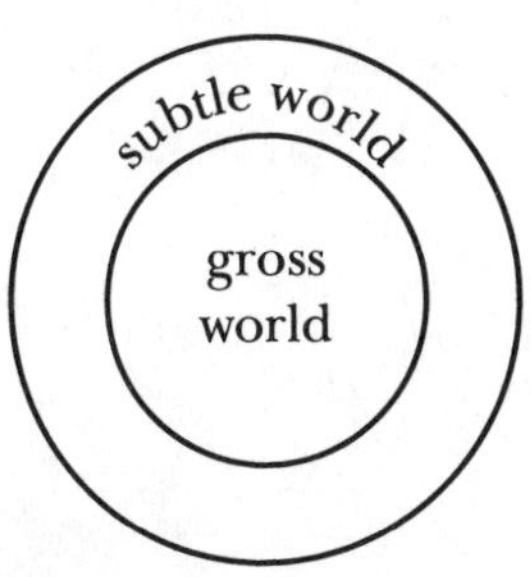

Fig. 1
The World of Nature

14. See F. Schuon, *Dimensions of Islam* (London: Allen & Unwin, 1970), p. 144.

The Sufis, basing their idea on the data provided by the Quran, formulated the doctrine of the "five Divine Presences" *(al-ḥaḍarāt al-ilāhiyyat al-khams)* to depict the hierarchy of the whole of Reality[15] (see Fig. 2). The above three states – the material, subtle and spiritual – in that order, are also the first three "Presences" in ascending order. The next higher level of reality or "Presence" in this hierarchy is the realm of the Divine Qualities *(asmā' ṣifātiyyah)*, that is to say, the Qualities of God, for example, those Qualities which refer to Him as Creator and Revealer. This fourth state, designated as *lāhūt*, is thus identifiable with the Creative Principle or Being. It is the ontological principle of the whole cosmos, and is therefore the Absolute with respect to the whole of creation. The next and the highest "Presence" is the Divine Essence *(al-dhāt)*. This "degree", termed *hāhūt*, is the infinite and Supreme Self, Beyond-Being which is the "non-qualified" and "non-determined" Principle, and is therefore the Pure Absolute[16].

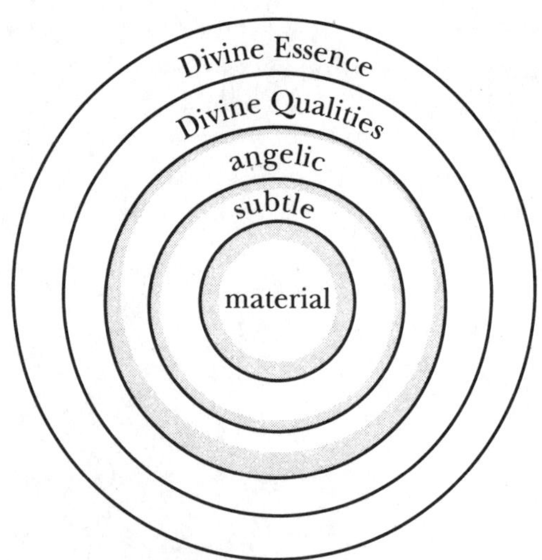

Fig. 2
Hierarchy of Reality

15. On the Quranic premises of the doctrine, see *ibid*, pp. 146-147.
16. *Hāhūt* is from *huwa* meaning He; thus, it may be translated as Quiddity or Ipseity. See *ibid*, p. 144.

The structure of Reality that is outlined above has been dealt with by Muslim philosophers, theologians and especially the Sufis. It is a generally accepted structure, although, in its detailed divisions and in the terminologies used, there are indeed differences not only between these distinct intellectual schools but even within the same school, as for instance among the Sufis. With these differences we are not concerned here. In the context of our present discussion the point which we wish to emphasize, however, is the fact that the above Islamic vision of Reality was very much present and operative in the minds of Muslim men of science, like Ibn Sīnā, al-Bīrūnī, Ikhwān al-Ṣafā', and so many others, in the course of their cultivating and developing the various sciences.

The cosmic reality thus envisaged, which represents the objective pole of Islamic epistemology, is always viewed in relation to its ontological principle, namely, the Divine Intellect or Pure Being. In fact, as asserted by Ibn Sīnā, *true science* is that science which seeks the knowledge of the essences of things in relation to their Divine Origin[17]. This is the knowledge of noumena, that which relates phenomena to their true Origin which is the source of all existence. Therefore it is only in the light of an awareness of such an hierarchy of Reality that true science is possible.

How is the essential relationship between the heirarchy of the subjective pole and that of the objective pole of knowledge envisaged? The relationship envisaged is one that involves the idea of a one-to-one correspondence between the two poles. Every level of cosmic existence has its corresponding existence in man. There is nothing in the macrocosm that does not derive from the metacosm, meaning the Divine Principle, and which is

17. Ibn Sīnā discusses true science or the real purpose of studying Nature in his *Ishārāt wa'l-tanbīhāt.* His conception of true science is aptly expressed by a contemporary author, F. Brunner, "La science véritable suspend la connaissance du monde a la connaissance de Dieu pour le monde dans son intégrale réalité et pour constituer l'expression légitime, au niveau du monde, de l'intellection transcendante qui est la fin de l'homme". See his *Science et réalité* (Paris, 1954), p. 13.

not to be found again in the microcosm[18]. Corresponding to the tripartite structure of the corporeal, the subtle, and the spiritual worlds of the traditional cosmos is the tripartite structure of body *(corpus)*, soul *(anima, psyche)*, and spirit *(spiritus)* of the traditional human microcosm (see Fig. 3). In Islamic terminology, these essential constituents of the microcosm are respectively called *jism, nafs* and '*aql*[19].

Viewed from the perspective of knowledge or consciousness *(shuhūd)*, *'aql* refers to the human intellect which is man's highest faculty of knowledge, and which may be identified with the eye of the heart *('ayn al-qalb)* for, in the language of the Holy Quran and prophetic ḥadīths, the heart means essentially the seat of knowledge, or the instrument for the attainment of knowledge. A knowledge of what the intellect is and does, that is to say, a knowledge of its nature, powers and functions, is the key to the understanding of the problem of the creative process, of the creation of ideas, concepts, and theories in man's scientific enterprise. Accordingly, we will deal with this important topic, albeit briefly.

The human intellect is of a spiritual substance whose source or principle is the Divine Intellect or the *Logos,* which is also the Principle of the macrocosmic Universe, and the source of the sacred Book, the Quran, which is the basis of religion[20]. As generally maintained by Muslims, the uncreated reality of the Holy Quran resides in the Divine Intellect. The fact that the individual human intellect, the macrocosmic Universe, and the Holy Quran all have the same metaphysical basis or source possesses an immediate significance for the methodology of

18. F. Schuon, *Esoterism as Principle and as Way* (Middlesex: Perennial Books, 1981), pp. 17-18.
19. Another possible set of Islamic terminology is *jism, khayal* and *rūḥ*.
20. According to many *ḥadīths,* God 'wrote' by the Pen *(qalam)* the inner reality of all things on the Guarded Tablet *(al-lawḥ al-mahfūẓ)* before the creation of the world. The Pen symbolizes the Universal Intellect, the Logos or the Word, "by which all things are made'. It is also by the Pen that God 'wrote' the eternal Quran upon the Tablet. Thus, metaphysically, the Quran contains the prototype of all creation.

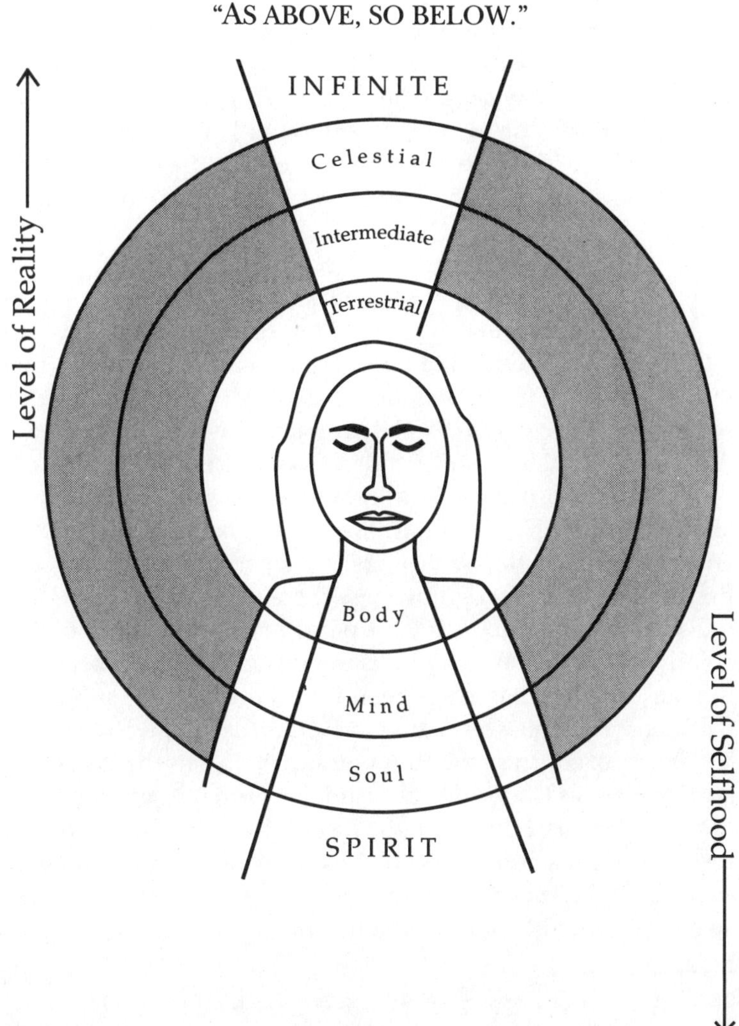

Fig. 3 Macrocosm and microcosm in one-to-one correspondence (this figure is reproduced from Huston Smith's *Forgotten Truth*).

science in Islam. In contrast to the motive that leads certain contemporary philosophers of science to consider sacred Scriptures as a possible source of scientific reference, there are profound metaphysical and intellectual reasons for the adoption of sacred Books by Muslim scientists and philosophers as an integral part of their overall methodology. In the latter case, it is a question of being in conformity with the nature of Reality as such.

The human intellect, the macrocosmic Universe, and the revealed Quran constitute three fundamental elements or aspects in the comprehensive idea of revelation in Islam. They are all integrally related to the central thesis in Islam, namely, that, by His nature, God creates and reveals[21]. According to one sacred ḥadīth *(ḥadīth qudsī)*, God desires to be known, so He creates the Universe. This implies that God's Creation is also His revelation, for otherwise it would not be possible for Him to be known through His Creation. The central being in this created Universe is man who, by virtue of the supernatural character of his intellect and its cognitive powers, and by virtue of being a universe in miniature[22], is in a position to know the Universe completely as well as to know its uncreated Principle. Thus the human intellect has often been referred to as the subjective, partial or particular revelation of God *(al-waḥy al-juz'ī)*.

By way of contrast, the Holy Quran, which is the basis of Islam, is referred to as God's objective and universal revelation *(al-waḥy al-kullī)*. Similarly, the created Universe is described as a cosmic revelation and a book of God, whose uncreated reality has been called *al-Qur'ān al-takwīnī* (meaning the Quran of creation). It is again the principle of *tawḥīd* which integrates these three forms

21. See Schuon, *Understanding Islam* (London: Allen & Unwin,1972), p. 13.
22. Man possesses within himself the complex faculties of the various souls: the mineral soul *(al-rūḥ al-'aqdiyyah)*, the vegetative soul *(al-nafs al-nabātiyyah)*, the animal soul *(al-nafs al-ḥayawāniyyah)*, and the rational soul *(al-nafs al-nāṭiqah)*. Through a complete knowledge, essentially speaking, of himself as the microcosm, he therefore knows the Universe the macrocosm. See Ibn Sīnā's treatment of this theme in Nasr, *Islamic Cosmological Doctrines*, Chap. 14.

of divine revelation into a total unity that is at once comprehensive and coherent.

How can the human intellect know completely the whole of the created order as well as know the uncreated Self? This knowledge is made possible through the actualization of all the possibilities latent within the intellect. But this actualization itself is possible only if the intellect, the subjective revelation in man, were to submit itself to the sacred Book, the objective revelation. Ibn Sīnā, for example, says that every human being possesses intelligence in a latent form, called material or potential intelligence *(bi'l-quwwah)*[23]. The process of actualizing all the possibilities of the intellect passes through several stages which represent different degrees of intellectual attainment.

The first stage is the attainment of habitual intelligence *(bi'l-malakah)*. A person acquires this intelligence when the first intelligible forms are present in his or her soul. The second stage is reached after full actualization of the intelligibles has taken place in the mind, and the corresponding intellect is called the actual intellect *(bi'l-fi'l)*. The third stage is the complete realization of this actual intellect, and this state of the intellect is called acquired intelligence *(mustafād)*. Then there is that supra-individual intellect which transcends this highest level of human intellect, and which renders this whole process of intellectual actualization possible. It is called by Ibn Sīnā the Active Intellect *(al-'aql al-fa''āl)*. The illumination, at various levels, of man's rational soul *(al-nafs al-nāṭiqah)* by the Active Intellect enables the various faculties and powers of knowing of the soul to be fully functional and receptive to "ideas" coming from the intelligible and spiritual worlds.

This doctrine concerning the intellect, expounded in detail by the school of philosopher-scientists in Islam, of which Ibn Sīnā is generally considered the greatest representative, but which we have presented here only in its main outlines, has important implications for all those who are genuinely concerned with the

23. See Nasr, "Intellect and Intuition," p. 39.

cultivation of the scientific mind, as this term is understood in its most universal sense. The problem of the creative process in scientific enterprise has been posed and debated rather extensively in contemporary philosophy of science. We have alluded earlier to this point at some stage of our discussion.

Questions have been asked whether creativity, that is to say, the question of the origin of ideas, concepts, and theories, is analyzable and reducible to any well-defined, step-by-step method, and whether creativity is something that is cultivable or not. Professor Nasr has posed the first question for Islamic science. He asks[24]: By what method did Muslim scientists arrive at their original ideas, concepts, and theories which were later tested against facts or the rigor of logical analysis? How did Ibn Sīnā arrive at his impetus theory, or Naṣīr al-Dīn al-Ṭūsī at his new model for planetary motion, or Ibn al-Haytham at the concept of momentum, one of the most fundamental concepts of modern physics, or Shihāb al-Dīn al-Suhrawardī at his theory of corporeal objects as being degrees of light? Professor Nasr affirms the view that such creativity, whether in the case of Muslim scientists or their modern counterparts, cannot be reduced to any well-defined, step-by-step method, but always involves an intuition, a jump of a creative nature.

Even though the above view is now widely shared by many modern scientists, the fact remains that the perspective in which the question of creativity or intuition is viewed in Islamic thought differs profoundly from that in which modern science seeks to understand the problem. The modern search for solutions to the problem of "origins", whether of ideas or otherwise, has remained a horizontal search bound to the terrestrial domain, for the perspective adopted is one that ignores or denies higher orders of reality beyond the world of matter and mind. The problem of the origin of ideas is sought to be resolved mostly at the level of the physics and chemistry of the human brain or consciousness. In such a perspective, the divine origin of man's creative ideas is denied, and in its place modern man invents

24. Nasr, "Reflections on Methodology . . .", p.8.

and popularizes the idea of human genius, a concept which is of minor importance to traditional civilizations.

Similarly, to the problem of how creativity or the intuitive dimension of man's thought processes may possibly be stimulated and enhanced, in true conformity to this secular and materialistic spirit of viewing the reality of human consciousness, the prescriptions sought are confined to those of the purely physical and psychological order. Sir Peter Medawar, British Nobel Prize winner for Medicine in 1960, provides a representative sample of this prevailing view of the problem when he says:

> That 'creativity' is beyond analysis is a romantic illusion we must now outgrow. It cannot be learned perhaps, but it can be encouraged and abetted. We can put ourselves in the way of having ideas, by reading and discussion and by acquiring the habit of reflection, guided by the familiar principle that we are not likely to find answers to questions not yet formulated in the mind. I am not offended by the idea that drugs may help us to formulate hypotheses, but I know of none which improves their quality ,and I should hesitate to use a drug which did not enhance the critical faculty in proportion to the rate of accession of ideas[25].

From the traditional point of view, the realm of creative or intuitive ideas to which modern scientific mind seeks to be receptive, as the above view so well illustrates, is not the same world of intellectual intuition as understood in Islamic science. The latter embraces a much wider realm, for it includes the world of the Spirit. That there are degrees of intuition has been amply demonstrated by Schuon, the greatest representative and exponent of the traditional perspective in the West today, in his numerous works[26]. The modern realm of intuitive ideas does

25. P. Medawar, *op. cit.*, pp. 109-110.
26. Examples of his works in which the question of intuition is dealt with in its various aspects are *Logic and Transcendence*; *Stations of Wisdom* (Middlesex: Perennial Books, 1980); *From the Divine to the Human* (Bloomington:World Wisdom Books, 1981).

not extend beyond that which, in the traditional perspective, is known as the imaginal world, the Latin *mundus imaginalis* or the Islamic *'ālam al-khayāl*, an objective reality that stands between the physical and spiritual realms of existence[27]. We are not here denying the fact that creative and intuitive ideas that are the concern of modern mind have a practical import of their own in the scientific enterprise.

But we are also fully aware that modern science is currently wrestling with many problems of such an order that it is only through being receptive to ideas of higher levels of reality that true solutions to these problems can be found. We have in mind such problems as the question of the origin of life in the biological sciences, the ultimate reality of matter in physics, or the question of the origin of the physical universe in modern cosmology. However, as rationally argued by Ibn Sīnā, reception of these "higher" ideas is possible only if the mind is illuminated by the Active Intellect, but to be so illuminated, the intellect must be already illuminated by the light of faith, and touched by the grace issuing from revelation, for "the Spirit bloweth where it listeth". Intellectual intuition, says Schuon, demands the submission of all the powers of the soul to the pure Spirit which is identified, ontologically, with the fundamental dogma of Revelation[28].

If, in modern science, the problem of creativity and intuition is reduced to that of the human genius and sought to be formulated in terms of biological categories alone, traditional science, on the contrary, seeks to formulate the problem in terms of divine origin and the actualization, through the aid of divine agencies, of all the potentialities of the human intellect as conceived in the Divine Plan. This does not mean that, in the traditional formulation of the problem, human factors, both natural (biological and psychological) and cultural, are denied of their legitimate roles and importance. On the contrary, in the

27. See H. Corbin, *Creative Imagination in the Sufism of Ibn 'Arabī* (Princeton,1969) and also his *Spiritual Body and Celestial Earth: from Mazdean Iran to Shi'ite Iran,* (Princeton, 1977).

28. Schuon, *Dimensions of Islam,* p. 76.

traditional perspective, the cultivation of creative minds calls for the creation of the kind of total environment – physical, social and cultural, intellectual and spiritual – which is most conducive to such an actualization. In the case of Islam, this total environment is defined by the whole of its religious and spiritual universe which flows directly from the Quran, that objective and universal revelation which is the indispensable link between man and the Universe.

Faith in the Quranic revelation unveils all the possibilities that lie before the human intellect. Submission to revelation at all levels enables the intellect to actualize these possibilities to the extent grace from revelation makes it possible. The cultivation of the Muslim intellect is based upon a complete awareness of this principle. Within this perspective, it is a meaningul thing for a scientist of the stature of Ibn Sīnā, certainly one of the best scientific minds in the whole history of mankind, to often resort to prayer to seek God's help in solving his philosophical and scientific problems[29]. And it is also perfectly understandable why the purification of the soul is considered an integral part of the methodology of knowledge.

We all know too well that the central concern of Islam is with the protection and correct functioning of the human intelligence. Islam's obsession with intellectual health has to do with the fact that it has made intelligence the point of departure for man's salvation[30]. Earlier, we made the remark that the Quran, as God's objective revelation, enables man to realize the full potentiality of his intellect. This remark needs further comments. The religious and spiritual universe created out of the Quran at once removes impediments to the proper and full growth of the intellect and sustains all the nourishments necessary for its wholesomeness and healthy *(salīm)* growth, and, thus, its correct functioning. This Quranic universe provides a constant reminder to man of the divine origin

29. Nasr, *Islamic Cosmological Doctrines,* p. 181.
30. On this theme, see Schuon, *Understanding Islam*; and Nasr, *Ideals and Realities of Islam* (London: Allen & Unwin, 1971).

of things, as well as provides him with an immediate background for reflection, meditation and contemplation, which therefore prepares the intellect to be very receptive to ideas from the world of the Spirit. Islamic science, in fact, with all its methodologies and technological applications, has been conceived within the womb of the Quranic universe, although its historical ingredients, especially during the initial phase of its growth and development, may have been supplied from diverse sources.

After Nature itself, which is already Islamic, the first level of the religious and spiritual universe of Islam is that of the *Sharī'ah* which, all jurists agree, has as one of its highest objectives the protection and the healthy growth of the intellect. Since the *Sharī'ah*, which pertains to both thought *(īmān)* and action *('amal)*, does not exhaust the total meanings of the Quran, there must be other levels of submission to this objective revelation. The *Sharī'ah* is extracted out of the Quranic reality by applying the method of *tafsīr*. However, the domain of *tafsīr* does not extend beyond the external *(ẓāhir)* meanings of the revealed Book. The aspect of the *'aql* that is operative in the method of *tafsīr* is the rational faculty (reason), which is its reflection or outward projection onto the mental plane. The power of the rational faculty is analysis or ratiocination, and its instrument is logic. However, the extensive use of the rational faculty in the *tafsīr* of the Holy Book by *fuqahā'* (jurists), *mutakallimūn* (theologians), and the *falāsifah* (philosophers) did not lead to the kind of rationalism rampant in the modern world.

Rationalism is false not because it seeks to express reality in rational mode, so far as this is possible, but because it seeks to embrace the whole of reality in the realm of reason, as if the latter coincides with the very principle of things[31]. In *tafsīr*, the rational faculty is placed at the disposal of faith or revelation in the sense that it is called upon to present and expound the contents of Revelation in a rational manner to the best degree possible, whereas in modern thought it has been used to rebel against truth claims which lie outside its cognitive competence.

31. Schoun, *Stations of Wisdom*, p. 36.

Such is the nature of logic[32]. It can put itself at the disposal of either truth or error. The validity of a logical demonstration does not depend on the epistemic status or truth-value of its premises, the "prior knowledge" which this demonstration aims at communicating. Rather, it depends on the correctness of its syllogistic reasoning. A possible role for revelation in the method of *tafsīr* is in furnishing data which might serve as the premises of rational or logical arguments, or as the criteria to judge the truth-value of conclusions established in such kinds of arguments.

The method of *tafsīr* is equally applicable to Nature, the cosmic text. In an analogous way, sciences of nature developed exclusively through this method necessarily remain at the level of external and literal meanings of the cosmic text, and as such cannot exhaust the reality of the cosmos, let alone the whole of Reality. In general, modern science, ever since its birth, has always been such a kind of science. Islam too had developed a science of the natural world based on a methodology which may be collectively referred to as *tafsīr.* But it developed this science alongside other sciences, which are based on some other methodologies. Moreover, limitations inherent in the methodology of *tafsīr* are duly recognized. As for modern science, it claims itself to be *the* science of nature, its methodology *the* methodology of knowledge, and, further, it harbors the illusion that, sooner or latter, through its very method of inquiry, nature will reveal its ultimate secrets to man, perhaps in the form of some mathematical formulae.

The methodology of *tafsīr* of the Holy Book, as it has been developed traditionally, including the method of linguistic analysis, must constitute an integral component of the overall methodology of Islamic science, which is sought to be revived in the modern world. The integration of *tafsir* methodology into Islamic science is justified on the ground that the Book of Nature is the macrocosmic counterpart of the Holy Quran. The 8th/

32. On this question, see *ibid,* Chap. 1.

15th century Sufi master, 'Azīz al-Nasafī, in his *Kashf al-ḥaqā'iq,* compares Nature to the Quran in such a way that each genus in Nature corresponds to a *sūrah,* each species to a verse, and each particular being to a letter[33]. A *tafsīr* of the Holy Book necessarily involves a *tafsīr* of the phenomena of Nature itself.

The Quran contains many verses which lie beyond the competence of the method of *tafsīr* to reveal their meanings. In the same way, Nature presents before man many phenomena which cannot simply be reduced to categories of formal logic with which rationalism has been identified. At the frontiers of modern science today, we encounter numerous examples of such phenomena. In modern physics, there is a breakdown of logic when it comes to the question of the nature of light. The nature of light as being both continuous and discontinuous, that is, existing as both waves and corpuscles, is indeed a paradox of modern physics. Then, we have the phenomena of nothingness in atomic physics, the birth and death of symmetrical particles from "nothing" and to "nothing"[34], and the behavior observed of the electron, which suggests that it possesses a kind of intelligence. These phenomena have led a number of physicists to turn to oriental mysticism to seek a meaningful explanation to the problem. In so doing, they get entangled in issues which can no longer be considered scientific as this term is currently understood, but rather in issues of a religious and philosophical nature. There is no doubt that modern physics has encountered a new level of reality, namely, natural phenomena of a supra-logical and supra-rational order, which call for the application of another kind of methodology.

As applied to the Holy Book itself, the method of *tafsīr* must at some point give way to the method of *ta'wīl. Ta'wīl* or hermeneutic interpretation refers to the knowledge of the inner meaning of a sacred text. It is therefore concerned with the esoteric dimension of the Quranic revelation. In Islamic spiritual

---

33. See F. Meier, "Nature in the Monism of Islam" in Joseph Campbell (ed.), *Spirit and Nature* (Princeton, 1982), pp. 202-203.
34. Nasr, *Knowledge and the Sacred* (New York: Crossroad, 1981), p. 115.

tradition, this dimension has generally been identified with *tasawwuf* (Sufism), which may be defined as submission to God's objective revelation at the level of *iḥsān,* with respect to both thought *(īmān)* and action *('amal)*[35]. As regards thought, *ta'wīl* is concerned with the intellectual dimension of *tasawwuf,* namely, the science of Reality whose central doctrine is the same principle of *tawḥīd* that is dealt with by *tafsīr,* but which is now understood and formulated at a higher level of meaning.

As regards action, *ta'wīl* is concerned with the spiritual dimension of *tasawwuf,* that is, a science of the soul or spiritual realization in which the ritual acts are basically the same as those prescribed and performed at the level of the *Sharī'ah,* but are sought to be interiorized at the deepest level possible. This is the level of submission of all the powers of the soul to the Pure Spirit. Traditional cosmology and traditional psychology[36], which are intimately related to each other, and which admit of various conceptual schemes, are formulated on the basis of this inner dimension of the Quranic revelation through the application of the method of *ta'wīl.*

The method of *ta'wīl* is employed not only in *tasawwuf,* but also in *fiqh* (jurisprudence) and *kalām* (theology) although with somewhat different connotations. As far as discussion of methodology of science is concerned, it is the method of *ta'wīl* as understood and applied in Sufism which is of particular interest to us. As it is understood in Sufism, *ta'wīl* is not opposed to *tafsīr,* but rather is an intensive form of the latter[37]. If the operational component of the *'aql* in the method of *tafsīr* is the rational faculty which exercises an analytical function by means of logic, then its component which is operative in the method of *ta'wīl* is

---

35. On the Quranic roots of *tasawwuf,* see Nasr, *Ideal and Realities of Islam.*
36. Huston Smith prefers to use the term 'pneumatology' for the science of the soul since the word 'psychology' as currently used denotes at best half the ground covered by traditional psychology. See his *Forgotten Truth,* p. 60.
37. For a treatment of *ta'wīl,* see, for example, al-Attas, S.M.N., *The Concept of Education in Islam* (Kuala Lumpur: ABIM, 1980); and Nasr, *Ideals and Realities of Islam,* pp. 58-61.

the intuitive faculty whose function is synthesis and unification, and whose chief instrument is symbolism. In the Sufi science of *ta'wīl* a symbol is distinguished from an allegory. A symbol is the "reflection", in a lower order of existence, of a reality belonging to a higher ontological status, a "reflection" which in essence is unified to that which is symbolized, while allegory is a more or less "artificial figuration" by an individual, having no universal existence of its own[38].

The dual aspects of the intellect, one rational, the other intuitive, are said to have manifested themselves at the level of the structure of the physical brain as well. Modern brain research has revealed a distinct separation or lateralization of cortical functions giving rise to an area of scientific investigation popularly known as "right and left mindedness". Carl Sagan describes this distinct separation as follows:

> The left hemisphere processes information sequentially, the right hemisphere simultaneously, accessing several inputs at once. The left hemisphere works in series; the right is parallel. The left hemisphere is something like a digital computer; the right like an analog computer[39].

The localization of intuitive aspects of thought in the right hemisphere of the brain is itself of great symbolic significance. It symbolizes the primacy of intellectual intuition over ratiocination. The famous French Egyptologist, Schwaller de Lubics, contends that intuitive vision was a major aspect of ancient science. Just as logical training can sharpen the mind, so can the cultivation of symbolic attitude sharpen intuitive vision. In several of his works on ancient Egyptian science, Schwaller de

---

38. In the words of al-Ghazzālī, there is not a single thing in this world of sense that is not a symbol of something in the higher world. It is through the science and method of symbolism, says he, that we comprehend the inner nature of the correspondence between the symbol and the symbolized. See his *Mishkāt al-anwār*, Englis trans. by W.H.T. Gairdner (Lahore: Muhammad Ashraf), pp. 121-125.
39. Carl Sagan, *The Dragons of Eden*, New York, p. 169.

Lubics shows that the ancient Egyptians, through their symbolic attitude, were able to cultivate the intellect to the extent of perceiving all of the phenomena of nature as a symbolic writing, revealing the forces and laws governing the physical as well as the spiritual aspects of our universe[40]. Islam, however, true to its manifestation as a religion of the middle way, was able to create within its civilization sciences of nature which extensively employed both the rational and intuitive faculties in a balanced manner and within a unified worldview.

We may speak of *ta'wīl* as an esoteric methodology which is inseparable from the question of spiritual transformation of man. The *ta'wīl* of the Holy Book, and correspondingly the *ta'wīl* of the cosmic text, both are linked to the *ta'wīl* of the human soul. The soul cannot return either text to its true, inner meaning unless the soul too returns to its transcendent source *(ḥaqīqah)*. What is implied here is a spiritual travail, the return of the soul to its Divine Origin. This doctrine served as the basis of purification of the soul, which is an integral part of the methodology of knowledge in Islam. This particular methodology has often been described as a higher kind of empiricism[41].

At this higher level of "empirical experience" the objects of observation and "experimentation" are no longer the external things, but the soul of the experimenter itself. What is now sought to be dominated and conquered is the animal nature within him. The experimentation consists of cleansing the rational soul from the impurities of nature and bodily forms, through asceticism and piety, until it becomes a pure substance. The soul then becomes illuminated and its highest faculty, the intellect, becomes functional. The intellect is then set to experience what we call intellectual intuition through which it perceives truth directly in the same manner the physical eye per-

40. Schwaller de Lubics, *Symbol and the Symbolic: Ancient Egypt, Science and the Evolution of Consciousness* (New York: Inner Traditions Int.,1978).
41. See al-Attas, S.M.N., *The Positive Aspects of Tasawwuf: Preliminary Thoughts on An Islamic Philosophy of Science* (Kuala Lumpur: Islamic Academy of Science, 1981), p. 6.

ceives the sensible world. There is a whole set of terms used in Islamic epistemology to describe this direct perception of the inner reality of things: *dhawq, ishrāq, mukāshafah, baṣīrah, naẓar, badīhah, ḥads* and *firāsah*[42], terms which all imply the knower's direct experience of the things known.

The application of the methodology of *ta'wīl* to the understanding of the natural world may help to reveal its divine roots. In this knowledge of the "divine roots" of physical things, are to be found the real answers to questions posed by modern science concerning the origin of the world of multiplicity.

Our whole discussion in this chapter may appear to some as too philosophical and mystical. However, we strongly believe that all the points we have raised are very much relevant to Islamic methodology of science. This methodology has to be deeply rooted in the revealed Book of Islam and in the spiritual tradition which issues forth from that revelation. In fact, it had been formulated and applied in history with remarkable success. This legacy is inherited by us today, although many Muslims are ignorant of it. It is not a mere historical coincidence that so many Muslim scientists were either practicing Sufis or intellectually attached to the Sufi perspective, as Professor Nasr's works have clearly demonstrated.

There is indeed a profound conceptual relationship between the inner dimensions of Islam, the depth and breadth of Muslim scientific minds, and sciences of nature that were cultivated in Islamic civilization. To revive Islamic science in the modern world requires that we once again pay due heed to that intimate link.

42. Nasr, "Intellect and Intuition . . .," pp. 36-37.

CHAPTER 3

The Place of Doubt in Islamic Epistemology : Al-Ghazzālī's Philosophical Experience

Authentic works attributed to Abū Ḥāmid Muḥammad al-Ghazzālī (450/1058–505/1111) are numerous, and they deal with a vast range of subjects. But the specific work of his which has given rise to many commentaries by scholars upon the problem of doubt in his philosophical system is *al-Munqidh min al-ḍalāl*[1] (Deliverence from Error).

This autobiographical work, written about five years before al-Ghazzālī's death and most probably after his return to teaching at the Maimūnah Niẓāmiyyah College at Naishapur in Dhu'l-qa'dah 499/July 1106, following a long period of retirement to a life of self-discipline and ascetic practices, has

1. The title of the book occurs in two readings. One is *Al-Munqidh min al-ḍalāl wa'l-mufṣiḥ 'an al-aḥwāl* (What Saves from Error and Manifests the States of the Soul); the other is *Al-Munqidh min al-ḍalāl wa'l-Muwaṣṣil (or: al-Mūṣil) ilā dhi'l-'Izza wa'l-Jalal* (What Saves from Error and Unites with the Possessor of Power and Glory).

For an annotated English translation of this work, based upon the earliest available manuscript, as well as translations of a number of al-Ghazzālī's other works that are specifically mentioned in the *Munqidh*, see R. Joseph McCarthy, *Freedom and Fulfillment: An Annotated Translation of al-Ghazzālī's al-Munqidh min al-ḍalāl and Other Relevant Works of al-Ghazzālī* (Boston, 1980). For references to translations of the *Munqidh* into various languages, see p. xxv.

been variously compared by some present-day scholars with the *Confessions of St. Augustine*, with Newman's *Grammar of Assent* in its intellectual subtlety and as an *apologia pro vita sua*, and also with Bunyan's *Grace Abounding* in its puritanical sense[2]. More important, from the point of view of our present discussion, is the fact that this work has often been cited to support the contention that the method of *doubt* is something central to al-Ghazzālī's epistemology and system of thought, and that, in this question, al-Ghazzālī therefore anticipated Descartes (1596-1650)[3]. In fact, a number of comparative studies have been made concerning the place and function of *doubt* in the philosophies of the two thinkers.

Our aim in this chapter is to discuss the meaning and significance of *doubt* in the life and thought of al-Ghazzālī, not as an anticipation of the method of doubt or the sceptical attitude of modern western philosophy, but as an integral element of the epistemology of Islamic intellectual tradition to which al-Ghazzālī properly belongs. We will seek to analyze the nature, function and spirit of the Ghazzalian doubt. In discussing the above question, we are mindful of two important factors. One is the specific intellectual , religious, and spiritual climate prevailing in the Islamic world during the time of al-Ghazzālī, which no doubt constitutes the main external contributory factor to the generation of doubt in the early phase of his intellectual life. The other concerns the whole set of opportunities which Islam ever places at the disposal of man in his quest for certainty, and what we know of al-Ghazzālī's life tells us that he was very much exposed to these oppor-

2. See M. 'Umaruddin, *The Ethical Philosophy of al-Ghazzālī* (Lahore, 1977), p. 286, note 2 to chap. IV; also, Wensinck, *La Pensée de Ghazzali*, p. 111.
3. See M. Iqbal, *The Reconstruction of Religious Thought in Islam* (Lahore: Iqbal Academy Pakistan & Institute of Islamic Culture, 1989), p. 102; M. Saeed Sheikh, "Al-Ghazzali: Metaphysics" in M. M. Sharif, *A History of Muslim Philosophy* (Wiesbaden, 1963), vol. 1, pp. 587-588; Sami M. Najm, "The Place and Function of Doubt in the Philosophies of Descartes and al-Ghazzālī"; and also W. Montgomery Watt, *The Faith and Practice of al-Ghazālī* (Chicago 1982), p. 12.

tunities. Further, the spirit of the Ghazzalian doubt can best be understood when viewed in the context of the true purpose for which *al-Munqidh* has been written, and also in the light of his later works.

In *al-Munqidh,* al-Ghazzālī informs us of how in the prime of his life he was inflicted with a mysterious malady of the soul, which lasted for nearly two months during which time he "was a sceptic in fact, but not in utterance and doctrine"[4]. He was a student in his early twenties at the Niẓāmiyyah College in Naishapur when he suffered from this disease of scepticism.

What is the nature of this Ghazzalian doubt? Al-Ghazzālī tells us that his doubt has been generated in the course of his quest for certainty, that is, for knowledge of the reality of things "as they really are" *(ḥaqā'iq al-umūr)*[5]. This knowledge of the reality of things "as they really are" is what al-Ghazzālī calls *al-'ilm al-yaqīn,* a sure and certain knowledge which he defines as "that in which the thing known is made so manifest that no doubt clings to it, nor is it accompanied by the possibility of error and deception, nor can the mind even suppose such a possibility"[6]. Something ought to be said here about this inner quest of al-Ghazzālī, because it is very much relevant to the theme of our present discussion. In fact, the meaning of this quest should never be lost sight of if we want to understand correctly the nature and significance of the Ghazzalian doubt.

In Islam, the quest for *ḥaqā'iq al-umūr* originated with the famous prayer of the Prophet, in which he asked God to show him "things as they really are". This prayer of the Prophet is essentially the prayer of the gnostic inasmuch as it refers to a supra-rational or inner reality of things. And for this reason, the Sufis have been the most faithful and consistent of the believers in echoing this prayer of the Prophet. The famous

---

4. McCarthy, *op.cit.*, p.66.
5. Al-Ghazzālī, *Munqidh min al-ḍalāl,* p. 11. The text cited here is the one published together with its French translation by Farid Jabre, *Erreur et Deliverance* (Beirut, 1969).
6. McCarthy, *op. cit.*, p. 63.

Sufi, Jāmī (d. 1492), had this prayer beautifully expanded, capturing in an eloquent manner the very spirit of the gnostic's inner quest:

> O God, deliver us from preoccupation with worldly vanities, and show us the nature of things "as they really are". Remove from our eyes the veil of ignorance, and show us things as they really are. Show us not non-existence as existent, nor cast the veil of non-existence over the beauty of existence. Make this phenomenal world the mirror to reflect the manifestation of Thy beauty, not a veil to separate and repel us from Thee. Cause these unreal phenomena of the Universe to be for us the sources of knowledge and insight, not the causes of ignorance and blindness. Our alienation and severance from Thy beauty all proceed from ourselves. Deliver us from ourselves, and accord to us intimate knowledge of Thee[7].

Al-Ghazzālī's quest for certainty, as he has defined it, is none other than this quest of the gnostic. Initially, however, it was a purely intellectual quest. There were both internal and external forces at work in fueling that quest to the point of generating a period of intense doubt in the youthful life of al-Ghazzālī. Internally, by his own admission, his natural intellectual disposition has always been to grasp the real meaning of things. As for external forces, we have already referred to the most important of these, namely, the various intellectual, religious and spiritual currents of al-Ghazzālī's times, all of which must have engaged his highly reflective and contemplative mind. It is quite clear from the *Munqidh* that these various currents were of great concern to him.

In fact, al-Ghazzālī traced the genesis of his famous doubt to these currents. He was struck by the diversity of religions and creeds, and by the fact that the followers of each religion

7. Jāmī, *Lawā'ih, A Treatise On Sufism*, trans. E.H. Whinfield and M.M. Kazvini, (London: Royal Asiatic Society, 1914), p.2.

cling stubbornly to their inherited beliefs. One consequence of his critical reflection upon this religious phenomenon was that he began to question uncritically inherited religious beliefs *(taqlīdāt)*. But living as he was in an age in which the idea of Transcendence was very much a living reality in the souls of men, the problem of diversity of religions did not lead al-Ghazzālī to the kind of relativism that is rampant in modern times as a response to the same problem[8]. On the contrary, it was to lead him to the search for the inner reality of human nature, that is, man's primordial nature *(fiṭrah)*, which on the earthly plane becomes the receptacle for the multiplicity of religious forms and expressions.

Contrary to the view held by some modern interpreters of his thought, al-Ghazzālī was not against *taqlīd* as such. He never advocated at any time for its total abandonment. In fact, he considered it necessary for the simple believers whose minds are free of the kind of intellectual curiousity one finds in philosophers and scientists, and who are therefore content to accept things based on the authority of the experts. Al-Ghazzālī's criticism of *taqlīd* must be seen in the context of his quest for the highest level of certainty, a quest which, in fact, though not in principle, is the concern, not of the majority, but of the few like him. From the point of view of this quest, *taqlīd* is certainly a great impediment to its realization. Consequently, al-Ghazzālī let himself loose from the bonds of *taqlīd (rābiṭat al-taqlīd)*.

Here, one needs to make a clear distinction between *taqlīd*, which is a particular manner of acquiring ideas, and *taqlīdāt*, which are the ideas themselves. This distinction is somehow seldom noted by many students of Ghazzalian thought. Al-Ghazzālī's rejection of *taqlīd* for himself stemmed from his methodological criticism of its inherent limitations, while in accepting it for the simple-minded he was simply affirming an

8. For a profound critique of the modern interpretation of the meaning of diversity of religions, see F. Schuon, *Gnosis: Divine Wisdom* (Middlesex: Perennial Book, 1978), chap. 1.

important aspect of the subjective reality of the human order, namely, that individual human beings differ from one another in intellectual capability. The unreliability of *taqlīd* stems from the fact that it is susceptible to lending itself to both true and false *taqlīdāt.* The solution to the problem of false *taqlīdāt,* however, is not sought through the complete eradication of *taqlīd,* which is practically impossible, but through addressing oneself to the question of the truth or falsity of the *taqlīdāt* themselves. Thus, in the *Munqidh,* al-Ghazzālī tells us how, after reflecting upon the problem of *taqlīd,* he sought to sift out these *taqlīdāt,* to discern those that are true from those that are false[9]. A lot of his intellectual efforts were indeed devoted to this task.

For al-Ghazzālī, the positive function of *taqlīd,* namely, the acceptance of truths based on authority, is to be protected by those who have been entrusted with true knowledge, who constitute the legitimate authority to interpret and clarify knowledge about religious and spiritual matters. As it pertains to knowledge, another aspect of the reality of the human order affirmed by al-Ghazzālī is that there are degrees or levels of knowledge and, consequently, of knowers. This view has its basis in the Quranic verse which al-Ghazzālī quoted: "God raises in degrees those of you who believe and those to whom knowledge is given"[10]. In Islamic theory of knowledge, there is a hierarchy of intellectual and spiritual authorities culminating in the Holy Prophet, and ultimately God Himself. Faith *(īmān),* which is a level of knowledge, says al-Ghazzālī, is the favorable acceptance *(ḥusn al-ẓann)*[11] of knowledge based on hearsay and experience of others, of which the most reliable is that of the Prophet.

There has been objection from certain modernist circles that the idea of admissibility of *taqlīd* for one group of people and its prohibition for another is socially unacceptable and even dangerous, for it can lead to the crystallization of a caste

9. Al-Ghazzālī, *Munqidh . . .,* p. 11.
10. *The Quran,* Chapter LVIII (The Woman who Pleads), Verse 11. See McCarthy, *op. cit.,* p.96.
11. Al-Ghazzālī, *Munqidh,* p.40.

system, which is against the very spirit of Islam. What has been said above is actually already sufficient to render this objection invalid. Nevertheless, we like to quote here the rebuttal of a scholar who has bemoaned the banishment of the Islamic idea of hierarchy of knowledge and of authorities at the hands of the modernists:

> "In respect of the human order in society, we do not in the least mean by 'hierarchy' that semblance of it wherein oppression and exploitation and domination are legitimized as if they were an established principle ordained by God . . . The fact that hierarchical disorders have prevailed in human society does not mean that hierarchy in the human order is not valid, for there is, in point of fact, *legitimate* hierarchy in the order of creation, and this is the Divine Order pervading all Creation and manifesting the occurrence of justice"[12].

It is this idea of the hierarchy of knowledge and of being which is central to al-Ghazzālī's epistemology and system of thought, and he himself would be the last person to say that such an idea implies the legitimization of a social caste system in Islam.

To sum up our discussion of al-Ghazzālī's methodological criticism of *taqlīd*, we can say that he was dissatisfied with it because it could not quench his intense intellectual thirst. It was obvious to him at that young age that *taqlīd* is an avenue to both truth and error, but as to what is true and what is false there was an open sea of debate around him, which disturbed him profoundly. It led him to contemplate upon one of the most central questions in philosophy, namely, the question of what true knowledge is, and this marked the beginning of an intensification of his intellectual doubt.

Besides the problem of the diversity of religions and creeds, in which a major issue was *taqlīd*, there was another, and more

---

12. al-Attas, S.M.N., *Islam and Secularism* (Kuala Lumpur: ABIM, 1978), p.101.

important, religious and spiritual current which contributed to the genesis of his doubt and which deeply affected his mind. This he mentioned as the existence of numerous schools of thought *(madhāhib)* and groups *(firaq)* within the Community of Islam itself, each with its own methods of understanding and affirming the truth and each claiming that it alone is saved. Al-Ghazzālī comments in the *Munqidh* that in this state of affairs of the Community, which he likens to "a deep sea in which most men founder and from which few only are saved", one finds the fulfilment of the famous promise of the Prophet: "My Community will split into seventy-odd sects, of which one will be saved".

The above religious climate was not peculiar to the times of al-Ghazzālī alone. A few centuries earlier, al-Ḥarīth b. Asad al-Muḥāsibī (165/781-243-837)[13], another famous Sufi, whose writings exercised a great influence on al-Ghazzālī, lamented the similar pitiful state of affairs into which the Islamic community has fallen. In fact, the autobiographical character of the *Munqidh* may have been modeled on the introduction to al-Muḥāsibī's work, *Kitāb al-wasāyā (or al-nasā'ih),* which is also autobiographical in character[14].

The following extract from this work reveals striking similarities to certain passages in the *Munqidh,* and gives some indication as to the kind of religious climate prevailing during the time of al-Muḥāsibī:

> It has come to pass in our days, that this community is divided into seventy and more sects: of these, one only is the way of salvation, and for the rest, God knows best concerning them. Now I have not ceased, not so much as one moment of my life, to consider well the differences into which the community has fallen, and

13. On the life and teaching of this early Sufi figure, see Margaret Smith, *An Early Mystic of Baghdad: A Study of the Life and Teaching of Ḥārith ibn Asad al-Muḥāsibī* (London, 1935).
14. See A.J. Arberry, *Sufism: An Account of the Mystics of Islam* (London: Unwin Paperback, 1979), p.47.

> to search after the clear way and the true path, whereunto I have searched both theory and practice, and looked, for guidance on the road to the world to come, to the directing of the theologians. Moreover, I have studied much of the doctrine of Almighty God, with the interpretation of the lawyers, and reflected upon the various conditions of the community, and considered its diverse doctrines and sayings. Of all this I understood as much as was appointed for me to understand: *and I saw that their divergence was as it were a deep sea, wherein many had been drowned, and but a small band escaped therefrom; and I saw every party of them asserting that salvation was to be found in following them, and that he would perish who opposed them . . .*[15]

It is interesting to note that, although al-Ghazzālī's autobiographical work is more dramatic and eloquent than that of al-Muḥāsibī, both men were led into an almost similar kind of intellectual crisis through similar external circumstances. Both sought the light of certainty and that knowledge which guarantees salvation, and they found that light in Sufism. In the process, they accomplished a philosophical as well as a sociological analysis of knowledge, the details of which remain to be studied. But having said this much, we may add that al-Ghazzālī's philosophical discussion of *doubt (shakk)* and certainty *(yaqīn)* can still claim originality in more ways than one.

Having discussed the main factors which contributed to the generation of the Ghazzalian doubt, and to his formulation of the fundamental idea of "true knowledge" we now proceed to investigate into the philosophical meaning and significance of this doubt. We have seen earlier how al-Ghazzālī defined the kind of certain and infallible knowledge *(al-'ilm al-yaqīn)* which he was seeking. It is that knowledge which is completely

15. *Ibid*, pp.47-48, italics mine. Compare the italics portion with McCarthy, *op. cit.*, pp. 62-63.

free from any error or doubt, and with which the heart finds complete satisfaction. Is such a kind of certainty or certitude possible? It is significant that al-Ghazzālī never explicitly posed that question. But, armed with the above criteria of certainty, he proceeded immediately to scrutinize the whole state of his knowledge. He found himself "devoid of any knowledge answering the previous description except in the case of sense-data *(ḥissiyyāt)* and the self-evident truths *(ḍarūriyyāt)*[16.]" He then set out to induce doubt *(tashkīk)* against his sense-data to determine whether they could withstand his test of infallibility and indubitability. The outcome of this effort, in which reason *('aql)* appeared as judge over the claims of the senses to certitude, was that his reliance on sense-data proved no longer tenable. The charge of falsity leveled by reason against sense-perceptions could not be rebutted by the senses.

With his reliance on sense-data shattered, al-Ghazzālī sought refuge in the certainty of rational data which "belong to the category of primary truths, such as our asserting that 'Ten is more than three', and 'One and the same thing cannot be simultaneously affirmed and denied', and 'One and the same thing cannot be incipient and eternal, existent and non-existent, necessary and impossible'"[17]. However, this refuge in the rational data *('aqliyyāt)* too was not safe from elements of doubt. This time, doubt crept in through an objection, made on behalf of sense-data, against the claims of reason to certitude.

As explained in the *Munqidh,* these claims of reason are not refuted in the same way reason itself has earlier refuted the claims of the senses. They are merely subjected to doubt by means of analogical argumentations. Still, it is a doubt which reason proves unable to dispel in an incontrovertible manner. Reason is reminded of the possibility of another judge superior to itself, which if it were to reveal itself would "give the lie to

16. McCarthy, *op. cit.,* p. 64.
17. *Ibid,* p.65.

the judgments of reason, just as the reason-judge revealed itself and gave the lie to the judgments of sense"[18]. The mere fact of the non- appearance of this other judge does not prove the impossibility of its existence.

This inner debate within the soul of al-Ghazzālī turned for the worse when its suggestion of the possibility of another kind of perception beyond reason was reinforced by various kinds of evidences and argumentations. First of all, an appeal was made to reason to exercise the principle of analogy to the phenomena of dreaming. Through this principle, reason would have realized that the relation of this suggested supra-rational state to our waking state, when the senses and reason are fully functional, is like the relation of the latter to our dreaming state. If our waking state judges our imaginings and beliefs in the dreaming state to be groundless, the supra-rational state likewise judges our rational beliefs.

This argumentation appears as if al-Ghazzālī, himself one of the most respected jurists, was addressing the jurists and other proponents of reason, who were well-versed with the principle of analogy. We are not suggesting here that these targeted groups were in al-Ghazzālī's mind at the time he was experiencing this inner debate. His indirect reference to them could well have surfaced at the time of his writing the *Munqidh* inasmuch as this work was written with a view of impressing upon the rationalists that Islamic epistemology affirms supra-rational perceptions as the real key to knowledge. Thus, al-Ghazzālī reproaches the rationalists in the *Munqidh*: "Therefore, whoever thinks that the unveiling of truth depends on precisely formulated proofs has indeed straitened the broad mercy of God"[19].

Next to confront reason in support of the possibility of a supra-rational state was the presence of a group of people called the Sufis, who claimed that they had actually experienced that state. They alleged that during their experience of these supra-

18. *Ibid.*
19. *Ibid*, p.66.

rational states, they saw phenomena which are not in accord with the normal data of reason. Finally, the last piece of evidence brought to the attention of reason is the prophetic saying, "Men are asleep: then after they die they awake", and the Quranic verse "Thou was heedless of this; now have We removed thy veil, and sharp is thy sight this day"[20]. Both the ḥadīth and the Quranic verse quoted refer to man's state after death, and reason is told that, may be, this is the state in question.

All these objections to the claim of reason to have the final say to truth could not be refuted satisfactorily by reason. The mysterious malady of al-Ghazzālī's soul, which lasted for nearly two months, is none other than this inner tussle or tension between its rational faculty and another faculty which mounts an appeal to the former, through the senses, to accept its existence and the possibility of those experiences that have been associated with its various powers, such as those claimed by the Sufis. This other faculty, which is supra-rational and supra-logical, is the intuitive faculty which, at this particular stage of al-Ghazzālī's intellectual life, had not yet developed beyond the mere ability to theorize and acknowledge the possibility of supra-rational experiences. Later, during a period of intense spiritual life, he claimed to have been invested with higher powers of the faculty, which disclosed to him innumerable mysteries of the spiritual world[21]. These powers al-Ghazzālī termed *kashf* (direct vision) and *dhawq* (translated as *fruitional experience* by McCarthy, and *immediate experience* by Watt)[22].

The gradational movement from sense-data to rational data presented no serious difficulty, but the first direct encounter between his rational and intuitive experiences proved to be a painful one for al-Ghazzālī. His two-month period of being

20. *The Quran*, Chapter L (*Qaf*), Verse 22.
21. McCarthy, *op. cit.*, p.94.
22. *Ibid*, p.95; Watt, *op. cit.*, p.62. On the various terms used in Islamic thought for intuition, and on the question of the relationship between intellect and intuition in the Islamic perspective, see Nasr, "Intellect and Intuition. . ."

"sceptic in fact, but not in utterance and doctrine" was the period of having to endure intense doubts about the reliability of his rational faculty in the face of certain assertive manifestations of the intuitive faculty. His problem was one of finding the rightful place for each of the human faculties of knowing within the total scheme of knowledge, and, in particular, of establishing the right relationship between reason and intuition, as this latter term is traditionally understood.

Thus, when he was cured of this sickness, not through rational arguments or logical proofs but through the effect of a light *(nūr)* which God cast into his breast, his intellectual equilibrium was restored, and he once again accepted the reliability of rational data of the category of *ḍarūriyyāt.* However, in this newfound intellectual equilibrium, reason no longer occupied the dominant position it used to have. In al-Ghazzālī's own words, that light which God cast into his breast is the key to most knowledge[23].

We do not agree with the view of certain scholars that the method of doubt is something central to al-Ghazzālī's epistemology and system of thought. The *Munqidh* does not support the view that al-Ghazzālī was advocating systematic doubt as an instrument in the investigation of truth[24]. And there is nothing to be found in it, which is comparable to Descartes' assertion that "it is necessary once in one's life to doubt of all things, so far as this is possible"[25]. This brings us to the question of the true nature of al-Ghazzālī's first personal crisis.

McCarthy describes al-Ghazzālī's crisis of scepticism as an epistemological crisis, which is of the intellect alone, in contrast to his second personal crisis which is a crisis of conscience, and of the spirit[26]. Father Poggi, whose *Un Classico della Spiritualita Musulmana* is considered by McCarthy to be one of the finest studies on al-Ghazzālī and the *Munqidh,* does not

23. Al-Ghazzālī, *Munqidh. . .,* p. 13.
24. This view is discussed in Sami M. Najm, *op. cit.*
25. Descartes, *Principles,* pt. 1, 1 in *The Philosophical Works of Descartes,* trans. E.S. Haldane and G.R.T. Ross, (New York, 1955).
26. McCarthy, *op. cit.,* p.xxix.

consider the youthful scepticism of al-Ghazzālī as real but purely a *methodical* one[27]. Another celebrated Italian Orientalist, Guiseppe Furlani, also agrees that the doubt of al-Ghazzālī is not that of a sceptic, but rather of a critic of knowledge[28].

We agree with the common view of these scholars that, at the time of his crisis, al-Ghazzālī was neither a philosophical nor a religious sceptic, and that the crisis was an epistemological or methodical one. The *Munqidh* provides ample evidence to support this view. Al-Ghazzālī was not a philosophical sceptic because he never contested the value of metaphysical certitude. He was always certain of the *de jure* certitude of truth. Thus, as we have earlier mentioned, he never questioned the possibility of knowledge of *ḥaqā'iq al-umūr.* His natural, intellectual disposition toward seeking that knowledge was, in a way, an affirmation of his personal conviction in the *de jure* certitude of truth.

According to Schuon, it is the agnostics and other relativists who sought to demonstrate the illusory character of the *de jure* certitude of truth by opposing to it the *de facto* certitude of error, as if the psychological phenomenon of false certitudes could prevent true certitudes from being what they are and from having all their effectiveness and as if the very existence of false certitudes did not prove in its own way the existence of true ones[29]. As for al-Ghazzālī, he never fell into the above philosophical temptation of the agnostics and relativists. His doubt was not of truth itself, but of modes of knowing and modes of accepting truth. But, since by truth, he meant here the inner reality of things, his quest for that reality also implied a quest for its corresponding mode of knowledge.

---

27. Vincenzo M. Poggi, *Un classico della Spiritualita Musulmana* (Rome: Libreria dell' Universita Gregoriana, 1967), p. 171.
28. Giuseppe Furlani , "Dr. J. Obermann, Der philos. und regligiose Subjektivismus Ghazalis," (Recensione) in *Revista trimestrale di studi filosoficie religiose,* vol.III, no.2, pp. 340-53, (Perugia, 1922). McCarthy in his above cited work provides an English translation of some excerpts from Furlani's above review, see pp. 388-390.
29. F. Schuon, *Logic and Transcendence,* p.44.

His criticism of all modes of knowing that were then within his practical reach was motivated by a real theoretical awareness of the possibility of another mode of knowing, which the Sufis claim as theirs. In the case of al-Ghazzālī, this possibility must have agitated his mind right from the time it was first impressed upon him through his direct personal encounter with the way of the Sufis. We may recall here the early educational background of al-Ghazzālī. It was an education which was permeated by a strong influence of Sufism. His father, says al-Subkī, was a pious dervish who spent as much time as he could in the company of the Sufis[30].

The first teacher to whom his early education was entrusted was a pious Sufi friend of his. Studying together with him then was his younger brother, Aḥmad al-Ghazzālī (d. 1126) who, though less famous, later made his mark as a great Sufi whose disciples include 'Abd al-Qāhir Abū Najīb al-Suhrawardī (d. 1168), the founder of the Suhrawardiyyah Order, and most probably, as believed by a number of scholars, al-Ghazzālī himself. As a student at Naishapur, one of the subjects he studied was Sufism. He also became a disciple to the Sufi, Abū 'Alī al-Faḍl ibn Muḥammad ibn 'Alī al-Fārmadhī al-Ṭūsī, who was a pupil of al-Qushairī (d. 465/1074). Al-Ghazzālī learnt from al-Fārmadhī (d. 477/1084) the theory and practice of Sufism and, under the latter's guidance, even indulged in certain ascetic and spiritual practices.

He was increasingly attracted to the idea of a direct personal experience of God emphasized by the Sufis. However, he felt a bit disheartened when, in these early attempts at following the Sufi path, he failed to attain that stage where the mystics begin to receive pure inspiration from "high above"[31]. In the light of this background, there is a strong reason to believe that Sufism plays a central role in leading al-Ghazzālī to his

30. Al-Subkī, *Ṭabaqāt al-shāfi'iyyah al-kubrā* (Cairo, 1324/1906), vol. IV, p. 102, quoted in M. Saeed Sheikh, *op. cit.*, pp. 582-283.
31. Ibn Khallikān, *Wafayāt al-a'yān*, English translation by de Slane, (Paris, 1842-1871), vol. II, p. 122.

epistemological crisis. Al-Ghazzālī's doubt of the trustworthiness of reason was not generated from "below" or by the reflection of reason upon its own self, but was suggested from "above" as a result of his acquaintance with the Sufi's mode of knowledge, which claims to be supra-rational and which "offers its own critique of reason". Likewise, the doubt was removed not through the power of reason, but from "above" as a result of the light of divine grace, which restores to each faculty of knowledge its rightful position and its validity and trustworthiness at its own level.

Al-Ghazzālī was also never at any time a religious sceptic. He tells us in the *Munqidh* that, throughout his quest for certainty, he always had an unshakable belief in the three fundamentals of the Islamic faith:

> "From the sciences which I had practiced and the methods which I had followed in my inquiry into the two kinds of knowledge, revealed and rational, I had already acquired a sure and certain faith in God Most High, in the prophetic mediation of revelation, and in the Last Day. These three fundamentals of our Faith had become deeply rooted in my soul, not because of any specific, precisely formulated proofs, but because of reasons and circumstances and experiences too many to list in detail."[32]

The above quotation is yet another evidence provided by the *Munqidh* that al-Ghazzālī's so called scepticism is not to be equated with the scepticism encountered in modern western philosophy. The doubting mind of al-Ghazzālī was never cut off from revelation and faith. On the contrary, it was based upon a "sure and certain" faith in the fundamentals of religion. As for the doubting mind of the modern sceptic, it is cut off from both the intellect and revelation and, in the pursuit of its directionless activity, it has turned against faith itself. Now,

32. McCarthy, *Munqidh* . . ., pp. 90-91.

what is the distinction between the "sure and certain" faith which al-Ghazzālī always had and that certainty which he was ever eager to seek? We will deal briefly with this question because in its very answer lies the significance of the Ghazzalian doubt and also because charges have been leveled against al-Ghazzālī by scholars like J. Obermann[33] that his haunting doubts of objective reality led him to find sanctuary in religious subjectivism.

The answer to the above question is to be found in the idea of certainty *(yaqīn)* in Islamic gnosis. There are degrees of certainty: in the terminology of the Quran, these are *'ilm al-yaqīn* (science of certainty), *'ayn al-yaqīn* (vision of certainty) and *ḥaqq al-yaqīn* (truth of certainty). These have been respectively compared to hearing about the description of fire, seeing fire and being consumed by fire[34]. As applied to al-Ghazzālī's quest for certainty, the "sure and certain" faith, which he claimed he had acquired from his inquiry into the various sciences, referred to *'ilm al-yaqīn,* since his acceptance of the truths concerned was inferential in nature, based as it was upon data furnished by revelation and the authority of the Prophet. In other words, at the level of faith, the particular truth which is the object of the faith is not known directly or with immediacy. Nevertheless, to the extent that in one's act of faith one participates in the truth through both reason and heart, faith already implies a particular level of knowledge and of certainty. Thus, from the beginning of al-Ghazzālī's quest for the true knowledge of the Real, a certain element of certitude was always present.

In the *Kitāb al-'ilm* (Book of Knowledge) of his *magnum opus, Iḥyā' 'ulūm al-dīn* (The Revivification of the Religious Sciences), al-Ghazzālī discussed the usage of the term *yaqīn* by the major intellectual schools of Islam up to his time. He

---

33. J. Obermann, *Der philosophische und religiose Subjektivismus Ghazzalis' Ein Beitrag zum Problem der Religions* (Wien und Leipzig, 1921), p. 20.
34. See Nasr, *Knowledge and the Sacred* (New York: Crossroad, 1981), p.325; also Abu Bakr Siraj al-Din, *The Book of Certainty* (New York, 1974).

identified two distinct meanings to which the term was being applied. In one group were the philosophers *(nuẓẓīr)* and the theologians *(mutakallimūn)*, who employed the term to signify lack or negation of doubt, in the sense that the knowledge or the truth in question is established from evidence which leaves no place for any possibility of doubt[35]. The second meaning of the term *yaqīn* was the one adopted by the jurists and the Sufis as well as most of the learned men. *Yaqīn,* in this case, refers to the intensity of religious faith or fervor which involves both the acceptance, by the soul, of that which "prevails over the heart and takes hold of it" and the submission of the soul to that thing in question.

For al-Ghazzālī, both kinds of *yaqīn* need to be strengthened, but it is the second kind of *yaqīn* which is the nobler of the two, since without it serving as an epistemological basis for the first kind of *yaqīn,* the latter would definitely lack epistemic substance and value. Moreover, it fosters religious and spiritual obedience, and praiseworthy habits. In other words, philosophical certainty is of no value if it is not accompanied by submission to the truth and by the transformation of one's being in conformity with that truth. Although the jurists and the Sufis both have been identified with the second kind of *yaqīn,* they are generally concerned with different levels of *yaqīn.* The Sufis are basically concerned with a direct or immediate experience of the Truth, and with submission to the Pure Spirit not merely at the level of external meanings of the *Sharī'ah* (Divine Law) but at all levels of the selfhood. For this reason, the degrees of certainty earlier mentioned properly belong to *ma'rifah* (Islamic gnosis) rather than to *fiqh* (jurisprudence). In al-Ghazzālī's popular terminology in the *Iḥyā'*, these belong to *'ilm al-mukāshafah* (science of revelation) and not to *'ilm al-mu'āmalah* (science of practical religion).

---

35. Al-Ghazzālī, *Kitāb al-'ilm,* English trans. by Nabih Amin Faris, (Lahore, 1974), pp. 193-194.

Reverting back to al-Ghazzālī's "sure and certain faith", there are, with respect to his ultimate goal, deficiencies both in his modes of knowing and in the submission of his whole being. Deficiency in the former was a root cause of his first personal crisis which, as we have seen, was epistemological in nature. Deficiency in the latter had a lot to do with his second personal crisis which was spiritual, although the two crisis are not unrelated. We have identified al-Ghazzālī's "sure and certain faith" with certainty at the level of *'ilm al-yaqīn* which refers to a particular manner of participation in the Truth. Objectively, if doubts could be generated about the trustworthiness of *'ilm al-yaqīn* as being the highest level of certainty, it is because a higher level of certitude is possible, for as Schuon profoundly says, if man is able to doubt, this is because certitude exists[36].

Al-Ghazzālī's acquaintance with the methodology of the Sufis made hime aware of the *de jure* certitude of truth of a higher level. At the time of his epistemological crisis, he was only certain of this certitude in the sense of *'ilm al-yaqīn.* After the crisis, as a result of the light of intellectual intuition which he received from Heaven, that certainty was elevated to the level of *'ayn al-yaqīn.* This newfound certainty was not the end of al-Ghazzālī's intellectual and spiritual quest. He had a longing for the mystical experience of the Sufis. He had indulged in some of their spiritual practices but without success in terms of fruitional experience. This must have been a lingering source of inner discontent in him. He was to realize later his major fault: he was too engrossed in worldly desires and ambitions such as fame and fortune[37], while the efficacy of spiritual practices presupposes a certain frame of mind and a certain level of spiritual virtues like the sincerity of one's intention.

Al-Ghazzālī mentions in the *Munqidh* that immediately after his first crisis was over, he proceeded to study with greater

36. Schuon, *op. cit.*, p.13.
37. McCarthy, *op. cit.*, p.91.

thoroughness the views and methods of the various seekers of the Truth. He divided the seekers into four groups. These were "the *mutakallimūn* (theologians) who allege that they are men of independent judgment and reasoning; the *bāṭinites* who claim to be the unique possessors of *al-ta'līm* (authoritative instruction) and the privileged recipients of knowledge acquired from the Infallible *Imām*; the philosophers who maintain that they are the men of logic and apodeictic demonstration; and finally the Sufis who claim to be the familiars of the Divine Presence and the men of mystic vision and illumination"[38]. There is no doubt that al-Ghazzālī had undertaken this comparative study of all the classes of seekers of the Truth with the view of exhausting all the possibilities and opportunities that were open to him in the pursuit of the highest level of certainty, although by then one could already detect in him a special inclination and sympathy toward Sufism.

At the end of this thorough study, he came to the conclusion that "the Sufis were masters of states *(arbāb al-aḥwāl)* and not purveyors of words *(aṣḥāb al-aqwāl)*"[39]. He also came to realize that there was a great difference between theoretical knowledge and realized knowledge. To illustrate the difference he gave the following example. There is a great difference between our *knowing* the definitions, causes, and conditions of health and satiety and our *being* healthy and sated, between our *knowing* the definition of drunkenness and our *being* drunk, and between our *knowing* the true nature and conditions of asceticism and our actually *practicing* asceticism. Certitude derived from realized knowledge is what *ḥaqq al-yaqīn* is. This knowledge is free from error and doubt because it is not based on conjecture or mental concepts, but it resides in the heart and thus involves the whole of man's being[40].

Realized knowledge, however, demands the transformation of the knower's being. The distinctive characteristic of the Sufi

---

38. *Ibid*, p. 67.
39. Al-Ghazzālī, *Munqidh* . . . p.35.
40. Nasr, *op. cit.*, p.325.

mode of knowledge, says al-Ghazzālī, is that it seeks the removal of deformations of the soul such as pride, passional attachment to the world and a host of other reprehensible habits and vicious qualities, all of which stand as obstacles to the realization of that knowledge, in order to attain a heart empty of all save God and adorned with the constant remembrance of God[41]. This led al-Ghazzālī to reflect upon his own state of being. He realized the pitiful state of his soul and became certain that he was "on the brink of a crumbling bank and already on the verge of falling into the Fire"[42] unless he set about mending his ways. Before him now lies the most important decision he has to make in his life. For about six months he incessantly vacillated between the contending pull of worldly desires and the appeals of the afterlife. This is al-Ghazzālī's second personal crisis which is spiritual and far more serious than the first, because it involves a decision of having to abandon one kind of life for another which is essentially opposed to the former. He tells us how, at last, when he has completely lost his capacity to make a choice, God delivers him from the crisis by making it easy for his heart to turn away from the attractions of the world. In the spiritual path of the Sufis, al-Ghazzālī found the light of certainty that he has tirelessly sought from the beginning of his intellectual awareness of what that certainty is.

It is therefore in the light of Islamic epistemology and, especially in the light of the idea of degrees of certainty *(yaqīn)* in Islamic gnosis that the famous Ghazzalian doubt should be studied and understood. When al-Ghazzālī turned to his own inner being to find the light of certainty, it was not an exercise in religious subjectivism or an act of disillusionment with objective reality, as maintained by scholars like Obermann and Furlani. On the contrary, al-Ghazzālī was drawn to the highest objective reality that is. The Ultimate Truth underlying objective

41. McCarthy, *op. cit.*, p.90.
42. *Ibid*, p.91.

reality is identical to the Supreme Self underlying human selfhood or man's subjective consciousness. The intellectual and spiritual tradition in which al-Ghazzālī lived and thought made him fully aware of the fact that what veils man from this highest reality is the darkness of his own soul. Therefore in turning to his own inner being, al-Ghazzālī was merely following that traditional path which alone could guarantee, by divine grace, the removal of that veil. This is the universal path of all the real seekers of the Truth, of which al-Ghazzālī was an outstanding example.

CHAPTER 4

The Unity of Science and Spiritual Knowledge: The Islamic Experience

Science, understood in the restricted sense of an organized, orderly and objective knowledge of the natural order, is not the product of the modern mind alone. Such forms of knowledge had also been extensively cultivated in pre-modern civilizations such as in the Chinese, Indian, and Islamic civilizations. These pre-modern sciences, however, differ from modern science with respect to goals, methodology, sources of inspiration, and their philosophical assumptions concerning man, knowledge, and the reality of the natural world.

Another major difference between pre-modern and modern sciences pertains to the place of science in relation to other kinds of knowledge. In pre-modern civilizations, science was never divorced from spiritual knowledge. On the contrary, one finds an organic unity of science and spiritual knowledge. The main aim of this chapter is to explain how this unity was achieved in pre-modern times. My specific reference is to the Islamic scientific tradition. However, many of the features of Islamic science mentioned here equally apply to the other pre-modern sciences.

By *spiritual knowledge* I mean knowledge pertaining to the spiritual order. The essence of spiritual knowledge is knowledge of the world of the Spirit. In Islam, this knowledge refers to the knowledge of the One, of God and His Unity. It is worth repeating that the principle of Divine Unity *(al-tawḥīd)* constitutes the central message of Islam. In Muslim classifications of knowledge composed over the centuries, the knowledge of *tawḥīd* was always held to be the highest form of knowledge as well as the ultimate goal of all intellectual pursuits.

Spiritual knowledge is not confined solely to the world of the pure Spirit. It is also concerned with the manifestations of the Spirit in the different orders of reality that make up the whole universe.

A fundamental component of a Muslim's knowledge of God is the knowledge of the universe as an effect of the divine creative act. Knowledge of the relationship between God and the world, between Creator and creation, or between the Divine Principle and cosmic manifestation constitutes the most fundamental basis of the unity of science and spiritual knowledge. In Islam, the most important sources of this type of knowledge are the Quran and prophetic *ḥadīths.* To understand the Islamic conception and experience of the unity of science and spiritual knowledge, it is necessary to refer to some of the key concepts and ideas embodied in this knowledge.

The Quran as Source of Both Science and Spiritual Knowledge

The Quran is the fountainhead of Islamic intellectuality and spirituality. It is the basis not only of religion and spiritual knowledge but of all kinds of knowledge. It is the main source of inspiration of the Muslim vision of the unity of science and spiritual knowledge. The idea of this unity is a consequence of the idea of the unity of all knowledge. The latter is in turn derived from the principle of Divine Unity applied to the domain of human knowledge.

Man gains knowledge from different kinds of sources and

through various ways and means. But all knowledge ultimately comes from God who is the All-knowing. In the Quranic view, man's knowledge of things corporeal as well as spiritual is possible because God had given him the necessary faculties of knowing. Many Muslim philosophers and scientists assert that in the act of thinking and knowing the human intellect is illuminated by the divine intellect.

The Quran is not a book of science. But it does provide knowledge of the principles of science, which it always relates to metaphysical and spiritual knowledge. The Quranic injunction to "read in the Name of Thy Lord" has been faithfully observed by every generation of Muslims. It has been understood to mean that the acquisition of knowledge, including scientific knowledge should be based on the foundation of our knowledge of God's Reality. Islam, in fact, gives legitimacy to a science only if it is organically related to the knowledge of God and of the world of the Spirit. Consequently, Islamic science possesses a religious and spiritual character. According to the famous Muslim scientist, Ibn Sīnā (Avicenna), that science is true science which relates knowledge of the world to the knowledge of the Divine Principle.[1]

Nature as Source of Scientific and Spiritual Knowledge

Nature is a source of many types of knowledge: mathematical, physical, and metaphysical; scientific and spiritual; qualitative and quantitative; practical and aesthetical. This is because, as a world and viewed in its totality, the reality of nature is comprised of many aspects. Each type of knowledge corresponds to a particular aspect of nature that is singled out for study. Modern science has chosen to study only some of these aspects. In conformity with its scientific conception of nature and its reductionistic and materialistic worldview, modern science ignores, belittles or denies altogether the metaphysical, spiritual, qualitative, and aesthetical aspects of nature. Eddington and

1. F. Brunner, *Science et realite,* p.13.

Whitehead have rightly asserted that modern science is a kind of subjectively-selected knowledge since it deals only with those aspects of the reality of nature which the so-called scientific method is competent to study.[2]

In Islam, the unity of nature is regarded as an image of the unity of the Divine Principle. The goal of Islamic science is to demonstrate the unity of nature, that is the interrelatedness of all its parts and aspects. Consequently, Islamic science seeks to study all the different aspects of nature from a unified and integrated standpoint. For example, the fundamentality of the mathematical aspect of the universe is well recognized in Islamic science. According to Ikhwān al-Ṣafā' (the Brethren of Purity), an eleventh-century brotherhood of Muslim scientists and philosophers, "the whole world is composed in conformity with arithmetical, goemetrical and musical relations."[3] But this mathematical content of the universe was never studied in Islam from a quantitative point of view alone. Muslim mathematics was both a qualitative and a quantitative science.

Following the Pythagoreans, whose mathematical conception of the universe found easy acceptance into the Islamic worldview, many Muslim mathematicians speak of the "virtues" and "personalities" of various geometrical figures. One of their declared aims in studying geometry is to help prepare the human soul in its journey to the world of the spirits and eternal life.[4] Similarly, the science of numbers is seen to be related to spiritual knowledge. Numbers are not merely quantitative entities on which may be performed the arithmetical operations of addition, substraction, multiplication, and division. Numbers are also qualitative entities. In its qualitative aspect, number is the spiritual image resulting in the human soul from the repetition of unity. Numbers are therefore regarded as the projection or as so many expressions of unity. Knowledge of the generation of

2. S.H. Nasr, *Man and Nature*, p.28.
3. See S.H. Nasr, *Islamic Cosmological Doctrines*, p.45.
4. *Ibid*, p.49.

numbers from the number one presents to the human mind a powerful illustration of the generations of all things from God. Ikhwān al-Ṣafā' compared the creation of the world by God to the generation of numbers from the number One.[5] The number zero, whose historical origin may be traced to the metaphysical speculation of the Hindus, is said to symbolize the Divine Essence which is beyond all determinations including Being.

Mathematics as cultivated by the Muslims emerges as a primary link between the physical world and the spiritual or metaphysical world of the Platonic archetypes. Arithmetic and geometry, the foundation of the mathematical sciences, find their application in the domain of the physical sciences as well as in the domain of metaphysical knowledge of *tawḥīd.* Muslim philosopher-scientists like al-Fārābī, Ikhwān al-Ṣafā' and Quṭb al-Dīn al-Shīrāzī considered mathematical training indispensable to having a sound knowledge of spiritual truths.[6]

Nature is also a source of spiritual and metaphysical knowledge because it is not merely 'natural'. Nature also possesses a 'supernatural' aspect. In Islam, the natural and the spiritual are closely intertwined. Spiritual reality manifests itself in the natural world while remaining independent of the latter. The two orders are connected by means of a vertical, metaphysical relationship. The natural world is variously described in the different religious

5. "Know, oh Brother (May God assist thee and us by the Spirit from Him) that God, Exalted Be His Praise, when He created all creatures and brought all things into being, arranged them and brought them into existence by a process similar to the process of generation (of numbers) from one, so that the multiplicity (of numbers) should be a witness to His Oneness, and their classification and order an indication of the perfection of His Wisdom in creation. And this would be a witness to the fact, too, that they (creatures) are related to Him who created them, in the same way as the numbers are related to the One which is prior to two, and which is the principle, origin and source of numbers, as we have shown in our treatise on arithmetic." Ikhwān al-Ṣafā', *Rasā'il* (Cairo: Arabiyyah Press, 1928), trans. by S.H. Nasr in his *Science and Civilization in Islam,* pp. 155-6.
6. I have dealt with the views of al-Fārābī and Quṭb al-Dīn al-Shīrāzī on this question in my *Classification of Knowledge in Islam* (Kuala Lumpur: Institute for Policy Research, 1991).

traditions as an effect, a manifestation, symbol, or reflection of the spiritual world. Conversely, the spiritual world is described as the cause, principle, root, or archetype of the natural world.

In the religious and intellectual history of the West, however, a sharp distinction has often been made between the natural and the spiritual in a manner which is not conducive to the realization of the unity of science and spiritual knowledge. The natural world is identified with the profane and the spiritual with the sacred. There was also a sharp line drawn between the natural and the supernatural or between nature and grace. In modern science, nature has lost its sacred character. The natural world has been emptied of its spiritual content. Consequently, nature is no longer seen as having a meaningful role in religious and spiritual life.

The fact that there is something of a spiritual order that resides in nature finds numerous expressions in Islamic philosophical and theological literature. In the language of the Quran, nature is said to bear within itself the imprints of God. The phenomena of nature, in the macrocosmic world as well as within the souls of men, are said to be the *āyāt* (signs) of God. The verses of the Quran are likewise called the *āyāt* of God. Nature is therefore regarded as a divine revelation, a counterpart of the Quran. It conveys to man its metaphysical and spiritual message of transcendence. In this religious and spiritual conception of nature lies the basis of unity of science and spiritual knowledge.

Nature is also said to be a book of symbols. According to al-Ghazzālī, everything that exists in the natural world is a symbol of something in the higher world.[7] As pointed out in an earlier chapter, symbol in its traditional sense is to be distinguished from allegory. As traditionally understood in Islam, symbol is the "reflection", in a lower order of existence, of a reality belonging to a higher ontological status. That higher world which is symbolized by the natural symbols is the spiritual world. For example, the sun symbolizes the Divine Intelligence; the empty vastness of

7. See his *Mishkāt al-anwār*, trans. by W.H.T. Gairdner, pp. 121-5.

space symbolizes the Divine All-Possibility and also the Divine Immutability; a bird symbolizes the soul; a tree symbolizes the grades of being; and water symbolizes knowledge and rain revelation. We can go on and on giving countless other examples.

There is an inner nexus between the symbol and the symbolized. This nexus is metaphysical and not physical in nature. Knowledge of the meaning of a symbol or of this inner nexus cannot be gained through logical or mathematical analysis or through empirical investigation. This knowledge belongs to that science traditionally called the science of symbolism, which is metaphysical in nature. The science of symbolism is of crucial importance to the quest for the unity of science and spiritual knowledge. For this reason, this science was cultivated in almost every pre-modern civilization. However, by its very nature, this science poses a certain difficulty to the modern scientific mind. This is because this science presupposes the acceptance of divine revelation and intellectual intuition as two fundamentally real sources of objective knowledge. It also presupposes the acceptance of other levels of existence than the physical and of the hierarchic reality of the universe. These presuppositions are found to be contrary to many of the basic assumptions of modern science.

The science of symbolism implies that natural objects are not to be regarded simply as facts as is done in modern science. Natural objects or phenomena that admit of empirical and mathematical study are also to be viewed as symbols. What this means is that the reality of a natural object is not exhausted by its scientific and mathematical content. Symbolic knowledge of natural objects is not only possible, but also is no less real than the corresponding scientific or mathematical knowledge. Muslim scientists of past centuries had shown that symbolic and scientific knowledge of natural things are not contradictory or unrelated. In fact, symbolic knowledge of nature helps to reveal the meta-scientific or metaphysical significance of scientific facts, theories and laws discovered through empirical study of the natural world. And in a number of known cases, it was the symbolic knowledge itself which inspired Muslim scientists to embark upon new areas of scientific study leading to original discoveries in those areas. A good example is of how Suhrawardī's twelfth-century metaphysics of light and cosmology based on light symbolism helped to bring about intense scientific activity in the field of optics in thirteenth-century Islam. Quṭb al-Dīn al-Shīrāzī and his student Kamāl al-Dīn al-Fārsī made important discoveries in this field.[8]

The harmonious relationship between scientific and symbolic knowledge of nature is well illustrated by Ibn Sīnā in his work known as *Oriental Philosophy*. In this work, scientific facts became transformed into symbols which were to act as guide posts for the traveler upon the path of spiritual perfection in his journey through and beyond the cosmos to the Divine Presence.[9] Ibn Sīnā had drawn the scientific facts in question from a wide range of sciences including mineralogy, biology, astronomy, physics, cosmology, sociology, and anthropology as these sciences were known to the medieval world of his time. Physical and astronomical realities of the universe of which this scientific knowledge is a description were no longer seen in this work as external objects and phenomena to be scientifically analyzed and manipulated. Thanks to the symbolic knowledge of nature, Ibn Sīnā was able to see these realities as part of a cosmos of symbols through which his spiritual journey to God must pass. Scientific knowledge of the physical world can, therefore, play an important role in the formulation of the idea of a spiritual journey through the cosmos provided that the traditional knowledge of symbols is present and accepted.

Since nature is regarded as a divine revelation it is a source for gaining knowledge of God's wisdom. Muslim scientists firmly believe that God's wisdom is reflected in innumerable ways

---

8. For a discussion of these discoveries, see E.S. Kennedy, "The Exact Sciences in Iran under the Seljuqs and Mongols," *Cambridge History of Iran*, vol. V, ed. by J.A. Boyle, (Cambridge, 1968), p.676.
9. See H. Corbin, *Avicenna and the Visionary Recitals*, trans. W.R. Trask, (Texas: Spring Publications, 1980).

in His creation. They study such things as natural forms, forces, energies, laws and rhythms not only to gain scientific knowledge as currently understood but also to arrive at a better knowledge of divine wisdom. Let us take the example of zoology. Muslim zoological studies were pursued with diverse ends in view. There was first of all the scientific study of the anatomy and classification of animals. Muslim classifications of animals were based on numerous criteria such as the nature of their habitats and the way they organize their defense from external attacks.

Muslim interest in animals also arose out of practical concerns, the most important of which is the medical. Considerable attention was given to both veterinary medicine and pharmacological uses of animals. Then, there was the study of animal psychology and physiology. Another major concern displayed by Muslim zoologists was with the spiritual, symbolic, and moral significance of animals.

What is of great significance from the point of view of our present discussion is the fact that there existed many individual scientists and treatises in Islam which testify to the unity of scientific and spiritual knowledge in the domain of zoology. In al-Jāḥiẓ, the ninth-century author of *The Book of Animals*, the most famous Arabic work on zoology, scientific, literary, moral, and religious studies of animals are combined. According to him, the primary goal of the study of zoology is the demonstration of the existence of God and the wisdom inherent in His creation. Al-Jāḥiẓ treated zoology as a branch of religious studies.

In the fourteenth-century zoological work of Kamāl al-Dīn al-Damīrī, entitled *The Great Book of the Life of Animals*,[10] we encounter another good example of the combining of spiritual, moral, religious and juridical, literary, scientific, and medical perspectives in studying animals. Al-Damīrī even dealt with the significance of animals in the interpretation of dreams, a discipline which is inseparable from spiritual knowledge. The injunctions of the *Sharīʿah*, the sacred Law of Islam, concerning dietary prohibi-

10. For a modern study of this work, see J. de Somogy, "Ad-Damiri's *Ḥayāt al-ḥayawān:* An Arabic Zoological Lexicon," *Osiris*, vol.9 (1950), pp.33-43.

tions related to animal flesh, have inspired the study of animals from a religious and juridical point of view. Muslim concern with religious and juridical status of animals according to the Divine Law of Islam provides one of the main frameworks for the unity of science and spiritual knowledge in zoology. Many Muslim scientists were interested in discovering the scientific justification for these religious dietary prohibitions.

Careful observation was made of animal behaviour and the inner qualities and the genius of a particular animal species with a view of deriving spiritual and moral lessons from that animal species. There is a metaphysical basis for the belief that animals have much to teach man concerning the divine wisdom and about his own inner nature. According to Islamic spiritual tradition, man is a total reflection of the Divine Names and Qualities, whereas the animals are only partial reflections. However, the reflections in animals are often more direct than those in man. Animals are symbols of cosmic qualities and of spiritual attitudes. By virtue of possessing both good and evil qualities, animals present themselves as moral teachers to man.

From the Islamic point of view, a true zoology or science of animals only emerges when all of these different aspects of animals are taken into consideration. There is unity of scientific and spiritual knowledge in this conception of zoology. The link between the two types of knowledge is preserved not only in zoological works but also in works of art. Muslim artists drew miniatures of various animal species, which successfully captured the inner qualities of these animals. By virtue of the link that exists between the inner qualities of animals and the spiritual world, these works of art serve a kind of spiritual function, namely to enable man to contemplate the visible world as a reflection of the spiritual world.

Nature as a Source of "Divine Laws"

One of the main features of modern science is its success in the discovery of more and more of what is called in Western intellectual history "laws of nature". The idea that the cosmos has its own laws is found in all civilizations. There is order and harmony in the universe. However, in modern science, the "laws of nature" have lost their spiritual and metaphysical significance. In fact, the "laws of nature" are seen by many people today as being opposed to the "laws of God" found in religion. This modern cleavage between the "laws of nature" and "the laws of God" has disastrous consequences for the unity of science and spiritual knowledge. If we wish to restore this unity in the modern world, then one of the possible avenues is through the reassertion of the metaphysical or spiritual status of the "laws of nature."

In Islam, there has never been any cleavage between the "laws of nature" and the "laws of God." The "laws of nature" too are divine Laws. All laws are reflections of the Divine Principle. God is the Law-Giver. He manifests His Will both in the cosmos and in the human domain through laws. In the human domain, God has prescribed a Law *(Sharīʿah)* for every people. The Islamic *Sharīʿah* is only the last to be revealed. While there are many different Divine Laws revealed to mankind in its history, which are spoken of in Islam as *nāwāmīs al-anbiyāʾ* (Laws of the prophets), there is only one Divine Law governing the whole of creation. This latter Law is called *nāmūs al-khilqah* (Law of creation).

Although we speak of a single Divine Law governing the whole cosmos, there are different sets of laws for different orders of creation. Even within the same order of creation, such as in the natural order, there exist different laws for different species of beings. The Quran itself speaks of each animal species as an *ummah* (religious community) implying that God has promulgated a law for each species of being. The Quran also speaks of each creature as possessing its own nature. The goal of Islamic science is to know the true nature of things as given by God. Islamic science also seeks to demonstrate the unity of the "laws of nature" as a reflection of the unity of the Divine Principle. To know the nature and law of each species of being is to know the *islām* or *manner of submission* of that species to the Divine Will. This is the Quranic way of looking at the unity of the "laws of nature" and the revealed Law of religion. According to the Quran, all creatures other than the human species are necessarily Muslims, understood in this universal sense, since they cannot rebel against their own nature. In the human order, those people are Muslims who submitted to the Divine Law which God has promulgated for them. Man alone among the creatures is capable of revolting against God's laws and his own nature. From the metaphysical point of view then, there is no difference in nature between the "laws of nature" and the revealed laws of religion.

The laws governing the different orders of creation are not of the same degree of fundamentality or universality. Some laws are more fundamental and universal than others. There is an hierarchy of universality of laws of creation corresponding to the hierarchy of the created order. For example, biological laws are more fundamental and universal than physical or chemical laws since the former laws concern the biological domain which possesses a higher ontological reality than the physical domain which gives rise to the latter kind of laws. But the biological laws themselves are subject to a higher set of cosmic laws which are spiritual in nature. If the attempt to unify all the known existing laws in physics and biology is progressively pursued and in an objective manner, then a point is reached whereby the higher, nonphysical orders of reality would have to be seriously considered and examined. In other words, there is a limit to the universality of physical laws.

Cosmological Knowledge as Source of Conceptual Framework for The Unity of Science and Spiritual Knowledge

In the foregoing discussion, I have dealt with some of the most important teachings of Islam, which provide the necessary philosophical and religious justification for the unity of science and spiritual knowledge. I asserted that this unity is realized when each of the particular sciences is organically related to the supreme knowledge of *tawḥīd.* But what is meant by this "organic relation" and the concrete manner in which it could be achieved need further clarification.

The various natural and mathematical sciences are particular sciences in the sense that they deal with particular domains of reality. The supreme knowledge of *tawḥīd* is a metaphysical science. It is the most universal science since it deals with the Supreme Reality which contains all things. Between the supreme knowledge of *tawḥīd* and the particular sciences there lies a body of knowledge called cosmological knowledge.

By cosmology, I do not mean the modern discipline known by the same name. Traditional cosmology, whether in Islam or in other civilizations, refers to that science which deals with the structure of the cosmos and its qualitative content. Insofar as cosmology deals with the whole reality of the cosmos, it is a universal science. In his famous treatise on the classification of the sciences entitled *Iḥṣā' al-'ulūm* (Enumeration of the Sciences), al-Fārābī considers cosmology a branch of metaphysics. He also maintains that from cosmology may be derived the principles of the particular sciences. Indeed, in Islam, cosmology plays an important role as a bridge between pure metaphysics and the particular sciences. Cosmology is a source of conceptual framework for the unity of science and spiritual knowledge.

What is meant by science being organically related to the metaphysical knowledge of *tawḥīd* is that the former is conceptually integrated into the latter type of knowledge. The particular sciences may be conceptually integrated into the metaphysical science of *tawḥīd* because the Divine Principle is the metaphysical source of the world of multiplicity dealt with by the particular sciences. However, the necessary "conceptual tools" for that integration need to be derived from cosmology.

Cosmology is competent to supply these "tools of conceptual integration" because its goal is "to provide a science that displays the interrelation of all things and the relation of the levels of the cosmic hierarchy to each other and finally to the Supreme Principle. Thereby it provides a knowledge that permits the integration of multiplicity into Unity."[11]

11. S.H. Nasr, "The Cosmos and the Natural Order," in *Islamic Spirituality: Foundation*, ed. S.H. Nasr, vol.19 of *World Spirituality: An Encyclopedic History of the Religious Quest* (London: Routledge and Kegan Paul, 1987), p.350.

Cosmologically speaking, the world of sense perception is only one of many levels of existence. Muslims develop many cosmological models, each of which having its basis on certain scriptural data. Each model may be identified with the use of one or more types of symbolism. For example, in the cosmological model of Muslim Pythagoreans, such as Ikhwān al-Ṣafā', a combination of numerical, alphabetical, alchemical, and astrological symbolisms is used to depict the levels and qualities of cosmic reality.

The Peripatetic model, such as that of al-Fārābī and Ibn Sīnā, makes use of the symbolism inherent in the geocentric scheme of Ptolemaic astronomy. The model of Ishrāqī philosophers employs the symbolism of light. The Sufi cosmological model of Ibn 'Arabī presents all cosmic qualities as reflections of the Divine Names and Qualities and each level of cosmic existence as a "Divine Presence." But regardless of the type of symbolism used, we may discern in all these models three fundamental levels of cosmic existence, namely the spiritual, the subtle, and the physical. This division of the cosmos is a qualitative or "vertical' one for it refers to three different levels of qualities.

Cosmology provides us with knowledge of how the three worlds are related to each other. The spiritual world is a principle of the subtle world and the latter a principle of the physical world. Cosmology therefore demands that the physical world be treated not as an autonomous domain which is cut off from higher orders of reality. It insists on the relevance of spiritual and subtle entities in the study of the physical world. For example, the traditional "ether" is a non-physical, subtle entity. Knowledge of this "ether" is essential to the understanding of the origin of the physical cosmos.

Similarly, living forms studied in the biological sciences are essentially related to the spiritual and subtle worlds. The question of the origin of life on Earth cannot be resolved in terms of physical entities alone no matter how deep we penetrate into the molecular world. Life is a non-physical entity. It is an animating principle or energy which has penetrated into the physical realm. Molecular activities associated with living forms are not the source of life. Rather, they are particular manifestation of life on the physical plane. The Islamic cosmological principle, which is essential to the understanding of the mystery of life, is the idea of the Universal Soul *(al-nafs al-kulliyyah)*. The Universal Soul is the "soul" of the natural order. It is to the natural order what the human soul is to the human body.

The Universal Soul, an entity which animates the whole cosmos, is what generates life in plants and animals. Plant and animal souls with their numerous respective powers or faculties are considered as so many faculties of the Universal Soul. The Universal Soul is itself created by God. Knowledge of the cosmic function, powers, and qualities of the Universal Soul, especially in relation to the natural order, is indispensable for the intergration of the biological sciences into the spiritual knowledge of *tawḥīd*.

It is beyond the scope of this essay to go into a discussion of all the relevant cosmological principles. The examples I have given are sufficient to demonstrate the importance of cosmology as a source of conceptual framework for the unity of science and spiritual knowledge.

Conclusion

There is a need to revive traditional cosmology in the modern world. This cosmology has an important role to play in any proposed project aimed at realizing the unity of science and spiritual knowledge. The revival of traditional cosmology does not call for the abandonment or neglect of the experimental method and modern tools of scientific research and inquiry, which have proved so successful in the quantitative study of nature. But it does call for fundamental changes in the modern attitude towards reality and knowledge. The acceptance of traditional cosmology has profound methodological consequences. It means that the modern scientific method has to drop its claim of being the sole way of knowing things. Other possible avenues to knowledge of the universe need to be acknowledged.

Moden science must come to terms with the historical fact

that there have been societies and civilizations which cultivated diverse ways of studying and knowing the natural world. This diversity of ways of knowing is not to be construed as a kind of "epistemological anarchy" as imagined by some contemporary philosophers of science. Such societies and civilizations have seen unity in this diversity, thanks to the traditional doctrine of the hierarchy and unity of modes of knowing.

The spirit of reductionism which has come to characterize modern science has impoverished the natural order. The revival of traditional sciences and the cosmological sciences on which they are based may help to bring about in modern man a consciousness of the richness of reality.

CHAPTER 5

The Atomistic Conception of Nature in Ash'arite Theology

Introduction

In Islamic intellectual history, we encounter several conceptions of nature, which differ from each other because they arose out of different perspectives of viewing and understanding nature. The most wellknown of these, and also the earliest to have been formulated, was the theory of nature associated with the theologians *(mutakallimūn)* of the Ash'arite school. It has been often referred to as the atomistic conception of nature, since it emphasizes the discontinuous and atomistic character of matter, space, and time. Our aim in this chapter is to provide an introductory discussion of several important features of this conception, including its treatment of the problem of causality and the related question of the meaning of "laws of nature."

General Remarks on Atomism

The idea of atomism had a long history in both Eastern and Western thought.[1] Out of the different philosophical and religious molds in which this idea has been conceived throughout that long history, have arisen such a wide variety of its formulations that, content wise, no single definition can adequately express and comprehend them.

From the classical atomic theory of Greek philosophical speculation to fifth-century atomism of Indian religious sects, from the atomism of *kalām* in ninth-century Islam to that of the European Renaissance and to the atomic theory of modern science, one fundamental idea, and the only one, that has remained common to all these theories is the idea of the finitude of the divisiblity of particles constituting the material world. This is assuming that those variants which convey the idea of the divisibility of substance *ad infinitum* are excluded. Otherwise, they have nothing in common, save the claim by each of them that it is the explanation of the nature and reality of the physical world.

Of course, one finds certain interesting similarities between some of them, as, for example, between Indian atomism and the atomic theory of *kalām,* or even between the latter and the atomic theory of modern quantum physics. Similarities in the former case have led certain scholars to postulate an Indian influence on *kalām* atomism,[2] in addition to an Epicurean origin for some of its ideas. However, neither of these claims has yet been conclusively established by modern scholarship. Similarities between *kalām* atomism and modern quantum physics have gained the attention of those contemporary historians of science, who are primarily interested in discovering the historical roots of modern scientific theories, or in examining in what way these earlier ideas anticipated the modern ones.

1. For the history of atomism, see L.L.Whyte, *Essay on Atomism — From Democritus to 1960* (London, 1961); also J.M. Baldwin, ed., *Dictionary of Philosophy and Psychology* (New York, 1940), vol. 1.
2. See Majid Fakhry, *A History of Islamic Philosophy*, pp. 32-34.

Whatever might have been the historical connections between *kalām* atomism and the various forms of atomism found in other cultures and civilizations, our main interest here is not in discussing it as a possible offshoot or as anticipation of one or more of the latter atomisms, but rather as an independent, integral philosophy of nature, which issues forth directly from the Islamic Revelation. More to the point, we are interested in understanding the atomic theory of *kalām* as one of several philosophies of nature formulated by Muslims.

The atomistic philosophy of nature is Islamic insofar as it has a Quranic basis. But it is only *a* and not *the* philosophy of nature in Islam, because it is based not upon the whole teachings of the Quran concerning nature, but rather upon a specific theological perspective contained in that revealed Book. There are other theological perspectives in the Quran, which, in fact, have been used by other intellectual schools to serve as the bases for expounding philosophies of nature distinct from that of *kalām*. This point is worth emphasizing. In essential terms, the debate between *kalām* and *falsafah* was not a debate between two world-views, one Islamic, the other unIslamic or less Islamic. On the contrary, it was a debate between two particular philosophical perspectives which both fulfill the fundamental criteria of Islamicity and which therefore equally qualify to be called Islamic.

Understandably, one may have a personal preference for one particular theologico-philosophical perspective over another. One's inclination and choice is influenced by one's intellectual constitution and background and a host of cultural factors. Thus there is the claim that *kalām*'s theological perspective is more in affinity with the psychological make-up of the Arabs who first originated this atomism.[3] This perspective of *kalām* will be dealt with further in a later section in this chapter.

3. S.H. Nasr, "Islamic Conception of Intellectual Life," in P. P. Wiener, ed., *Dictionary of the History of Ideas* (New York: Charles Scribner's Sons, 1973), vol. II, p. 642.

Muslim Atomism in Historical Perspective

The theory of atomism was first developed in Islam by the Mu'tazilah theologians during the first half of the third/ninth century. It is possible that the idea of atomism had already been discussed as early as the beginning of the second/eighth century, in relation to the fundamental problem of substance *(jawhar)* and accident *('araḍ)*. This possibility is suggested by certain arguments put forward by Ḍirār b. 'Amar, one of the earliest Mu'tazilite theologians, and a contemporary of Wāṣil b. 'Aṭā' (d. 131/748), the founder of the Mu'tazilah school. Ḍirār's arguments appeared to have been directed against the very basis of *kalām*'s atomic theory. He was said to be one of the few dissidents of this theory. He rejected the doctrine of the body as consisting of two distinct elements, atoms and accidents, and instead reduced the body to "an aggregate of accidents, which, once constituted, becomes the bearer (or substratum) of other accidents."[4]

However, it is quite certain that by the middle of the third/ninth century, atomism had become firmly established in the theological circles of Islam as a theory which commended itself as the antithesis of Aristotelianism. According to an account of early *kalām* atomism, as given by Abu'l-Ḥasan al-Ash'arī (d.330/941), the founder of the Ash'arite school of *kalām*, in his *Maqālāt al-islāmiyyīn*, such early ninth-century Mu'tazilite figures as Abu'l-Hudhail al-'Allāf (d. 226/840), al-Iskāfī (d.241/855), Mu'ammar ibn 'Abbād al-Sulāmī (d. 228/842), Hishām al-Fuwaṭī (a contemporary of Mu'ammar), and 'Abbād ibn Sulaymān (d.250/864) all accepted the atomic theory in one form or another.[5]

This atomism begun by the Mu'tazilite theologians was later refined and extensively developed by the Ash'arite school, especially by Abū Bakr al-Bāqillānī (d. 403/1013) who may be consi-

4. Fakhry, *Islamic Occasionalism* (London: Allen and Unwin, 1958), p. 33; also his *op. cit.*, p. 53.
5. Fakhry, *Islamic Occasionalism*, p. 34.

dered its outstanding "philosopher of Nature." After the fourth/tenth century it was the atomism of Ash'arite *kalām* which flourished in Islam, having as its exponents such famous names as al-Ghazzālī and Fakhr al-Dīn Rāzī (d.606/1209).[6] It has remained to this day the dominant 'philosophy of nature' in Sunni theology.

The science of *kalām* has its roots in the earliest theological and political debates in the Islamic community concerning such problems as free will and predestination, the question of whether the Quran is created or uncreated, the relation of faith to works, the definition of a believer, and many more.[7] All these issues arose out of specific internal factors and developments then existing within the community, that were both religious and political in nature.[8] These debates led to the emergence, during the first/seventh century, of various sectarian groups with distinct, definable views which distinguished them from the majority of the community. The most famous of these groups were the Murji'ites, Qadarites, and Khawārij. It was out of these early theological trends and manifestations that the first systematic theological school emerged, namely, the Mu'tazilah.

If *kalām* owes its origin to factors that were internal to the Islamic community, its development owes much to external factors. The first major external factor was the theological attacks against the very tenets of Islamic faith, carried out by such religious groups as Jews, Christians, and Manichaeans, as well as the Materialists, who were all intellectually armed with the tools of Greek logic. Another major factor was the introduction of Greek philosophical ideas into the community through translations of Greek works into Arabic. The challenge to Muslim thought posed by these two factors was already manifest as early as the beginning of the second/eighth century. It added a new dimension to the whole problem of thought, which had to be grappled with by the newborn *kalām*.

The nature of the new challenge is twofold, one methodo-

6. M.M. Sharif, *A History of Muslim Philosophy*, p. 226.
7. Fakhry, *A History of Muslim Philosophy*, pp. 42-44.
8. *Ibid*, pp. 37-41.

logical, the other doctrinal. At the methodological level the challenge involved finding rational answers to the fundamental problem of relationship between revelation and reason, of which the question of legitimacy of the use of logic or dialectical methods in theological discussions was but just one aspect. At the doctrinal level, the challenge involved the problem of identifying and formulating authentic criteria of orthodoxy or Islamicity in the face of conflicting claims to Islamicity.

As in the case of earlier Muslim responses to their internal challenges, there emerged a wide spectrum of reactions and responses from within the Islamic community to its external challenges. Within the Mu'tazilite school itself, which dominated the theological scene from the second/eighth century to the fourth/tenth century, the response underwent a transformation from what was initially simply a rationalization of faith to an adoption of rationalistic tendencies that were inherent in Greek philosophy of the Aristotelian school. Mu'tazilite rationalism was to lead, among other things, to a denial of the reality of Divine Attributes with the consequence that God was viewed more as an abstract philosophical concept than as a Reality Who is the fountainhead and basis of revealed religion.[9]

At the other end of the spectrum were the extremists of the literalist tradition, who were wholly opposed to any kind of rationalization of faith.

General Remarks on Ash'arite Theology

Ash'arite *kalām* originated as a reaction against these two diametrically opposed schools of thought, a reaction in which it sought to strike a middle course for the community. On the problem of the relationship between revelation and reason, al-Ash'arī succeeded in safeguarding the rights of interpretative intelligence, to use Schuon's words, without minimizing those of Revelation. Similarly, he presented a reconciliation between *tashbīh* (comparison or analogy) and *tanzīh* (abstraction or

9. Nasr, *op. cit.*, p. 641.

incomparability) in his conception of the Divinity by giving anthropomorphic qualities to God, while maintaining that these qualities should be abstracted, and were not to be understood in their literal sense. Likewise, as regards human freedom, he defined it in a way which was acceptable from the theological point of view, safeguarding both divine determinations and human responsibility.[10]

In fact, this spirit of "theological reconciliation" runs through most of his other doctrines, and thereby distinguishes him from both the Mu'tazilites and the literal traditionists. In our previous brief reference to the development of Ash'arite atomism, we have mentioned al-Bāqillānī, a student of al-Ash'arī, as one of the followers of this school most responsible for its refinement and detailed formulation. As regards the other Ash'arite doctrines, apart from al-Bāqillānī, it was al-Ghazzālī and also Fakhr al-Dīn Rāzī, who further elaborated on them to produce a more refined rational exposition.

Although the Ash'arites accepted the necessity of rationalization of faith, they were generally opposed to the rational methodology and speculation of the philosophers *(falāsifah)*. Undoubtedly, this attitude of theirs was mainly influenced by their desire to preserve the fundamentality and supremacy of revelation over reason. As they saw it, this important principle had been compromised by the philosophers, as a consequence of their rationalistic approach to even metaphysical (spiritual) knowledge.

In one respect, the Ash'arites possessed an independent spirit of intellectual speculation. Unlike the philosophers, they were not bound to any particular school of Greek philosophy. This spirit was productive of some of the severest criticism of Aristotelian physics. Consequently, the Ash'arites were able to develop many original ideas pertaining to the sciences of nature, particularly in the theory of atomism.

10. This whole passage is a paraphrase of Schuon's excellent summary of the Ash'arite theological position contained in his *Islam and the Perennial Philosophy*.

Ash'arite Atomism and Conception of Nature

Ash'arite atomism was the fruit of the direct application of a particular theological perspective embedded in the Islamic Revelation to the domain of nature. That application involved ideas and concepts drawn from many sources besides the Islamic ones. These "foreign" ideas and concepts were easily integrated into the theological perspective in question.

It is now time to explain what this "particular theological perspective" is all about. As the word "theology" necessarily implies, a theological perspective must be concerned with God. God has many Names, Attributes, and Qualities. The particularity of *kālam*'s theological perspective stems from the fact that out of so many Divine Names and Qualities, it chose to concentrate on just one of them for the purpose of constructing a religious worldview. *Kalām* seeks to depict the unlimitedness of Omnipotence almost to the point of ignoring all other Divine Qualities. The overwhelming motive for God's actions, according to al-Ash'arī, is "what He wills" and "because He wills."

Applied to God's activity in nature, this perspective gave rise to that important idea known in the West as *occasionalism* which has been defined as the belief in the exclusive efficacy of God, of whose direct intervention the events in nature are regarded as the overt manifestation or occasion.[11] Occasionalism implies that all things and all events in nature are substantially discontinuous by nature. The world is a domain of separate, concrete entities which are independent of each other. There is no connection whatsoever between them, save through the Divine Will. If *A* is connected to *B*, it is not because it is in their nature to be connected, but rather because God has willed them to be so. Every effect observed in nature is exclusively caused by God. Hence occasionalism also implies a denial of causality in the sense understood by the philosophers and scientists.

Atomism is therefore a direct consequence of this principle of substantial discontinuity of things. Thus Muslim atomism can

11. Fakhry, *Islamic Occasionalism*, p.9.

be said to have its basis in specific theological principles of Islam, which, in its intellectual history, have been mainly identified with the school of *kalām*. This answers Wolfson's amazement as to how atomism, "a discredited theory which has been rejected by most of the Greek schools of philosophy as well as the Church Fathers, could have found acceptance among the mutakallimūn."[12]

Atomism was taken very seriously by the *mutakallimūn*, because it was inseparably linked to their theology, so much so that, in Ash'arite *kalām*, its doctrinal status was transformed by al-Bāqillānī and other fellow theologians from being a mere premise in support of specific religious beliefs to being an essential part of the creed. Their interest in atoms and accidents was not scientific but theological. This was to "vindicate the absolute power of God and to ascribe to His direct intervention not only the coming of things into being, but also their persistence in being from one instant to another."[13] If it happened that certain elements of foreign atomisms fitted nicely into their theological framework, it was well and fine. Otherwise, those atomisms in themselves were of little or no interest to them.

How did the Ash'arites justify, religiously speaking, their rational speculation into the "metaphysics of atoms and accidents," as well as the particular atomistic doctrines which they had adopted? In his work, *Risālah fī istiḥsān al-khauḍ fi'l-kalām*, al-Ash'arī replies to criticisms made by the literal traditionists who considered discussion about such questions as motion, rest, body, accident, atom, and space an innovation and sin. He argued that the Prophet was not unaware of all these things, only that he did not discuss them, since problems concerning them did not arise during his lifetime. Moreover, there was no explicit injunction in the Quran, or from the Prophet, which prohibits discussion of such matters. On the contrary, al-Ash'arī reminded his critics, one can find the general principles *(uṣūl)* underlying

12. See Harry A. Wolfson, *The Philosophy of the Kalam* (Cambridge, MA: Harvard University Press, 1976), p. 467.
13. Fakhry, *A History of Muslim Philosophy*, p. 54.

these physical issues and problems explicitly mentioned in the Quran and the ḥadīths.[14] We may infer from these remarks of al-Ash'arī that the above problems, which we associate today with physics, were widely discussed during his lifetime. Since the discussions were not merely scientific, but involved issues that clearly touched upon the religious beliefs of Muslims, they necessitated the active participation of the religious scholars. And attempts had to be made to find answers to these problems on the basis of the general principles contained in the Quran and the ḥadīths.

In fact, wherever possible, al-Ash'arī quotes verses from the Quran and ḥadīths to prove his contention that rational discussion of atomism is religiously (scripturally) justified. For example,[15] he invokes the following Quranic passage to show that there is a scriptural basis for their definition of the accident *('araḍ)* as "that which cannot endure . . . but perishes in the second instant of its coming-to-be":

> Ye look for the transient things *(a'rāḍ)* of this world, but God looketh to the Hereafter
>
> (Chapter VIII, verse 67)

Generally, the whole Ash'arite approach to the problem of atomism was guided by religious considerations. Their approach may be summarized as follows. In the first place they formulated a general theoretical framework based on the two most important sources of Islam, namely, the Quran and ḥadīths. It was within this general framework that they sought to offer formulations of conceptual problems related to atomism, as well as their solutions. As regards the details, there were two possible sources or avenues open to them. The first of these were works on atomism from non-Islamic sources that were known to them.

---

14. Sharif, *op. cit.*, p. 225.
15. For more information on the various Quranic verses and prophetic ḥadīths quoted by al-Ash'arī, see his *Maqālāt al-islāmiyyīn* and *Risālah fī istiḥsān al-khauḍ fi'l-kalām.*

The second avenue was through their own speculative minds, relying on their reflective power and rational methods of inquiry, including elements of logic adopted from Greek philosophy. The necessary data for reflection and analysis came from the Islamic Revelation and non-Islamic atomisms. The result of this whole theoretical approach to the problem of the fundamental basis and structure of the world was an atomism which, in its totality, was unique, although, elementwise, we see similarities to, as well as divergence from earlier forms of atomism.

Nature and Characteristics of Ash'arite Atoms

The Ash'arites postulate the existence of indivisible particles which they express in Arabic (sing.) as *al-juz' alladhī lam yatajazza'*, literally meaning "the part that cannot be divided." These particles are the most fundamental units that could exist, and out of which the whole world is created. Accordingly, we will refer to them as the 'Ash'arite atoms.'

The world, which the Ash'arites define as everything other than God, consists of two distinct elements, atoms and accidents *(a'rāḍ)*. The atom is the locus which gives subsistence to the accidents. An accident cannot exist in another accident but only in an atom or a body composed of these atoms. Conversely, a body cannot be stripped of accidents, positive or negative, such as color, smell, life, knowledge, or their opposites.

The first major characteristic of the Ash'arite atoms is that they are devoid of size or magnitude *(kam)*, and are completely homogeneous. In other words, they are entities without length or breadth, but which combine to form bodies possessing dimensions. They therefore differ from the atoms of Leucippus and Democritus or those of Epicurus in Greek philosophy, which are always presented as having magnitude. This is an important divergence of Ash'arite atomism from its Greek antecedents.

Not surprisingly, Wolfson poses the following question: where did such a conception of unextended atoms come from?

For Wolfson, this "new idea" could not have arisen spontaneously in *kalām*, since "there is no conceivable reason, religious or rational, why Arabic philosophy should have departed on such a fundamental issue from its parent source."[16] And he finds it difficult to accept the view of such orientalists as Mabilleau and Pines, who have ascribed its origin to Indian atomism.

Wolfson is right in dismissing this view as mere conjecture, since it is lacking in historical evidence. But his own answer to the problem is no less conjectural. He could not throw away his suspicion that *kalām* must have inherited the idea in question from a Greek source. Unable to find support in the authentic writings of the Greek philosophers, he rests his hope in the spurious doxographies such as those preserved in Shahrastānī's Doxography of Greek Philosophers. However, the strongest claim he could finally come up with is to say that it was on the basis of these doxographies that the *mutakallimūn* were most likely to have made wrong inferences about the nature of Greek atoms![17]

In our view, there is no reason why we should deny *kalām* of originality in its formulation of the idea of unextended atoms, even if a similar idea existed earlier in Indian atomism. Contrary to Wolfson, we think that the Ash'arites had strong reasons, both religious and rational, for insisting on the above idea. The following argument is sufficient for the purpose at hand. The atoms cannot have magnitude because extension is a property of physical space, involving the idea of boundary or surfaces. But since space too is atomized, and their theology demands that the atoms be completely independent of one another, there can be no question of the atoms occupying physical space. The atoms, themselves non-material entities, exist in an imaginary space or void. Further, the Ash'arite theology necessitates the existence of atomic substances that could adequately serve as a basis for explaining the originatedness, ever-newness, and absolute independence upon God, of all things, physical as well as non-

---

16. Wolfson, *op. cit.*, p.473.
17. *Ibid*, p. 475.

physical, including all the qualities predicated of substances. In our view, the extended atoms, with all that are implied in the idea of extension, are not fundamental enough to meet this theological requirement.

The second main characteristic of the Ash'arite atoms is that they are determinate or finite in number. Thus, in opposition to all schools of Greek atomists, who believed in the infinite divisibility of matter, and who maintained that atoms are infinite in number, the Ash'arites rejected the infinity of atoms on the basis of the Quranic verse: 'And He counteth all things by number' (Chapter LXXII, verse 28). Here Wolfson agrees that there is a definite scriptural basis for *kalām*'s departure from Greek atomism.

The third important characteristic of the Ash'arite atoms is that they are perishable by nature. The Ash'arites maintain that the atom cannot endure two instants of time. At every moment of time the atoms come into being, and pass out of existence. Each atom's duration *(baqā')* is instantaneous. Its momentary existence is made possible through God's supervention upon it of the accident of duration, which, like all other accidents, is perishable. In the words of al-Bāqillānī, the accident "perishes in the second instant of its coming-to-be." This perishability of atoms and accidents is a direct consequence of their theological belief that God directly intervenes not only in the coming of things into being, but also in their persistence in being from one instant to another.

If the atoms and accidents are created and annihilated at every instant, then how do we explain the fact that, as far as our ordinary experience tells us, it is the same world that continues to exist? *Kalām's* answer to this question has been well summarized by Professor al-Attas:

> The world, after its initial existence, does not endure or continue to exist *(baqā')*, but passes out of existence *(fanā')*; it ceases to exist at every moment of time, and what we observe of its continuance in existence is in reality the continuous renewal of its similars. Thus at

> every moment of time the world is in need of existence, and what we observe of the world as such is that it is ever dependent for its existence upon the Truth most Exalted, Whose act of creation is perpetually bringing forth similar worlds from non-existence into existence. In this way we imagine the continuance of the same world in existence, whereas in reality such is not the case.[18]

The divine activity of "perpetually bringing forth similar worlds from non-existence into existence" takes place at the atomic level, and may be explained as follows. When God creates an atom of a body, He also creates in it the accidents that cast it into being. The moment this atom passes out of existence He replaces it with a similar atom by creating in it similar accidents, that is, accidents of the same species as the one subsisting in the preceding atom, so long as He wills the same body to continue in existence. If He wills otherwise, then He would cease creating the accidents in question.

All that we observe of generation and corruption, and change and motion in the meso world, including, for the Ash'arites, miracles, are the results of 'atomic phenomena' that are directly produced by this divine activity. One of the reasons why the Ash'arites adhered fervently to their atomism is that its theoretical framework is comprehensive enough to allow for a rational explanation of miracles.

If God wills a miracle to happen, for example, the instantaneous transformation of a body *A* into a body *B*, then He would cease creating the atoms bearing the accidents or qualities predicated of the body *A*. What He brings instantaneously into existence instead are the atoms bearing the accidents or qualities predicated of the body *B*.

One other aspect of Ash'arite atomism, which we have chosen to discuss here, is the atomic nature of time and motion. Corresponding to the bodily atoms are the atoms of time. The

18. Syed Muhammad N. al-Attas, *A Commentary on the 'Ḥujjat* al-*ṣiddiq' of Nūr al-Dīn al-Rānīrī* (Kuala Lumpur: The Ministry of Culture, Youth and Sports, 1986), p. 256.

general Ash'arite view of motion is that both motion and rest are 'modi' of substances. A substance which moves from one point of space to another is at rest in relation to the second point, but in motion in relation to the first. This is so because motion supervenes upon the body only when it has settled in its second position[19]. For at the atomic level we cannot speak of the translation *(intiqāl)* of the same atom from one point of space to another. Rather we should speak of its recreation at the second point, since it is annihilated in between. This means that the concept of distance in Newtonian physics is not applicable here. A corollary of this theory of motion is the affirmation of the existence of vacuum or the voids.

Causality in the Atomistic Perspective

As we have seen, the Ash'arites atomize matter, space, and time, as a result of which the universe becomes a domain of separate, concrete entities which are independent of each other. There is no connection between one moment of their existence and the next. The Ash'arites therefore deny that there is any horizontal nexus between things. In other words they deny the Aristotelian notion of causality. How does this segmented, divided, and discontinuous reality then find its connection and unity? It is through the Divine Will which creates all things at every moment, and which is the direct and sole cause of their existence and qualities.[20] There is unity and harmony in Nature because it is brought into being and governed by the single will of the One.

The Ash'arite idea of God as the sole cause of all things and of all events negates the role of secondary causes in nature. No finite, created being can be the cause of anything. It is not in the nature of things to possess a causal power or quality. The so-called power which natural objects, including human beings, seem to possess is not an effective power, for it is a derived power. The following passage from al-Ghazzālī's *Tahāfut al-*

19. Fakhry, *op. cit.*, p. 40.
20. Nasr, *Islamic Life and Thought* (Albany: SUNY Press, 1981), p. 96.

falāsifah (*The Incoherence of the Philosophers*) summarizes the views of the Ash'arite theologians concerning causality, in opposition to the philosophers:

> According to us the connection between what is usually believed to be a cause and what is believed to be an effect is not a necessary connection; each of two things has its own individuality and is not the other, and neither the affirmation nor the negation, neither the existence nor the non-existence of the one is implied in the affirmation, negation, existence, and non-existence of the other — e.g., the satisfaction of thirst does not imply drinking, nor satiety eating, nor burning contact with fire, nor light sunrise, nor decapitation death, nor recovery the drinking of medicine, nor evacuation the taking of a purgative, and so on for all the empirical connections existing in medicine, astronomy, the sciences and the crafts. For the connections in these things is based on a prior power of God to create them in a successive order, though not because this connection is necessary in itself and cannot be disjoined — on the contrary, it is in God's power to create satiety without eating, and death without decapitation, and so on with respect to all connections.
>
> The philosophers, however, deny this possibility and claim that, that is impossible. To investigate all these innumerable connections would take too long, and so we shall choose one single example, namely the burning of cotton through contact with fire; for we regard it as possible that the contact might occur without the burning taking place, and also that the cotton might be changed into ashes without any contact with fire, although the philosophers deny this possibility.[21]

21. Al-Ghazzālī, *Tahāfut al-falāsifah.* This whole passage is taken from S. Van den Bergh's translation of Averroes' *Tahāfut al-tahāfut,* E.J. Gibb Memorial Series, New Series 19 (London: Luzac and Co., 1954), pp. 316-317. One may also refer to N. A. Kamali's translation in al-Ghazālī's *Tahāfut al-falāsifah* [*The Incoherence of the Philosophers*] (Pakistan Philosophical Congress, 1963).

The concept of cause and effect and the idea of the necessary connection that exists between them is important to science and philosophy. In classical Greek philosophy as well as in medieval Jewish, Christian, and Islamic philosophy and science the Aristotelian notion of causality was widely accepted. In this notion explicit recognition was given to the role of finite, created beings as horizontal or secondary causes in nature. The philosophers distinguished between four kinds of causes, the material, the formal, the efficient, and the final. Even in modern science the idea of causality is of great importance, although it is no longer as comprehensive a concept as its medieval antecedent in that the efficient and the final causes are no longer taken into account in the explanation of natural phenomena.

The Aristotelian doctrine of causality is claimed to be based upon the nature of things. Each thing has its specific nature which determines its specific functions in the cosmic order. To summarize the views of the philosophers concerning causality we quote here a passage form Ibn Rushd's *Tahāfut al-tahāfut (The Incoherence of the Incoherence)*, which was written as a response to al-Ghazzālī's critique:

> To deny the existence of efficient causes which are observed in sensible things is sophistry . . . For he who denies this can no longer acknowledge that every act must have an agent. The question whether these causes by themselves are sufficient to perform the acts which proceed from them, or need an external cause for the perfection of their act, whether separate or not, is not self-evident and requires much investigation and research.
>
> And if the theologians had doubts about the efficient causes which are perceived to cause each other, because there are also effects whose cause is not perceived, this is illogical. Those things whose causes are not perceived are still unknown and must be investigated, precisely because their causes are not perceived . . .
>
> And further, what do the theologians say about the

> essential causes, the understanding of which alone can make a thing understood? For it is self-evident that things have essences and attributes which determine the special functions of each thing and through which the essences and names of things are differentiated. If a thing had not its specific nature, it would not have a special name or definition, and all things would be one — indeed not even one; for it might be asked whether this one has one special act or one special passivity or not, and if it had a special act, then there would indeed exist special acts proceeding from special natures, but if it had no single act, then the one would not be one. But if the nature of oneness is denied the nature of being is denied, and the consequence of the denial of being is nothingness.
>
> Further, are the acts which proceed from all things absolutely necessary for those in whose nature it lies to perform them, or are they only performed in most cases or in half the cases? This is a question which must be investigated, since one single action-and-passivity between two existent things occurs only through one relation out of an infinite number, and it happens often that one relation hinders another. Therefore, it is not absolutely certain that fire acts when it is brought near a sensitive body, for surely it is not improbable that there should be something which stands in such a relation to the sensitive thing as to hinder the action of the fire, as is asserted of talc and other things. But one need not therefore deny fire its burning power so longs as fire keeps its name and definition . . .[22]

So here we have the classic encounter of two minds, two perspectives, and two philosophies within Islam, one theological, the other scientific. Faced with this confrontation of perspectives, one is easily tempted to take sides as the past intellectual history of the Muslim peoples in the last seven hundred years or so has

22. Averroes, *op. cit.*, pp. 318-319.

clearly shown. We try hard here to resist this temptation. As far as we are concerned, both men were great thinkers. Both were honest, sincere, and devout Muslims. Both, in their own ways, made significant contributions to the past glory of Islam. More important still, both views on causality can be defended by appealing to the Quran.

Each perspective has a positive function to play within the intellectual universe of Islam, and each perspective caters to the intellectual needs of a specific sector of thinking people in the Islamic community. Together the two perspectives enriched Islam's intellectual culture. Both are living perspectives in the sense that in every age we can always find the two types of minds, the theological and the scientific, here typified by al-Ghazzālī and Ibn Rushd respectively, existing side by side and interacting with each other, sometimes creatively and at other times negatively, depending on the level of their intellectual tolerance. We may find them not only among Muslims but also among people of other cultures as illustrated, for example, by the existence of the Humean and Einsteinian minds in the intellectual culture of the West.

The theological perspective on causality seeks to explain the world and all phenomena, the "natural" and the "supernatural" or the miraculous, in terms of the divine omnipotence alone. In order to safeguard or glorify divine omnipotence, it denies the objective reality of causal powers in creatures, given to them by God as part of their respective natures. Apart from the phrase "God has power over all things", which one finds repeated in almost every page of the Quran, there are numerous verses which provide a clear scriptural basis for the Islamicity of the theological perspective. We produce here a few examples: "It is God Who causeth the seed-grain and the date-stone to split and sprout" (6:95); "It is He Who sendeth down rain from the skies" (6:99); "It is not ye who slew them; it was God: when thou threwest (a handful of dust), it was not thy act, but God's" (8:17).[23]

23. Further relevant verses include 56:63-64; 67:19.

In all these verses secondary, horizontal, or immediate causes appear to be negated by being absorbed into the Ultimate Cause which is presented as the direct and sole cause of all the phenomena in question. The last verse, which refers to divine help given to Muslims at the battle of Badr, is the most explicit in its denial of the power of causation in created beings.

The scientific perspective on causality seeks to explain the world and all phenomena, including the miraculous, in terms of "natural causes" or by appealing to the natures of things, given to them by God. The Muslim philosophers never denied the reality of God as the Ultimate Cause of all things, nor did they ever deny the possibility of miracles, as often alleged by their opponents. But as men of science, they emphasized the importance of immediate and secondary causes, without, however, forgetting their divine origin. Their doctrine of a vertical causal chain, beginning with physical causes and ending up finally with the Necessary Being (God) as the First or Ultimate Cause, appears to its opponents as compromising or undermining the idea of God as absolute determination and freedom.

It can be said that in the perspective of philosophers like al-Farābī and Ibn Sīnā the world is dependent not only upon God's Will but also His Being. It is clear, however, that the aspect of God which they glorified is His Being and Intelligence (Knowledge and Wisdom). In order to safeguard and glorify this aspect of Divine Reality, they emphasized the objective reality of the essences and attributes of created things. "Creation," they maintained, "is the giving of being by God and the shining of the rays of intelligence so that each creature in the Universe is related to its Divine Source by its being and its intelligence."[24]

The attitude of the philosophers toward miracles or "supernatural" events may be best illustrated by the following anecdote. It was reported in traditional Muslim sources that in a meeting between Ibn Sīnā and Abū Sa'īd, a Sufi, in a bath house, the latter asked our philosopher-scientist if it were true that a heavy body seeks the center of the earth. Ibn Sīnā replied

24. Nasr, *Islamic Cosmological Doctrines*, p. 213.

that this was absolutely true. Abū Sa'īd subsequently took up his metal vase and threw it into the air, whereupon instead of falling down it stayed up in the air. "What is the reason for this?" he asked. Ibn Sīnā answered that the natural motion would be the fall of the vase but that a violent force was preventing this natural motion. "What is this violent force?" asked Abū Sa'īd. "Your soul!" replied Ibn Sīnā, "which acts upon this."[25]

Ibn Sīnā's answer is most instructive. Here we have the typical traditional Muslim scientific mind at work! He did not attribute the miraculous event to the direct intervention of divine power. He explained it instead as the effect of a "natural" cause in the form of an invisible, violent force. Obviously then, by "natural cause," we do not mean here the same thing as it is understood in modern materialistic philosophy. In contrast to their modern counterparts who seek to explain the "higher" in terms of the "lower," traditional Muslim scientists identify the essential causes of things with principles that are higher, on the ontological scale, than the things explained. To explain miracles "naturally" or scientifically, they extend the domain of natural causal powers beyond the physical and subtle worlds to include entities described as having superior natures and of which the miracles are perceived as the immediate effects. Thus in the anecdote Ibn Sīnā identifies the cause of Abū Sa'īd's miracle with an invisible force radiating from the latter's soul, whose nature is superior enough to subdue the gravitational pull of the earth.

The philosophers' treatment of the phenomenon of revelation experienced by the Prophet provides another good illustration of their "scientific" attitude toward miracles and, more generally, causality. The revelation of the Quran is generally regarded by Muslims as the Prophet's greatest miracle. And yet, as explained by the philosophers in their treatises on faculty psychology,[26] this "greatest miracle" is to be attributed to the

25. *Ibid*, p. 194.

26. For a detailed discussion of the philosophers' theory of revelation within the framework of faculty psychology, see O. Bakar, *Classification of Knowledge in Islam*, chapters 2 and 3.

superior nature of the Prophet's intellect. They maintained that, by nature, the prophetic intellect is superior to all other human intellects, and is in constant, inner contact with Gabriel, the Archangel of Revelation. It is by virtue of its perfect nature that the prophetic intellect becomes the recipient of divine revelation.[27]

To many Muslims, the attempt by the philosophers to formulate a scientific theory of revelation on the basis of psychological principles could only mean the downgrading of the miraculous status of this greatest miracle. In the perspective of the philosophers, however, what greater miracle can there be than the fact that a human intellect is in direct communication with God's archangel. And who can blame the philosophers for emphasizing the intermediary role of Gabriel, when no less an authority than the Quran itself provides a clear support for their standpoint. Says the Quran: "Verily this is the word of a most honorable messenger (i.e. Gabriel), endowed with power, with rank before the Lord of the Throne," (81:19-20).

The scientific perspective on causality too may claim its Islamicity on the basis of scriptural support. We produce below some of the relevant verses[28] from the Quran: "Glorify the name of thy Guardian-Lord Most High, Who hath created, and further, given order and proportion, and Who hath ordained laws and granted guidance" (87:1-3); "By the (winds) that scatter broadcast; and those that lift and bear away heavy weights; and those that flow with ease and gentleness; and those that distribute and apportion by command" (51:1-4); "God is He Who created seven firmaments and of the earth a similar number; *through the midst of them (all) descends His command:* that ye may know that God has power over all things, and that God comprehends all things in (His) Knowledge" (65:12).

27. Philosophers like al-Fārābī and Ibn Sīnā placed the prophetic intellect in the highest position in the hierarchy of the faculties of the human soul. They identified the prophetic intellect with the "acquired intellect" *(al-'aql al-mustafād)* in its highest perfection. See *ibid.* p. 64.
28. For more of the relevant verses, see, for example, 48:7; 82:10; 82:19.

The first and second passages confirm the philosophers' belief in the objective reality of natures, essences, or attributes of created things, and of their intermediary powers of causation. In particular, the second passage reminds us of one very important point. In the Quran God swears in the names of the natures or realities of things, implying that He Himself acknowledges their objective reality. The last passage is perhaps the most significant of all. It would not be an exaggeration if we were to claim that the whole passage provides the best possible summary of the philosophers' theory of causality. That part of the passage in italics, which refers to the "descent of the divine command" *(yatanazzal al-amr)* through the different levels of reality, provides a clear scriptural confirmation of their doctrine of "vertical causal chain." Moreover, it is made perfectly clear in the passage that the whole idea of this vertical causal chain is so that through it man will finally be led to acknowledge divine omnipotence and divine omniscience. This is the philosophers' way to the glorification of divine power and intelligence.

The foregoing discussion clearly shows that both positions are grounded on solid religious and rational foundations. There are some who think that the philosophers' perspective on causality has been dealt a serious blow by al-Ghazzālī's wellknown "counter-example of the fire." In denying fire its nature as a burning agent, al-Ghazzālī was no doubt influenced by the story of the miracle of Prophet Abraham mentioned in the Quran. Abraham was thrown into the fire by his polytheist enemies, but was not burnt. We were once personally reminded by Schuon that the same Quranic verse can be used as an argument against the theologians in favour of the philosophers.

The verses in question read as follows: They said, "Burn him and protect your gods, if ye do (anything at all)!" We said, "O Fire! Be thou cool, and (a means of) safety for Abraham!" (21:68-69). Schuon answers on behalf of the philosophers that if indeed fire is not a burning agent, then God would not have commanded the fire to cool!

In the light of the denial, by the theologians, of the Aristotelian notion of causality, it is pertinent to ask whether the idea of "laws of nature" has any meaning for them, for in natural science it is inseparably linked to the idea of causality. By "laws of nature," we mean the regular relationships, qualitative as well as quantitative, that exist between individual things in nature, as manifested in the uniformity of sequence of cause and effects. The Ash'arites do not deny the fact that natural phenomena display a remarkable uniformity. But in their view this uniformity is only apparent, not real, in the sense that it has no objective existence. It is no more than a mental construct or a habit of the human mind.

It is the habit of the mind to connect two phenomena together as cause and effect. For example, by observing the phenomenon of heat connected with fire, the mind thinks that it is the fire which causes the heat, whereas in reality it is God who wills the fire to be hot. Therefore in the perspective of the Ash'arites, "laws of nature" are not objectively real. They are mental constructs determined by the will of God and given the status of "law" by Him.

The Place and Significance of Ash'arite Atomism

As we have noted, Ash'arite atomism occupies an important place in Sunni theology. As a philosophy of nature, it differs from those conceived by the Peripatetic philosophers and the Shi'ite theologians in that the latter emphasize the substantial continuity of things and the importance of the causal chain in nature. However, it has many similarities to the Sufi conception of perpetual creation and annihilation of the world.

The occasionalism of Ash'arite *kalām* had a great impact upon Latin scholasticism as well as upon post-Renaissance philosophy of Descartes, Malebranche, and Hume. The man credited with the transmission of *kalām* to the Latin West was the famous Jewish philosopher and theologian, Mūsa b. Maimūn (Maimonides). His *The Guide for the Perplexed*, which provides a comprehensive account of *kalām*, was translated into Latin as early as 1220, and later served as the basis of Thomas Aquinas' critique of Islamic occasionalism. Interestingly enough, in his repudiation of causality, Hume presented arguments very similar to those offered by the Ash'arites, but without positing the Divine Will as the nexus between two phenomena which the mind conceives as cause and effect. Moreover, some of his examples were the same as those of the Ash'arites. This led certain scholars to assume that Hume must have been acquainted with Ash'arite atomism through the Latin translations of Averroes' *Tahāfut al-tahāfut* and the above mentioned work of Maimonides (its Arabic title: *Dalālat al-hā'irīn*).

Ash'arite atomism also possesses a great significance for contemporary historians and philosophers of science. This is because of its many similarities to the atomic theory of modern physics. One important consequence of this is that we are forced to re-examine some of the assumptions underlying the currently accepted views concerning the epistemological foundation of scientific methodology and scientific theories. For Ash'arite atomism suggests to us the possibility of another way of viewing and understanding nature, which is different from the one adopted in modern science, but which was successful in formulating a unified atomic theory that shares several common features with contemporary quantum physics.

CHAPTER 6

An Introduction to the Philosophy of Islamic Medicine

Introduction

By *Islamic medicine* is meant that system of medicine, which was conceptualized and cultivated by the Muslim peoples of diverse racial and ethnic origins and climes for more than a millennium since the birth of the first Islamic community until the present times. Like everything else which deserves to be called Islamic, Islamic medicine is primarily based upon principles which are derived from the basic teachings of the religion of Islam. It is the fruit of a conscious attempt by some of the best of Muslim minds at finding the solution to the problem of medical and health care of the Muslim community in conformity with the Islamic worldview in which God, man, nature, and society are closely intertwined and harmoniously interrelated. Islamic medicine is indeed one of the most important cultural manifestations of the spiritual, moral, and ethical values of Islam.

In speaking of medicine as a system modern scholars usually wish to refer not only to the body of medical knowledge proper and its numerous branches, but also to such related things as the organization of medical practice and health care in the form of various institutions. Viewed in this sense of a medical system, Islamic medicine must be ranked amongst the most developed and the most effective medical systems the world has ever known. During the long period of its history, Islamic medicine initiated new medical practices and gave birth to new medical and health institutions which made possible a more systematic organization and development of preventive medicine, medical education, medical ethics, drug production, registration and distribution, and therapeutic administration than ever seen before.

These new practices and institutions remain to this day a part and parcel of the very organization of the modern medical system. This is especially true in the field of pharmacy. In the words of Cyril Elgood, a noted contemporary historian of medicine,

> so soundly did the Arabs establish their Materia Medica that their pharmacy has survived longer than any other section of their whole system. Their method of distribution of drugs is virtually unchanged today. The Pharmacy is still a most important part of the hospital.[1]

Thanks to the scholarly efforts of several prominent Muslim physicians, most notably Ibn Sīnā, the whole body of medical knowledge known to the Muslims was put into systematic writing in works which have been widely acknowledged as among the greatest medical encyclopedias of all time. Especially with the help of classifications and the novel features of diagrams and illustrations, these medical encyclopedias facilitated learning and instruction, and consequently served as popular textbooks not only in the medical schools of the Islamic world but also in

1. C. Elgood, *Safavid Medical Practice (The Practice of Medicine, Surgery and Gynaecology in Persia Between 1500 A.D. and 1750 A.D)* (London: Luzac & Company Ltd.,1970), p. 30.

those of the West until as late as the nineteenth century.[2]

The Islamic medical system, at least during its Golden Age, has also demonstrated its remarkable power of synthesis and its flexibility or dynamic nature as reflected in its adaptability to change, as well as its scientific character through its ability to absorb what was best of the doctrines, methods, and techniques in the various traditional medical systems with which the Muslims came into contact. For example, when Islamic medicine spread to the Indo-Pakistani sub-continent beginning in the fourteenth century it got enriched by its encounter with the Ayurvedic medicine and other traditional Indian systems of medicine.

What is noteworthy, however, is the fact that during all these periods when the process of enrichment of the Islamic medical system was taking place the basic philosophical framework and foundation of Islamic medicine remained practically unchanged. The general principles on which the theories of Islamic medicine were based were viewed by Muslim physicians as philosophically and scientifically valid and applicable at all times. Unfortunately, the philosophy and theories of Islamic medicine have been largely forgotten or they are hardly understood by present-day Muslims save in the few places like the Indo-Pakistani sub-continent where Islamic medicine still exists as a living system of medicine. In fact, what we observe today is that while many of the external (physical) and organizational aspects of the Islamic medical system have survived to form an integral part of the modern medical system, the underlying philosophy of Islamic medicine is ridiculed and rejected by many men of science, including Muslims, as unscientific. Their reductionistic notion of science has led them to entertain the idea that modern medicine alone is scientific medicine. Consequently, they dismiss Islamic medicine as irrelevant to the medical and health needs of a modern society.

In this chapter, we take up the position that the principles underlying the Islamic theories of medicine need to be restated,

2. The two most famous medical textbooks of the Middle Ages are Ibn Sīnā's *al-Qānūn fi'l-ṭibb* (*The Canons of Medicine*) and al-Zahrāwī's *Kitāb al-tasrīf* (*The Book of Concession*).

popularized and given fresh application in the light of the crisis in contemporary medical and health care. The main consideration in rediscovering and reviving the Islamic philosophy of medicine is not theoretical or academic. Rather, it is the firm conviction that the Islamic medical system would be the system most suited to the Islamic way of life and the most effective in meeting the overall medical and health needs of the Muslim Community of every age. However, no significant revival of Islamic medicine could be expected unless there is a prior intellectual acceptance, at least by the scientific community, of its philosophy and the scientific theories which arise from that philosophy.

1. Medicine as a Branch of Knowledge within Islamic Culture

In Islamic as in Western culture, medicine is regarded as both a science and an art. More specifically, it is a practical or non-syllogistic art placed in the same category as architecture, agriculture, and navigation.[3] As a science, medicine appears in many Muslim classifications of the sciences as a branch of natural science (or philosophy) since it deals with particular aspects of the human body.

1.1 The subject-matter of medical science

As defined by Ibn Sīnā in his celebrated work, *The Canon of Medicine*, the medical profession's final authority for eight centuries, medical science is that "branch of knowledge which deals with the states of health and disease in the human body, with the purpose of employing suitable means for preserving or restoring health."

Thus, the most fundamental concepts of medical science

3. The notion of practical or non-syllogistic art as understood by many Muslim philosopher-scientists would embrace the modern idea of applied science. We have discussed the nature of this category of branches of knowledge in our *Classification of Knowledge in Islam*.

are the concepts of health and disease. There are many different philosophies and theories of health and disease in the history of medical thought of the human race. Each philosophy is based on a particular conception of the human body,[4] and more specifically on a particular physiological perspective. Also, each philosophy has given rise to a distinct system of medicine. The Islamic theory of health and disease, including its physiological basis, is explained below.

1.2 The goal and role of medical science

The general aim of medical science, according to Muslim physicians, is to secure and adopt suitable measures which, with God's permission, help to preserve or restore the health of the human body. The normal state of the human body is the state of health. This is the state in which all the functions of the body are carried on normally, and which is characterized by the harmony, balance, and equilibrium of all the constituent elements and systems of the body. Illness or disease results from the disruption of this harmony and equilibrium when one or more functions or forms of the bodily organs are at fault. The role of medical science and the physician is to find and employ suitable means for the preservation of that normal state of health or for its restoration in cases where the body has been afflicted with disease.

The preservation of health brings into focus the importance of preventive medicine or prophylaxis. The restoration of health on the other hand pertains primarily to the task of therapeutic medicine. Thus, there are two main areas of concern of medical science: preventive medicine and therapeutic medicine. The Islamic medical system places great emphasis on both.

1.3 Religious valuation of medical science

Of all the practical sciences and arts cultivated by Muslims,

4. For a detailed discussion of the Islamic conception of the human body, see Chapter 9 of this book.

none had been accorded a more noble and esteemed position than medicine. Many among both religious and medical authorities in Islam considered the art and practice of medicine as "a religious vocation of the first order because it helps men and women to help others preserve and restore their health."[5] Human well-being is the goal of Islam. The Islamic notion of well-being incorporates the ideas of safety, wholeness, and integrality of both the human individual and the human collectivity, of which physical health is clearly a necessary and inseparable element.

Health is viewed in Islam in a holistic way with the consequence that Islamic medicine too is holistic in nature. One of the names of the Quran is *al-Shifā'* meaning "that which heals" or "the restorer of health." Muslims understand this health to refer to spiritual, intellectual, psychological, and physical health. All these different dimensions of human health were integrated and unified within the religious worldview of Islam. Thus, the goal of medicine is fully in harmony with the Quranic vision of human well-being.

Medicine has generally been r egarded by Muslims as a science whose roots are clearly established in the Quran and the Sunnah of the Prophet. The nobility and prestige of medicine in traditional Islamic society was further enhanced by the belief that this art was originally revealed to mankind through Prophet Idris.[6]

The high religious value accorded to medicine is also clearly reflected in that Muslim classification of knowledge, which is based upon ethico-legal considerations. According to the ethico-legal criteria of the Islamic *Sharī'ah,* medicine belongs to the category of *farḍ kifāyah* sciences. It is not incumbent upon every Muslim to learn this category of knowledge. Rather, it is obligatory upon the Muslim community as a collective entity to

5. F. Rahman, *Health and Medicine in the Islamic Tradition* (New York: Crossroad, 1987), p.39.
6. This belief was accepted by many Muslim medical authorities and historians of ideas like Sā'id al-Andalusī and Ibn al-Qifṭī, as well as by religious scholars, including al-Ghazzālī.

learn it. The principle asserted by the *Sharī'ah* is that it is necessary that there exist a sufficient number of Muslims who learn medicine to meet the medical and health needs of the community. If this principle is faithfully observed by Muslims, then they would be spared of the acute medical and health problems which befall them at the present moment.

By virtue of this special religious recognition given to medical science the physician came to occupy a highly influential and respectable position in Islamic society. But it is also true to say that the personality and intellectual traits and standing of the Muslim physicians have in turn helped to maintain and enhance the prestige of medical science and the medical profession. The Muslim physician is not a specialist like his modern counterparts. He is generally a person of wide learning, and he takes a great interest in many of the sciences. He is an intellectual in every sense of the word. He is generally the very embodiment of Islamic intellectuality. For as asserted by Nasr,

> the wise man or *ḥakīm*, who has been throughout Islam's history the central figure in the propagation and transmission of the sciences, has usually also been a physician. The relationship between the two is in fact so close that both the sage and the physician are called *ḥakīm*; many of the best-known philosophers and scientists in Islam, such as Avicenna and Averroes were also physicians.[7]

Befitting the great religious honour conferred by Islam on the medical profession it is only natural and appropriate that the Muslim society should have a high expectation of the physician. In general, the physician was expected to be "a man of virtuous character, who combined scientific acumen with moral qualities, and whose intellectual power was never divorced from deep religious faith and reliance upon God."[8] It goes to the credit of the Islamic medical system that the Muslim physicians generally succeeded in living up to that expectation.

---

7. S.H. Nasr, *Science and Civilization in Islam*, p.184.
8. *Ibid*, p.185.

2. The Scope and Divisions of Islamic Medical Science

Muslim physicians divide medical science into two main parts, namely the theoretical and the practical (see Chart I).

2.1 Theoretical medicine

Theoretical medicine is comprised of five major branches. These are:

2.1.1 **Physiology**

This science whose name *'ilm umūr ṭabī'iyyah* literally means the "science of natural affairs" (of the human body) is concerned with the functioning of all structures, organs, and parts of the human body viewed as a living organism. Muslim physiology which is based upon the humoral theory is fundamentally different in many respects from the physiology of modern medicine. The humoral theory will be discussed later.

2.1.2 **Anatomy**

This science (*'ilm al-tashrīḥ*) is mainly concerned with the structures of the human body and of its parts. However, as understood and defined by Muslim physicians, anatomy was a very much wider subject than the modern discipline known by the same name. Ṣadr al-Dīn 'Alī Isfahanī, a famous Persian teacher of medicine of the fifteenth century, defined anatomy as "the science of the individual parts of the body of animals and men, of the purpose for their creation, and of the signs of divine power and wisdom manifested in them."[9]

Thus, anatomy is closely related to physiology. In fact, the Muslim physicians refused to make anatomy a subject separate from physiology or even theology as clearly implied in the above definition. Anatomy was perhaps the most popular branch of medicine among Muslims in the sense that it was taught not only to medical students but also students of philosophy, theology, Sufism and law *(fiqh)*.

---

9. C. Elgood, *op. cit.*, p.129.

CHART I

CHART SHOWING WHAT ARAB (UNANI) SYSTEM OF MEDICINE DEALS WITH

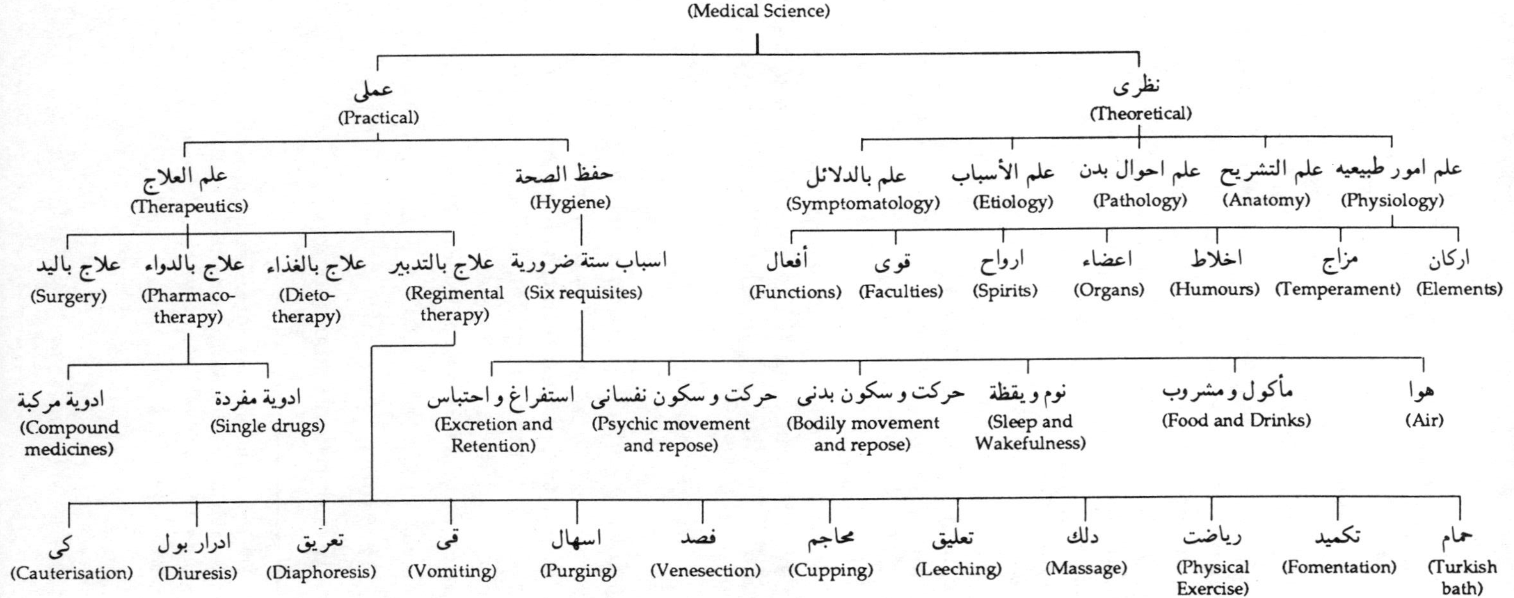

2.1.3 **Pathology**

Understood in its broadest sense, this science *('ilm aḥwāl badan)* deals with the states of the body. It is the study of the nature and manifestations of disease and of changes in function and structure in the human body.

According to Muslim physicians, there are three states of the body: (1) state of health, (2) state of disease, and (3) state of neither health nor disease. What is meant by this last category is that state of the body in which there is absence of both disease and complete health as in the case of old people or those who are convalescing, that is those who are in a state of recovery after an illness, operation or injury.

In his *Canon of Medicine,* Ibn Sīnā gives a detailed classification of diseases.[10]

2.1.4. **Etiology**

This science *('ilm al-asbāb)* is specifically concerned with the study of the causes of diseases or abnormal states of the body. It is therefore very closely related to pathology.

2.1.5 **Symptomatology**

This science *('ilm bi'l-dalā'il)* is concerned with symptoms of diseases. Muslim physicians relied a great deal on external symptoms such as pulse *(nabḍ)*[10] and complexion. Their ability to diagnose a disease through these symptoms, especially the pulse, was extraordinary. Ibn Sīnā refers to the ten features of pulse to which Muslim physicians usually pay great attention during the diagnosis of a disease. These are:[11]

(1) quantity

(2) force

(3) duration of movement

---

10. The most basic division of diseases is the division into simple and complex diseases. See Hakim Mohammed Abdur Razzack and Ummul Fazal, *Report on Arab (Yunani) Medicine and the State of Kuwait,* 1977, p.12.
11. *Ibid.*

(4) condition of vessel wall, whether it is soft or hard
(5) volume
(6) duration of rest period
(7) palpitation of the pulse
(8) equality and inequality
(9) balance of the pulse
(10) rhythm

Muslim physicians were also greatly aware of the importance of the digestive system in internal disorders. They therefore carried out physical examination of urine and stool in the diagnosis of such cases as urinogenital disorders, pathogenesis of blood, metabolic disorders and liver diseases.

2.2 Practical medicine

Practical medicine is comprised of two branches, namely hygiene *(ḥifẓ al-ṣiḥḥah)* and therapeutics *('ilm al-'ilāj)*.

2.2.1 Hygiene

The term *ḥifẓ al-ṣiḥḥah* means the preservation of health. The branch of Islamic medicine known by this name constitutes a very wide domain of study since the Islamic idea of the preservation of health is a very comprehensive one, certainly far more comprehensive than the one conceived in modern medicine. It embraces personal hygiene and public health and that which constitutes the domain of concern of social and preventive medicine.

From the practical point of view, hygiene, understood in the comprehensive sense indicated above, is the most important branch of Islamic medicine since this medicine is primarily concerned with the prevention of illness rather than with cure. The great emphasis placed on the prevention of illness in the Islamic medical system is a direct consequence of the teachings of the *Sharī'ah*. For Muslims, as we have already remarked, health is the natural or normal state in which God has created man. One prophetic ḥadīth gives the advice that one should preserve and value one's health, which is a divine gift, before one is afflicted with illness. Such a response involves all aspects of one's existence, spiritual, psychological, and physical.

Similarly, Islamic social philosophy, with its emphasis upon the wholeness and integrality of the human collectivity, has prescribed duties and responsibilities to be honored by society toward those of its citizens who are in illness. Thus, in Islam, illness is never viewed as a mere medical problem with perhaps certain economic implications, as it is, unfortunately, regarded by so many people today. Illness is a multi-dimensional phenomenon which should never be reduced to its medical aspect alone. There are many ḥadīths which emphasize the positive value of illness, and which point to its spiritual and social significance.[12]

Islamic teachings concerning illness in all its dimensions, especially the spiritual, psychological, medical, and the social have enabled traditional Muslim society to produce a healthy human ecology or sociocultural environment in which the sick and the suffering were relieved of much of the kind of psychological and economic burden which many of their modern counterparts have to painfully bear, particularly those in industrialized western societies. Islamic spirituality and its faith tradition, its social relationships and institutions, particularly the family, and the popular nature of the Islamic medical system all played a role in delivering the sick from this "psychological and economic" burden. There is even nobility in the way they responded to failures in finding medical cures.

As the appearance of many modern diseases has clearly shown, there is a very close link between life style and health. Chronic and degenerative diseases such as heart disease and cancer, stress-related ailments, including what modern Japanese call *karoshi*[13], sexually transmitted diseases (STD) such as syphilis,

---

12. For a discussion of the spiritual and social significance of illness in Islam, see F. Rahman, *op. cit.*, especially the chapter entitled "Wellness and Illness in the Islamic worldview," pp. 11-28. See also Chapter 9 of this book.
13. *Karoshi* is the modern Japanese name for death from overwork. See the article "Living to Grips with *Karoshi*" in *Time*, Jan. 30, 1989.

chlamydia, genital herpes, genital warts, gonorrhea and now the latest addition, namely AIDS, diseases related to drug abuse, and iatrogenic diseases, that is diseases produced by diagnostic or therapeutic procedures, all have to do with a life style associated with modern industrialized societies.

The fundamental constituents of any life style are (1) dietary habits and modes of food production and consumption, (2) sex habits, (3) work habits, (4) organization of the environment, and (5) general attitude toward health, illness, disease and therapy. Each of the categories of diseases mentioned above is related to one or more of these aspects of modern life style. STDs are clearly related to sex habits. Stress-related ailments, including heart attacks and strokes, are direct consequences of modern work habits. Iatrogenic diseases result from the lack of a holistic attitude toward health, disease, and treatment among the moderns. Some of the consequences of this lack of integrated approach to the causes and treatment of diseases are "the prevalence of unnecessary and often risky surgery, doctors' over-readiness to prescribe inappropriate or dangerous drugs, and overuse of dangerous diagnostic procedures."[14] It is widely known that some 80 percent to 90 percent of all cancers are caused by such environmental hazards as air pollution, smoking, food additives, pesticides and radiation. And overweight-related diseases, not mentioned above and which are today a major medical concern in the West, are closely related to the problem of diet and dietary habits.

In the light of this close link between modern life style and many of the modern diseases, one should perhaps reflect more on the wisdom embodied in the Islamic life style. The Islamic life style as a whole, which is based upon the teachings of the *Sharīʿah,* may be viewed as a form of preventive medicine. In fact, to all faithful Muslims, the various rules and injunctions of the *Sharīʿah* concerning such things as ritual cleanliness, food

14. John Ehrenreich (ed.), *The Cultural Crisis of Modern Medicine* (New York: Monthly Review Press, 1978), p.14.

and drinks, dietary, sex, and work habits, the organization of the environment, and medical treatment are all ordained by God so that men and their society can preserve health and prevent diseases and illness to the best extent possible. For this reason, Islamic medicine incorporates these religious teachings into its literature to become an integral part of the medical curriculum, or more specifically of the subject called hygiene and public health. In this connection, it should be noted the whole body of prophetic ḥadīths dealing with medical questions had been systematized by many Muslim writers under the name of the *Medicine of the Prophet (Ṭibb al-Nabī)*.[15] This body of knowledge serves as the religious basis of Islamic medicine. Medical education in Islam must always begin with the study of this book.

Islamic medicine has laid down six essential pre-requisites for the preservation of health. These six principles, usually referred to as the "Six Necessities" *(Sittah ḍaruriyyah)*, form the subject of discussion by many authors.[16] These are:

(1) Air

(2) Food and drinks

(3) Bodily rest and movement

(4) Sleep

(5) Emotional rest and movement

(6) Excretion and retention

(1) **Air**

Good and clean air is necessary for health. Included in the Muslim exposition of this principle is the question of the influence of climates and soils up on the health of the individual. According to Ibn Sīnā, a change of environment can help relieve patients of many diseases. To ensure that good and clean

15. See, for example, C. Elgood's English translation of this work in *Osiris*, 14 (1962), pp.33-192.

16. C. Elgood, *Safavid Medical Practice*, pp.17-18.

air is available to city dwellers, Ibn Sina strongly recommended that the city should have plenty of gardens and that the architectural design of city buildings be ecologically harmonious with its climatic conditions.

(2) **Food and drinks**

A discussion of this second necessity involves, among other things, the following: (1) what is good to be eaten and drunk, and by extension what food and drink to be avoided, (2) the amount that should be eaten and drunk, and (3) the proper times of meals.

Muslim physicians maintain that we should only consume fresh food which is free from putrefaction and disease producing matters. Drinking water should be pure. Ibn Sīnā, for example, recognized the medical value of natural water obtained from certain kinds of wells thanks to its mineral content. On the other hand, polluted water was recognized as a carrier of disease. According to Hakim Abdul Razzack, Ibn Sīnā was the first to recognize this fact.[17] Muslim physicians further maintain that what is good to be eaten and drunk is relative to the individual since each person has a unique humoral constitution.

Concerning religiously prohibited food and drink such as pork and alcoholic drinks, many treatises were written by Muslim p hysicians, which specifically discuss or contain discussions of medical and scientific justifications for the prohibitions. For example, al-Razi (d. 925), the greatest of Muslim clinicians, wrote the following concerning drunkenness and the effects of alcoholic drinks on both the soul and body of man:

> Chronic and habitual drunkenness is one of the evil dispositions that bring those indulging it to ruin, calamity and all kinds of sickness. This is because the excessive drinker is imminently liable to apoplexy and asphyxia, that filling of the inner heart which induces sudden death, rupture of the arteries of the brain, and stumbling

17. H.M.A. Razzack & U. Fazal, *op. cit.*, p.15.

> and falling into crevices and wells; not to mention various fevers, bloody clots and bilious swellings in the intestines and principal parts, and delirium tremens and palsy especially if there be a natural weakness of the nerves. Besides all this, drunkenness leads to loss of reason . . . Drink weakens the rational soul and stultifies its powers, so that it is scarcely able to undertake careful thought and deliberation.[18]

These kinds of treatises clearly demonstrate the unity of religious and scientific principles governing Muslim dietary habits.

(3) **Bodily rest and movement**

Perfect health requires both bodily rest and bodily movement, especially in the form of physical exercises. Also, the treatment of certain kinds of diseases and physical afflictions depends on either bodily rest or bodily movement. For example, Muslim physicians maintain that inflammation and fractures require complete rest to get properly cured whereas paralysis requires specific kinds of movement. The medical value of physical exercises was very much emphasized.

(4) **Sleep**

Sleep is viewed as an ideal form of rest, physical as well as mental. Lack of sleep will bring about dissipation of energies, mental weakness and digestive disturbances.

(5) **Emotional rest and movement**

Muslim treatment of this principle involves primarily a discussion of which emotional states of a person help or harm his health. Happiness is to be encouraged because it helps to keep a person healthy. Sorrow or suffering, anger, and emotional strain generally are to be avoided because these emotional states can

---

18. S.H. Nasr, *op. cit.*, p.206.

give rise to many diseases. Some of the diseases mentioned by Muslim physicians were tuberculosis, hysteria, and mental disorder resulting from a disruption in the functioning of the neurophysiological system.

Diseases which are caused by psychological factors are usually treated with psychological means. This method of treatment forms a part of the branch of Islamic medicine called "psychological therapy" which is known today under the name "psychosomatic medicine." Muslim physicians recognized the therapeutic value of music, pleasant company, and beautiful natural scenery in dealing with diseases generated by psychological ill health.

(6) **Excretion and retention**

Proper and normal functioning of the excretory system is essential for sound health. Included in the discussion of this principle is the effects of sexual intercourse on health. Any irregularity in the excretion of waste products of the body, whether this be excess, dimunition or blockage, can lead to disease. Examples of the natural means of excretion of body waste products are diuresis, diaphoresis, vomiting, faeces, excretion through the uterus in the form of menses, and respiration.

2.2.2 **Therapeutics**

The term *'ilm al-'ilāj* means the science of treatment or curative procedures.

The science is divided into four main branches:

(1) regimental therapy *('ilāj bi'l-tadbīr)*

(2) dietotherapy *('ilāj bi'l-ghidhā')*

(3) pharmacotherapy *('ilāj bi'l-dawā')*

(4) surgery *('ilāj bi'l-yad)*

According to a famous ḥadīth of the Prophet, "God has sent down a treatment for every ailment." Another version reads:

"There is a medicine for every ailment such that if a right medicine hits a corresponding ailment, health is restored by God's permission." In the practice of Islamic medicine, the search for the "right medicine" went hand in hand with a deep reliance on divine help. Muslim physicians were guided by the principle that the treatment of a particular ailment depends very much upon its nature and causes. Centuries of experience based upon careful observation and systematic rational deliberations have enabled Islamic medicine to accumulate a staggering wealth of knowledge concerning therapeutics, which deserves to be studied by contemporary Muslims. In many areas and aspects, there is much that the modern world could benefit from Islamic therapeutics.

(1) **Regimental therapy**

This category of treatment covers a wide range of special techniques and physical means, and processes of a generally simple nature. These include venesection or phlebotomy, cupping, sweating, diuresis, the use of turkish baths, massage, exercise, purging, vomiting and even leeching.[19]

(2) **Dietotherapy**

Diet plays a more important role in Islamic medicine than in modern medicine. As already pointed out, consuming the right food and drink and in the right amount as well as in the right manner is one of the six essentials of sound health. In the view of Muslim physicians, the effect of diet on both health and illness is generally more powerful than that of drugs.

The scientific basis of dietotherapy, according to Islamic medicine, is the theory of correspondence between the natures within the humors of the body and the natures in food. Like drugs and the humors, food possesses various natures in different degrees, thereby affecting the humoral constitution of the person

19. For further discussion of these methods of treatment, see H.M.A. Razzack & U. Fazal, *op. cit.*, pp.16-17.

who consumes it. Accordingly, Islamic dietotherapy seeks to cure certain diseases by regulating the dietary habits of the patient. Since the fundamental idea of therapeutics in Islam is to find a medicine which can aid the body's natural power of self-preservation, traditionally called *medicatrix naturae*, to fight off the disease in question, the task of a dietotherapist is to prescribe a diet whose nutritive and pharmacological properties are capable of strengthening the body's natural power or what we now call immune system. The following remarks by a contemporary nutritionist and naturopath are very much in the spirit of Islamic medicine:

> We know that the human body has all sorts of weapons at its disposal to fight off invading germs. There are many factors affecting how well these various weapons function, including previous exposure to similar germs, heredity, stress, emotions and *nutrition*.[20]

There are many Muslim works on dietotherapy which contain discussions of nutrition and pharmacological properties of food.[21]

(3) **Pharmacotherapy**

This is a field in which Muslims possess a remarkable wealth of knowledge and made many outstanding contributions to the advancement of medicine. In Islam, the principles of pharmacology and pharmacotherapy are very closely related to the humoral theory of medicine. The use of a particular drug is governed by three main factors: (1) the nature of the drug in question, (2) the nature of the ailment in question, and (3) the temperament of the patient. The guiding principle is that the drug to be prescribed should possess qualities opposite to those present in the disease in question.

---

20. Eu Hooi Khaw's article "Science and Health: Eating Right for Stronger Resistance" *New Straits Times*, 19th May, 1989.
21. Several of these works are mentioned by H.M.A. Razzack and U. Fazal, *op. cit.*, p.18.

Islamic literature on pharmacology contains a detailed treatment of the following:

(1) The nature, qualities and temperament of drugs

(2) Gradation of the potency of drugs

(3) Division of drugs according to quality

(4) Action of drugs on various systems or organs of the body

(5) Use of purgatives

(6) Administration of drugs dealing especially with

  (a) dosage and timings

  (b) modes of administering drugs

  (c) forms and shapes of drugs

(7) Correction of harmful effects of drugs

(8) Drugs substitute

Islamic pharmacology is very much concerned with the classification of drugs. We have already referred to the classification according to their qualities. On this basis, drugs are classified into four groups:

(1) drugs with hot temperament

(2) cold drugs

(3) moist drugs including lubricants

(4) dry drugs

However, the most wellknown classification is the distinction between simple *(mufradāt)* and compound drugs *(murakkabāt)*. The simples are those drugs which occur in their natural and simple state. This branch of pharmacology is today known as pharmacognosy. The compounds are drugs as they are usually understood today. The branch of Islamic pharmacology dealing with compounds is usually discussed under the topic *aqrabadhin* which means drugs catalogue, pharmacopoeia, or medical formulary.

It is important that the full significance of Islamic pharmacology be made better known to the modern world, especially in the light of the threat to human health posed by many allopathic drugs. As aptly pointed out by Nasr,

> Islamic pharmacology is the depository of the experience and observation of countless generations of human beings extending over aeons of prehistory. It seems even from the empirical point of view absurd that such a wealth of knowledge acquired through experience and observation should be so easily discarded by many, even when there is a clear choice, in favour of drugs the ill-effects of many of which are often forced upon the public without a close study of their long-term consequences for the human body as a whole.[22]

(4) **Surgery**

In Islamic medicine, surgery is usually disapproved unless it is considered absolutely necessary. Muslim surgery was limited to the various forms of cauterization, caesarean and eye operations, oral surgery and dentistry. Traditional osteology, which is still widely practiced today in many parts of the Muslim world, is not really a part of surgery (unlike in modern medicine) since the treatment of broken or disjointed bones in Islamic medicine generally does not involve operations.

3. **The physiology of Islamic medicine**

Much of what we have discussed concerning preventive medicine and therapeutics in Islamic medicine may be best understood and justified by referring to the physiology upon which the whole of that medicine is based. Both health and illness are defined in terms of the fundamental concepts underlying this physiology.

---

22. S.H. Nasr, *Islamic Science*, p.185.

Muslim physiology is based on the humoral theory which presupposes a knowledge of the four elements and the four natures.[23]

3.1 **Humors as "elements" of the body**

In the world of Nature, there are four elements and four natures. The four elements are fire, air, water, and earth; the four natures are cold, hot, dry, and humid. The elements are not to be taken as being identical to the physical substances of the same names, which are found in the physical world. Rather, they are principles of which the physical substances in question are manifestations on the physical plane in the same sense that we speak, for example, of angels as being cosmological principles of the natural world. Similarly, the four natures are to be viewed as principles of the physical natures or qualities of the same names, which can be sensually experienced by man in his environment. Each element has two natures: fire is hot and dry, air hot and humid, water cold and humid, and earth cold and dry.

The humors, which constitute the "elements" or the "building units" of the body are the primary body-fluids produced from digested food. There are four such humors present in the body: blood, phelgm, yellow bile and black bile. These humors, like everything else in the world of nature, are composed of the elements and natures in different mixtures, proportions, and combinations.

Like the elements, each humor has two natures: blood is hot and humid, phelgm cold and humid, yellow bile hot and dry, and black bile cold and dry. There is thus a correspondence between the natures in the human body and the natures in things found in the world of nature.

In the human body, the humors mix together to produce a certain humoral constitution or temperament. Each person pos-

23. For a discussion of the theory of the four elements, the four natures and four humours in a more detailed manner, see O.G. Gruner, *A Treatise on the Canon of Medicine, Incorporating a Translation of the First Book* (London, 1930); Hamdard Institute, *Theories and Philosophies of Medicine,* (New Delhi, 1962); S.H. Nasr, *op. cit.*, pp. 159-161; H.M.A. Razzack & U. Fazal, *op. cit.*

sesses a unique temperament which represents his healthy state. Thus, in each individual, health means the harmony of the humors relative to his own constitution. Illness means the disturbance of that harmony. To restore health the physician must therefore re-establish the state of equilibrium of the humors.

It is not just the body as a total entity, which possesses a unique temperament. Each organ of the body too possesses a unique temperament. The health of each organ, which is so essential to the health of the whole body, is likewise defined as that state in which its constituent substances are in the correct proportion to each other, both in strength and quantity, and are well mixed.

According to Ibn Sīnā, the diversity of temperaments is what accounts, biologically speaking, for the different durations of creaturely lives, that is, the differences in longevity. This diversity of temperaments is determined by many factors apart from the particular nature of each human body. Ibn Sīnā mentioned race, climate, age, and sex as among the factors.

The nature and characteristics of Islamic therapeutics is largely determined by the above theory of the humors. The fact that the temperament of each person is unique means that no two people suffering from the same kind of disease or illness can be given the same mode of medical treatment. It also means that the defense mechanism of the body or the responsiveness of the immune system varies from individual to individual. The correspondence between the natures in the human body and the natures in the external world of nature further means that, for the sake of his health, man must live in harmony with his natural environment. Serious attention was therefore given in Islamic medicine to the understanding of the actual temperament of each patient, to the factors which determine the uniqueness of the temperament of each body, as well as to the external factors which affect health and illness, like the six necessities earlier discussed.

In the light of the above definition of health and illness, diagnosis for illnesses then consists in searching for the ways in which the balance of the humors has been disturbed.

3.2 The biological systems of the human body

In speaking of the biological systems of the human body, we are referring to what the Muslim physicians call the faculties or powers *(quwwah)* of the body and the various organs and physiological functions connected with them. The three fundamental systems of the body are the physical *(ṭabī'iyyah)*, nervous *(nafsāniyyah)*, and vital *(ḥayawāniyyah)* systems. The unity of these systems is made possible by the presence in the body of a vital force or spirit *(rūḥ)* which, according to Muslim physicians, has its centre in the left ventricle of the heart.

The medical and biological use of the term *rūḥ* is to be distinguished from the theological use of it. The latter refers to the purely spiritual substance which is identified with the angelic world. The vital spirit is neither a physical nor a spiritual substance. Rather, it is a subtle body or a form of subtle energy which stands intermediate between the physical body and the spirit in its theological sense. The function of the vital spirit is to direct the organization of life of the body. The possibility of this function presupposes a certain level of refinement and perfection in the mixtures of the humors of which the body is comprised.

The vital spirit is of three kinds:

(1) **the natural spirit**

This is the vital spirit as located in the liver. It is hot and moist. It is associated with the functions of nutrition and growth and reproduction, which are performed by faculties of the same names and subservient faculties. It travels within the veins.

(2) **the psychic spirit**

This spirit which is cold and moist has its centre in the brain. It produces sensation and perception through the cognitive faculty and movement through the motive faculty. It travels within the nerves.

(3) **the vital spirit proper**

This spirit is hot and dry. Functioning through the heart,

which is its centre, it preserves life by preparing suitable conditions for the functioning of the biological systems associated with the natural and psychic spirits, and by traveling within the arteries to all organs and tissues.

The natural spirit gives rise to the physical system, the psychic spirit to the nervous system and the vital spirit to the vital system. Health of the body depends on the proper functioning of each system and its constituent elements and the interrelation of the three systems within the total unity of the body. Consequently, Islamic medicine gives much importance to knowledge of these biological systems.

3.3 The metaphysical and cosmological basis of Muslim physiology

The historical origin of the above physiological theory may be traced to the Greek medical theories of Galen and Hippocrates. However, the theory was easily accepted by Muslim philosopher-scientists to become an essential component of the general theory of Islamic medicine, because it is in conformity with the following metaphysical and cosmological teachings of the Quran and Ḥadīth:

(1) that there are hierarchic levels of reality, from the lowest, namely, the physical world, to the highest, namely, God who is the Creator of the universe, including man. The three fundamental qualitative divisions of the universe are the physical, the purely spiritual, and the intermediate world which stands in between, namely, the subtle world. In the Quran, these three divisions are represented respectively by creatures of light, creatures of fire, and creatures of earth.

(2) order, justice, balance, harmony, and equilibrium pervade the whole universe

(3) the unicity of the universe, which is a cosmological consequence of the metaphysical idea of the unity of God.

(4) man, who has been created in the "best of moulds" is a microcosm of the universe; he is a multi-dimensional and

multi-layered creature with numerous natures, faculties (Chart II), and qualities, and yet a unified living entity characterized by wholeness and integrality; he is body, soul, and spirit.

(5) human felicity, well-being, and health, understood in its all-embracing sense, is the fruit of a way of life, which is in harmony with God, the natural and social environment, and with oneself.

4. The need for a new synthesis

Islamic medicine in both theory and practice is the product of the application of the above metaphysical and cosmological principles to the study of health, illness, and cessation of life. There is no doubt that the philosophy of Islamic medicine is very much different from, and even opposed to, that of modern medicine. Islamic medicine, like many other traditional systems of medicine, is holistic in nature whereas modern medicine is reductionistic.[24] But like the latter, Islamic medicine is also scientific.

Reviving Islamic medicine in the contemporary world does not entail a total rejection of modern medicine. Islamic medicine, as is true also of the other aspects of the Islamic system of life, has never been outright rejectionistic in its spirit. Its spirit is one of synthesis. Obviously, many essential elements of the philosophy of modern medicine have to be rejected. The traditional philosophy of medicine we have just presented would be the one which best conforms to the beliefs and values of Islam.

---

24. Fritjof Capra has well summarized this reductionistic nature of modern medicine: "Modern scientific medicine has overemphasized the reductionist approach and has developed its specialized disciplines to a point where doctors are often no longer able to view illness as a disturbance of the whole organism, nor to treat it as such. What they tend to do is to treat a particular organ or tissue, and this is generally done without taking the rest of the body into account, let alone considering the psychological and social aspects of the patient's illness." *The Turning Point,* p.157.

CHART II

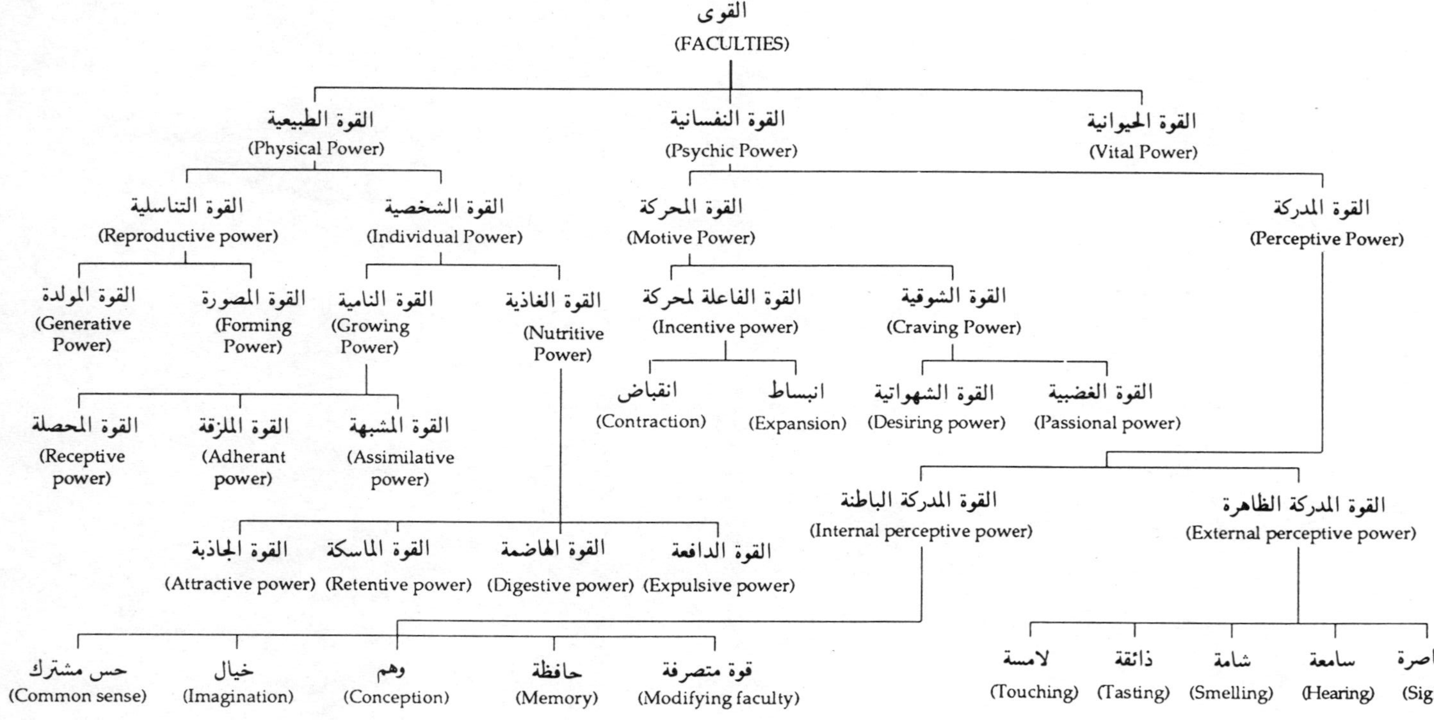

القوى
(FACULTIES)
القوة الطبيعية
(Physical Power)
القوة النفسانية
(Psychic Power)
القوة الحيوانية
(Vital Power)
القوة التناسلية
(Reproductive power)
القوة الشخصية
(Individual Power)
القوة المحركة
(Motive Power)
القوة المدركة
(Perceptive Power)
القوة المولدة
(Generative Power)
القوة المصورة
(Forming Power)
القوة النامية
(Growing Power)
القوة الغاذية
(Nutritive Power)
القوة الفاعلة لمحركة
(Incentive power)
القوة الشوقية
(Craving Power)
انقباض
(Contraction)
انبساط
(Expansion)
القوة الشهواتية
(Desiring power)
القوة الغضبية
(Passional power)
القوة المحصلة
(Receptive power)
القوة الملزقة
(Adherant power)
القوة المشبهة
(Assimilative power)
القوة المدركة الباطنة
(Internal perceptive power)
القوة المدركة الظاهرة
(External perceptive power)
القوة الجاذبة
(Attractive power)
القوة الماسكة
(Retentive power)
القوة الهاضمة
(Digestive power)
القوة الدافعة
(Expulsive power)
حس مشترك
(Common sense)
خيال
(Imagination)
وهم
(Conception)
حافظة
(Memory)
قوة متصرفة
(Modifying faculty)
لامسة
(Touching)
ذائقة
(Tasting)
شامة
(Smelling)
سامعة
(Hearing)
باصرة
(Sight)

But Muslims should derive the maximum of benefits from the achievements made by modern medicine in biological and medical knowledge, as well as in medical technology, to the extent that these are permissible. In other words, Muslims are called upon today to produce a new synthesis in the field of medicine within the framework of Islam. We believe that it is possible to integrate biological and medical knowledge discovered by modern scientists, insofar as these are true knowledge and not just hypotheses or even theories, into the philosophical framework of Islamic medicine since Islamic medicine is by nature synthetic, holistic, and scientific.

CHAPTER 7

The Influence of Islamic Science on Medieval Christian Conceptions of Nature

Introduction

Modern scholarship has furnished evidence[1] to prove beyond any doubt that the influence of Islamic science in the West began to manifest itself as early as the fourth/tenth century, and extended well into the post-Renaissance period. In our present discussion, we wish to restrict ourselves to its influence on thirteenth century Europe for two main reasons. Firstly, this period marked the peak of activity in the translation movement of the medieval period, which sought to render Arabic texts of Muslim scholars into Latin. And secondly, it was during this century that major intellectual changes took place in the West, changes which had a great bearing upon the subsequent development of western scientific thought. It was the golden age of scholasticism, which saw the synthesis of St. Thomas and men like Albertus Magnus, Roger Bacon, and Robert Grosseteste, who, within the matrix of Christian philosophy, were intensely

1. See D. M. Dunlop, *Arabic Science in the West* (Karachi: Pakistan Historical Society, 1958).

interested in the sciences of nature. The study of major intellectual changes during this active period of western learning would enable us, it is hoped, to be more appreciative of the extent and significance of the influence of Islamic science on medieval Christian conceptions of nature.

In order to establish the extent and significance of the influence of Islamic science on the thirteenth-century views of nature in the West, it is necessary to deal first, albeit briefly, with the following questions. Firstly, we must ask how much of Islamic science was transmitted to the Latin West by the thirteenth-century, and how that which was transmitted was received, interpreted and understood by its Latin audience. Secondly, we must consider what the dominant philosophies of nature in the Christian West were, prior to the entry of Islamic learning into its intellectual universe in the tenth century. The answers to these questions, which contemporary scholarship has made available to us, though certainly not the last words on the subject, provide us with the necessary materials to evaluate the extent and significance of Islamic influence. Accordingly, we will proceed to discuss these two questions beginning with the second.

Philosophies of Nature in the Christian West Prior to Islamic Influence

Every intergral religious tradition possesses both a theological dimension and a gnostic and metaphysical one, Christianity being no exception. In any study pertaining to the knowledge of nature in early medieval Christianity we feel it is important to bring out the clear distinction between these two dimensions which are termed respectively the exoteric and the esoteric. The type of science of nature which was profoundly Christian, both in its aims and presuppositions, was associated more with the contemplative and metaphysical dimension of Christianity than with the theological. It needs to be emphasized here that by gnosis we do not mean that kind of gnosticism which was banned as a heresy by the Christian Councils, but rather that unitive and illuminative knowledge which has a saving function and is inseparable from the love of God as a religious and spiritual experience.

By theology we mean a rational defense of the tenets of faith. Accordingly, if we wish to use the same term "theology" to denote both dimensions, as, in fact, many people tend to, then we insist on distinguishing between contemplative and metaphysical theology on the one hand and rational and philosophical theology on the other. In the history of Christianity, the first kind of theology is to be identified with many of the early Church Fathers among both Greeks and Latins, the metaphysicians and mystics of the Middle Ages such as Johannes Scotus Erigena and Hugh of Saint Victor, or with the sixteenth/seventeenth century German mystic, Jacob Boehme.

Eminent representatives of the second kind of theology include figures like St. Anselm of Canterbury, William of Auvergne, and St. Thomas Aquinas, the nominalist theologians of the fourteenth century such as William of Ockham, and also the leading spokesmen of the school of Neo-Thomism of the present century such as Jacques Maritain. The distinction between these two kinds of theology lies not so much in the realm of spiritual and religious truths which they seek to affirm as in the mode of their affirmations. On the question that is of particular interest to us here, both dimensions of Christianity were known to have produced conceptions of nature, which, although different from each other, were all characteristically religious. However, as we have previously asserted, it was within the contemplative and metaphysical dimension of Christianity that the greatest interest in nature, completely seen from Christian points of view, was to be found.[2] It does not mean that all the major theologians identified with this dimension have dealt with conceptions of nature in their theological formulations. For example, St. Bernard of Clairvaux and St. Francis of Assisi were two great theologians who certainly belong to this category, but the former, unlike the latter, was not at all interested in the study of nature.

2. See E. Gilson, *History of Christian Philosophy in the Middle Ages* (New York: Random House, 1955).

Conversely, we have a number of important figures in medieval Christianity who do not pass as theologians as this term is usually understood, but who were at once intensely interested in nature and deeply religious, and whose philosophical views best fit into that mystical and metaphysical dimension of Christianity we have in mind. One such figure was Roger Bacon, whose views on nature will be touched upon later. We have, therefore, considered their conceptions of nature as being no less Christian in spirit and content than those of the "pure" theologians.

Having identified where within medieval Christianity the greatest interest in nature was to be found, it would perhaps be pertinent to mention here the observation made by one scholar regarding the cultivation of the sciences of nature within the general religious matrix of Christianity as a whole. According to B. Bavink, except for a few Teutons, St. Francis of Assisi, the German mystic, Boehme, and Luther, Christianity has neglected the study of nature outside of the human being[3]. Certainly, the study of nature from a theological point of view did not occupy a central place in Christianity for reasons that were deeply rooted in that fateful historical encounter between early Christianity and the "cosmic religion" of the Greeks,[4] an encounter in which Christianity, in order to safeguard the transcendence of God in the face of rampant naturalism, had to draw a sharp line between the supernatural and the natural, or between grace and nature.

It is equally certain, however, that the field of natural study in medieval Christianity was not as barren and sterile as many modern historians of science have portrayed it to be. Prof. J. Oman, in his fully justified criticism of Alfred N. Whitehead for seriously ignoring religious interest in nature as an important factor in the origin and development of scientific interest, reminds us of the fact that centuries before the Reformation the

---

3. B. Bavink, "The Natural Sciences" in *Introduction to the Scientific Philosophy of Today* (New York, 1932), p. 576.
4. On this encounter, see J. Pepin, *Théologie cosmique et théologie chrétienne* (Paris, 1964).

north of Europe had witnessed the carving of natural objects and the daring feats of architecture in the forms of medieval cathedrals.[5] These achievements imply two things: firstly, the existence of a cosmology, and secondly, the existence of the science of natural objects and the techniques of making things, or art in its most universal sense. Scholars of traditional art and cosmology maintain that there exists a profound conceptual relationship between sacred art and cosmology. In their view, the medieval cathedrals represent a microcosmic model of the cosmos seen through a Christian vision.[6]

In contemporary history of science, it is seldom noted that medieval Christian knowledge of nature and of things natural, as was also true of classical Islam, existed on two different levels. First of all, there was the knowledge of nature at the popular level. This knowledge was based on survivals of such works as the *Historia Naturalis* of Pliny the Elder (A.D. 23-79) and other late popular encyclopaedias such as *Homiliae Novem in Hexaemeron* of Basil the Great (331-379) and the *Six Orations on the Creation of the World* of Basil's younger contemporary, Severianus, Bishop of Gabala. Also significantly contributing to this whole body of popular knowledge of nature were the writings of Basil's younger brother, Gregory of Nyssa, Isidorus (570-636), the Bishop of Seville, the great English monk, Bede (673-735), to whom posterity had given the title of "Venerable" in token of its admiration, and other similar medieval authors. It was also based on elements of Platonic cosmology derived from the *Timaeus* and often cited in the writings of some of the Fathers as well as by more popular writers.

On another level is the knowledge of nature associated mainly with figures like the mysterious Dionysius the Areopagite, who traced his lineage to Saint Paul and whose writings are considered by modern scholars as belonging to the fifth and

5. J. Oman, *The Natural and the Supernatural* (Cambridge University Press 1931), p. 479.
6. See Buckhardt, "Nature de la perspective cosmologique" in *Études Traditionnelles,* vol. 49 (1948), pp. 216-219.

sixth centuries, and the ninth-century Irish scholar, Johannes Scotus Erigena (810-877). There were also the sciences of nature and cosmologies associated closely with secret societies, the craftmen's guilds and organizations connected with the esoteric aspect of Christianity. It is partly because of the hidden and secret nature of this latter kind of knowledge, and partly because of its deeply spiritual character, that it is of little interest and consequently very little known to the mainstream of contemporary historians of science. Anyhow, the dominant philosophies of nature in the early medieval West, up to the times of its encounter with Islamic science and philosophy beginning in the tenth century, are to be sought from the body of writings and traditions associated with those two levels.

One important conception of nature which found general acceptance among men of learning of the time was that expounded by Dionysius. It was a conception based on the idea of the great chain of being and the idea of the universe as being hierarchic. It also viewed cosmology as being essentially linked to angelology in almost the same manner that Ibn Sīnā was to formulate and popularize in the Islamic world about six centuries later. It presented a view of the world in which elements of Neoplatonic cosmology were fully harmonized with scriptural data and Church doctrines. It was therefore a religious and spiritual conception of the universe. According to the Platonic and Aristotelian theories, the heavens consisted of nine concentric spheres which required movers of a more noble and spiritual character than the bodies moved, hence the idea of a hierarchy of spirits in the heavens. Dionysius identified these spirits with the various angelic beings mentioned in the Scriptures.[7] He arranged the angelic beings into a hierarchy of nine orders, grouped into three subsidiary hierarchies, and took these orders of angelic beings to be the movers of nine celestial spheres themselves. Above this hierarchy of angelic be-

7. S.F. Mason, *A History of the Sciences* (New York: Collier Books, 1962), pp. 68-69.

ings is God. Below it are the creatures of the earth: first man, then animals, plants, and finally the very dregs of the universe.

Dionysius's picture of the universe as hierarchical reality is indeed an elaborate one. Not only is the universe constituted of various orders of creatures in a hierarchy, but each of those orders is itself hierarchically arranged so that, for example, in the case of the first order of angelic beings, there is a chief Seraph and lesser Seraphim arranged in rank, just as on earth, says Dionysius, there is the Patriarch of the Church, his bishops, and so on, down a certain scale. Furthermore, the chain of creatures is a continuous one in the sense that the highest creature of one order is directly contingent upon the lowest creature of the next order above it, and the highest angelic being is itself contingent upon God. Although this Dionysian angelology as wedded to Neoplatonic cosmology was attacked by certain figures like John Philoponos ("the Grammarian") of Alexandaria, who instead of ascribing the motion of the heavenly bodies to the angelic beings postulated the existence of an inherent power or impetus originally given by God, it was to remain influential, especially within the sapiential dimension of Christianity.

With the name of Dionysius we may associate another important view of nature. This is the symbolic and contemplative view which was taken up in a more detailed exposition in the ninth century in the work of his Latin translator, Erigena. This is an important conception because, in contrast to modern science, it does not view natural phenomena as mere facts and as independent realities totally cut off from their divine roots or source. The reality of a thing is defined by its degree of separation from God,[8] or by its ontological status on the universal scale of beings. Creation is the very revelation or manifestation of God through his works. Dionysius calls this manifestation a "theophany" of the Divine Names. Since nature is a "theophany", it follows that our knowledge of it should enable us to know something about God. Creatures participate in various

8. Gilson, *op. cit.*, p. 83.

degrees in the reality of the Divine Names. For example, the whole of the created order is described as a circulation of the good from the Good, which is one of the Divine Names, and toward the Good. Similarly, divine love pervades the whole of creation, and it is through this love that all beings which radiate from God strive to return to Him. In this very perspective then, the cosmos becomes the theater wherein are reflected the Divine Names and Qualities. It thus serves as an icon to be contemplated and as a symbol of metaphysical truth.

The above perspective is the sapiential one. The corresponding doctrine of nature is metaphysical and cosmological, not scientific as understood in the modern sense. This perspective and these kinds of doctrines have been attacked by some theologians and philosophers as being pantheistic. Thus, both Dionysius and Erigena were accused of having expounded pantheistic views. This accusation appears, however, to be unjustified when one considers the fact that Erigena was fully aware of, and very emphatic on, the transcendent origin of the universe. Erigena, who is an important figure in any study on the relation between the sapiential perspective and the study of nature in the West, presented a comprehensive and detailed conception of nature and creation in his major opus, *De divisione naturae* (*Periphyseon* in its Greek title). This conception does not merely represent the personal views of Erigena, but rather represents a universal perspective of permanent value in the history of man's understanding of nature.

In this work, Erigena seeks to apply fundamental Christian doctrines to the study of nature and creation. For him, all things in the universe come from God and are created through Christ understood as the Logos. He interprets the opening phrase of the Scriptures, "In the beginning God made the heavens and the earth," to mean the creation of all the primordial causes in Christ.[9] For him also, the trinity manifests itself not only in the spiritual world but through all realms of creation: the *essentia* of

9. H. Bett, *Johannes Scotus Erigena, A Study in Medieval Philosophy* (Cambridge, 1925), p. 32.

the Father as the source of existence, the *sapientia* of the Son as the source of wisdom and the *vita* of the Spirit as the life of all things in the universe. Consequently, every creature is defined by a constitutive trinity[10], and hence the triune nature of man is comprised of the intellect *(nous)*, reason *(logos)* and sense *(dianoia)*. Man is also, for Erigena, a microcosm in whom is contained the whole of creation, not in a material or substantial but essential sense.[11] This spiritual and symbolic conception of nature is to influence even his astronomical system. He gives a more eminent place to the Sun because of its symbolic nature as the source of all existence and vitality and as the universal efficient cause in the cycle of the world.[12]

One more conception of nature which we will briefly consider here is the one associated with the popular view, and which is based more on the literal interpretation of the Scriptures. We may describe it as a theological conception of nature because it is the fruit of a deliberate attempt by theologians to give a rational defense and explanation to the various scriptural statements about nature in the face of contrary views enunciated by the "pagan" philosophers. In this "theological" explanation, which deals mainly with questions of cosmogony and cosmography, the scriptural data in point are for the most part not understood allegorically or symbolically but rather as the faithful depiction of the true physical reality. In this lies the seeds of the future conflict between theology and science in the West beginning with the Renaissance. How Islamic science and learning, or more precisely that component of it which reaches the West, helps to bring about the fertilization of those seeds is, in fact, our basic concern here.

Regarding the possibility of conflict between a religious Scripture and science on the question of knowledge of certain aspects of nature, the point to be noted is – apart, of course, from

10. Gilson, *op. cit.*, p. 120.
11. Bett, *op. cit.*, p. 58.
12. R. von Siebold and Erhardt, *The Astronomy of Johannes Scotus Erigena* (Baltimore, 1940).

the truly irreconcilable conflicts – not that a Scripture is false and science right or vice versa, but that each seeks to describe nature from its own point of view. A religious Scripture is above all a religious and not a scientific book, meant for a whole religious collectivity in which are to be found all categories of men. Its central function is to address the immediate needs of man as an immortal being in a kind of language that is easily understood by the average mind. It is therefore necessary that the description of Reality in Scriptures conform more to the exoteric view of things or to their immediate appearance than to the esoteric picture while at the same time conveying and revealing other levels of meanings that are of particular interest to the intellectually and spiritually gifted minds.

In fact, scriptural statements about nature are based upon the immediate appearance of things rather than on their true nature. So, if in the popular understanding of nature, theologians maintain such ideas as the tabernacle shape of the universe and the earth as the center around which revolve other planetary bodies, they are in a sense right. Moreover, it is religiously desirable since only by appealing to the normal human experience of reality can the religious and spiritual message of the Scripture be made transparent to all. That the earth is flat is obvious to all but that it is spherical is more difficult to grasp in the case of many people. Furthermore, the idea of the earth as the floor and of the heaven or the sky as the roof speaks powerfully of God as the All-Caring Creator and the Protector of human life. Men of science need to understand this particular religious motive and perspective. Among theologians who defended the popular views of nature, some were tolerant toward the scientific picture of the world depicted by the philosophers. St. Augustine, whose theology dominated early medieval Christianity, is one such figure. Others like St. Jerome and the followers of the Kosmos school of cosmographers were violently opposed to it.[13]

---

13. J.L.E. Dreyer, *A History of Astronomy from Thales to Kepler* (New York: Dover Publications, 1953), pp. 220-221.

Transmission of Islamic Science into the Latin West

We now turn to the other question, namely, concerning the extent of the transmission of Islamic science into the West between the tenth and the thirteenth centuries, and how this science was generally understood and interpreted. D.M. Dunlop, in his important survey[14] on the various studies carried out by scholars on the transmission of Islamic learning into the West, provided us with the following general picture of the translation movement in the West.

During the first period of the transmission, that is, in the tenth and the eleventh centuries, only certain texts of astronomy and mathematics were translated from Arabic into Latin. The source of these texts was Spain and the translation activity itself was linked with the schools of Lorraine in Germany. Concerning these schools the late J.W. Thompson wrote, upon reviewing the various evidences at his disposal, "I am convinced that the schools of Lorraine in the last half of the tenth century were the seedplot in which the seeds of Arabic science first germinated in Latin Europe, from which this knowledge radiated to other parts of Germany, to France, and especially into England."[15] In Spain itself, there appeared to have been an activity of translation and adaptation in Catalonia. Also in the eleventh century, but associated with a different center of transmission, namely South Italy, we saw the translation of various medical texts by Constantine Africanus.

The next period, which may be termed the middle period and which covers the whole of the twelfth century, saw the extensive publication and dissemination of all kinds of Arabic scientific works, including those of alchemy. It also witnessed the beginning of the translations of Muslim philosophical works. The main center of the translation activity were Spain and Italy and the major figures associated with it were Gundisalvi,

14. Dunlop, *op. cit.*
15. J.W. Thompson, "The Introduction of Arabic Science into Lorraine in the 10th Century" in *Isis,* XII (1929), pp. 184-193.

Gerard of Cremona and Plato of Tivoli. The names of Adelard of Bath and Stephen of Pisa should also be mentioned.

Then, we have the final period which stretches from the thirteenth century onwards. This was the period of continuous reproduction of Muslim works in almost all branches of learning until practically every writing valued by the West was rendered into Latin. During this period, the translation school at Toledo, which was one of the most important in the twelfth century, became even more active and emerged as the leading school for some time. Michael Scot was probably the leading figure during this period.

There is no doubt that the body of scientific and philosophical works being translated from Arabic into Latin during this period was considerable.[16] Many great scientists and philosophers of Islam, such as al-Kindī, al-Fārābī, Ibn Sīnā, al-Ghazzālī, al-Rāzī, to mention just a few, had some of their works translated, and they became famous in the Latin world under various Latinized names. From the point of view of our discussion in this chapter, it is very important to mention here the fact that most of these Islamic figures, as well as others not mentioned but who shared the privilege of having their works translated into Latin, belong in the Islamic intellectual universe to the school of philosopher-scientists *(falāsifah)*. This was only one of several intellectual schools which existed in the Islamic world up to the end of the thirteenth century, and which were known to have formulated definitive and distinctive views of nature.

Thus, one can say that the Latin West had known only one out of so many conceptions of nature to have been formulated in Islam, namely that of the Peripatetic school. The distinguishing feature of this school was its close identification with the Greek philosophical tradition, especially the philosophies of Plato and Aristotle, as seen, of course, through Muslim eyes. It is not surprising, therefore, that one of the major intellectual changes to have accompanied the acquaintance of the Latin West with

---

16. See Gilson, *op. cit.*, chap. on Greco-Arabian influences.

Muslim Peripatetic philosophy and science was the Aristotelianization of Christian theology. This in turn had several consequences upon the general Western view of nature.

The Peripatetic perspective seeks to integrate the cosmos into a pervasive rational system. Nature is viewed as a domain which must be analyzed and understood. Its knowledge is arrived at through the very method of ratiocination whose chief instrument is logic. In Islam, this school may therefore be identified with rationalism although Muslim rationalism is never divorced from faith and revelation. Observation and experimentation, which is at the heart of modern empiricism is, however, not a distinguishing feature of this school. On the contrary, as Prof. Nasr has shown in his numerous studies,[17] observation and experimentation stood for the most part on the side of the gnostic and mystical elements of the Islamic tradition while logic and rationalistic thought usually remained aloof from the actual observation of nature. There was, to be sure, much experimental activity coming from the Peripatetic school, but not to the extent that one can clearly associate this activity with the rationalism of that school in the same way one associates empiricism with rationalism in seventeenth-century science. Moreover, there were figures associated with this school, such as Ibn Sīnā, who also formulated conceptions of nature that were different from the characteristically Peripatetic or Aristotelian ones. These non-Peripatetic conceptions were contemplative and symbolical in character, and have always been identified with the metaphysical and mystical dimension of Islam.

We may sum up our discussion concerning the extent of the transmission of Islamic science into the West up to the end of the thirteenth century by saying that the sciences as developed by the Illuminationist school of Suhrawardī, the various schools of Sufism such as that of Ibn 'Arabī, and the neo-Pythagorean and Hermetic school of The Brethren of Purity *(Ikhwān al-Ṣafā')*, were almost unknown to the Latin West. Even the sciences of the

17. See, for example, his *Man and Nature*, p. 94.

Peripatetic school itself were only partially transmitted.

General Response to Islamic Science

Most of the transmitted scientific and philosophical works was rationalistic in nature. The non-rationalistic elements, such as alchemy and other occult sciences, did find their way into the West, but were confined to the various secret organizations like the Order of the Temple.[18] Consequently, a general impression was created in the Latin West that Islamic science and philosophy as a whole embodied a rationalism of the classical Greek type. This kind of understanding and portrayal of Islamic science helped to promote the rise of rationalism in thirteenth century Europe.

Within Islam, however, the place of rational philosophy was viewed somewhat differently. The Peripatetic school was certainly seen as expounding rationalistic tendencies. Al-Ghazzālī, for example, severely attacked these tendencies, as a result of which the intellectual life of Islam turned more and more toward the gnostic and illuminationist dimension associated with Sufism. Ibn Sīnā himself, toward the end of his life, "disowned" his rationalistic Peripatetic writings, and began to expound an "Oriental Philosophy" of a symbolic and contemplative nature. Ibn Rushd (the Latin Averroes) was regarded by many Muslims as the greatest exponent of rationalism among the scientists and philosophers. Still, they would say he was somewhat over-rationalized by his Latin interpreters. Not only was he over-rationalized but, as shown by Professor Harry Austin Wolfson in his interesting essay entitled "The Twice-Revealed Averroes,"[19] he was also misunderstood in his theological views to the extent that he was seen as expounding heretical views within Islam as well as being anti-religious in the general sense. Anyhow, he was instrumental, more than any other Muslim figure, in bringing about

18. See P. Ponsoyye, *Islam et le Graal* (Paris, 1957).

19. H.A. Wolfson, "The Twice-Revealed Averroes" in *Speculum*, XXXVI (1961), pp. 373-392.

the revival of Aristotelianism in the medieval West. Speaking of this influence, Professor Wolfson wrote:

> Despite the repeated condemnation of Averroes for his real or imaginary heresies, his commentaries were widely read and studied and copied. Moreover, they were imitated. The very same persons who damned him for his heresy – Albertus Magnus, Thomas Aquinas, and even Giles of Rome – followed his example and wrote commentaries on Aristotle in his style and manner; and they constantly quoted him. These new commentaries on Aristotle by Schoolmen, despite their freedom from religious error, did not replace Averroes. *They only created a greater interest in Aristotle, and with it in Averroes . . .* [20].

Influence of Islamic Science on Thirteenth Century Conceptions of Nature in the West

Having discussed the question of the extent of the diffusion of Islamic sciences in the medieval West and of how these sciences were generally received by the latter, we now finally turn our attention to the specific question of their influence upon the thirteenth-century conceptions of nature. We have already identified the dominant conceptions of nature in the West just prior to the entry of Islamic science. We wish to investigate how Muslim Peripatetic science and philosophy as interpreted by its Latin audience came to affect the development of those conceptions of nature. The overall picture of the development of intellectual thought in the thirteenth century West is by no means straightforward or easy to describe. David Knowles[21] speaks of the massive influx of various streams of thought into the intellectual universe of this century. Neoplatonic doctrines, Dionysian writings, Augustinian theology, and Aristotelian scholarship of the Jews,

20. *Ibid*, p. 382.
21. D. Knowles, *The Evolution of Medieval Thought* (Baltimore, 1962), p. 221.

Christians, and Muslims all contributed to this complexity. Their interactions resulted in major intellectual changes and, in the words of Knowles, in the "revolutionization of all existing modes of thought." There is no doubt, however, that the dominant stream of thought in this intellectual "revolution" was Aristotelian scholarship and philosophy. These interactions also resulted in various syntheses, the most important being that of Thomas Aquinas. In most of these syntheses significant traces of Islamic influence were clearly present.

Let us first consider the position of the symbolic and contemplative view of nature, which we have associated earlier with the names of Dionysius and Erigena. No Muslim writing dealing with this particular view of nature was known to have been transmitted to the Latin West. To the extent that this view of nature was prevalent and cultivated in the West, it hardly received any additional support and nourishment from Islamic sources in the way that thirteenth century Western rationalism received its external support from Muslim Peripatetic science and philosophy.

There never appeared in the West a school with which we may identify this vision of nature. But there arose, from the tenth to the thirteenth centuries, occasional figures like St. Hildegarde of Bingen (1099-1179), Hugh of Saint Victor (1096-1141), St. Francis of Assisi (1182-1226), and St. Bonaventure (1217-1274), all of whom expressed in various ways and in the most profound manner the Christian contemplative and symbolic vision of nature. Although these figures were great men who exercised much influence in other domains, the contemplative view of nature remained peripheral to the intellectual consciousness of this period. Indeed, it was increasingly pushed aside as the gnostic and metaphysical dimension of Christianity became ever more stifled in an increasingly rationalistic environment.

There was a new diffusion of Dionysian writings and Erigenian doctrines around the end of the twelfth century or the beginning of the thirteenth century. It was associated with such figures as Amaury of Bene (d. 1206 or 1207), a professor of logic and theology at Paris, David of Dinant, and a certain Mauritius of Spain.[22] They were said to have revived, among other things, the Erigenian doctrine of nature as "theophanies." We do not know whether their exposition of the symbolic and contemplative view of nature was authentic, since no original writings of theirs have survived. We presume their ideas had begun to gain currency in Paris in view of the fact that they warranted prohibitions from the provincial synod of Sens in 1210 and the University of Paris in its specially proclaimed sets of statutes in 1215. The latter prohibited at the same time the teaching of Aristotle's *Metaphysics*, his writings on natural philosophy, and commentaries on the subject.

The intellectual circle centering on these figures has been accused of expounding pantheistic views. Whatever the real merits or demerits of their ideas[23] might have been, the intellectual current associated with them was only a secondary one compared to the great tidal wave of Aristotelian philosophy. As to whether they were acquainted or not with some of the Muslim scientific and philosophical works, Gilson points out that there is evidence of an Avicennian influence, at least in the domains of psychology and ontology. The same appears to apply to St. Bonaventure who was aware of Ibn Sīnā's idea of the Agent Intellect as the illuminator of the human intellect. St. Francis of Assisi was known to have visited Muslim lands, but he showed little interest in the intellectual sciences.

Thus, we can say that, due to the accidents of translation, Islamic literature on the symbolic and contemplative conceptions of nature never became known to the medieval West so as to influence the latter's formulation of this important conception. Whatever authentic expositions there might have been, they were of purely Christian inspiration.

As far as metaphysical and cosmological doctrines of nature were concerned, however, there was a considerable influence of

22. See Gilson, *op. cit.*, pp. 240-243.
23. Gilson is of the opinion that this question is yet to be resolved in a definitive manner by contemporary scholarship.

Islamic science, especially of Ibn Sīnā's metaphysical cosmology. In the twelfth century, the Avicennian corpus provided the Latin world with a rich metaphysical cosmology, a branch of knowledge dealing with the metaphysical description of the structure of the universe. Central to this cosmology is the doctrine of the hierarchy of beings and of their emanation from the One. The corresponding cosmogony consists of a system of emanations of separate Intelligences, each producing a celestial sphere having a soul and a body, originating from the Primary Cause and descending right to the sublunary world and human souls. Scientifically and metaphysically speaking, all that the Latins had at their disposal before reading Ibn Sīnā was a partial knowledge of the *Timaeus*. The *Celestial Hierarchy* of Dionysius was also known, but appeared to have posed certain difficulties which they were unable to solve.

It was this cosmology of Ibn Sīnā that enabled the Dionysian angelology to be interpreted in a new cosmological light for, as we have seen earlier, the cosmologies of both men are essentially linked to angelology. All the different forms of Platonism diffused through the twelfth century found Ibn Sīnā's cosmology scientifically and metaphysically attractive. As Gilson puts it, the biblical notion of creation disappeared under the luxuriant metaphysics of the emanation of the world.[24] The response of the Christian theologians to this new development was to attempt at a synthesis of Avicennian metaphysics and cosmology and Augustinian theology. As clearly shown by Gilson, there indeed existed an "Avicennizing Augustinism" whose most important exponent was perhaps William of Auvergne (1180-1249).

In the above synthesis, the Avicennian cosmology was accepted in its outline but several of its important elements had to be eliminated in order to preserve the Christian theological perspective, or more precisely that of Augustine. The idea of eternal and necessary emanation was rejected for that would have compromised the idea of the creative act as the preroga-

24. Gilson, *ibid*, p. 240.

tive of God alone. Moreover, the idea is contrary to the biblical notion of creation *ex nihilo* in time. In opposing the idea of an eternal emanation of possibles governed by the necessity of the divine understanding, William of Auvergne argues that the will of God is eternal but free; His decisions are eternal but it does not follow that their effect is also eternal. God has eternally and freely willed that the world should begin in or with time. This was exactly the position taken up by the theological school of *Kalām* in Islam about two centuries earlier in its dispute with the philosophers.

Also significantly eliminated was the doctrine of the Active Intelligence as the illuminator of men's souls. It is perhaps more accurate to say "a modification of this idea", since the "Avicennizing Augustinians" sought to identify this Active Intelligence with God himself whereas Ibn Sīnā identified it with the Archangel Gabriel or the Holy Spirit. The criticism of William of Auvergne and other theologians of similar persuasion against these fundamental doctrines of Ibn Sīnā led eventually to the destruction of his angelology and cosmology.

Thus, paradoxically, it was among the theologians influenced by Ibn Sīnā that his harshest critics were to arise. Corbin tries to explain this paradox by saying that the representatives of "Avicennizing Augustinism" were not really aiming at a true synthesis of Ibn Sīnā's cosmology and Augustinian theology. Rather they were theologians who, under the influence of Ibn Sīnā, borrowed the terminology of Aristotle to formulate the Augustinian theory of illumination.[25]

In short, there were two principal Latin interpretations of Ibn Sīnā's cosmological doctrines. In the first, identified with that milieu of theologians called "Latin Avicennism" by Father Roland de Vaux, both doctrines mentioned were accepted as being in harmony with the cosmology and angelology of Dionysius. Among those identified with this group were the Archdeacon of Toledo and Dominicus Gundissalinus, the celebrated translator of Ibn Sīnā. In the second, identified with the "Avicennizing

25. H. Corbin, *Avicenna and the Visionary Recital* (Irving, 1980), p. 104.

Augustinism", the two doctrines were rejected for the sake of defending the Augustinian theological position as they had interpreted and understood it. Other famous figures representing this intellectual perspective include Albert the Great (Albertus Magnus) and Roger Bacon. Regardless of the differences that exist between these two principal interpretations, the corresponding conception of nature that resulted was still of a spiritual and religious nature.

Roger Bacon's view of nature deserves a special mention. In his scientific and philosophical views Bacon was greatly influenced by Ibn Sīnā whom he explicitly acknowledged as " the leader and the prince of philosophy after Aristotle", thus preferring him above Averroes. He undertook to integrate the Avicennian corpus, to the extent possible, into the Christian perspective. He was an illuminationist and a Pythagorean who tried to cultivate the sciences of nature in the matrix of supernatural knowledge. He conceived of mathematics in a symbolic sense. He has often been called the founder of the experimental method. But, for him, experiment is of two kinds. The first kind of experiment is the one made on external nature. This is the source of certainty in natural science. The second kind of experiment refers to a person's "experimental acquaintance" with the work of the Holy Spirit within his or her soul. This is the source of the knowledge of heavenly things which culminates in the vision of God.[26] His cosmogony, influenced partly by Muslim works on optics, constitutes another important conception of nature, and resembles that of the Illuminationist school of Suhrawardī earlier mentioned.

Finally, we will briefly discuss certain important developments affecting theological conceptions of nature associated with the popular view. In a way, we have already touched upon it when we were describing the attempt of the "Avicennizing Augustinism" to defend such ideas as the biblical notion of creation *ex nihilo* as understood in popular theological teaching.

---

26. A. E.Taylor, *European Civilization* (London, 1935), Vol. III, p. 827.

But this theology was illuminative, being Augustinian. In the thirteenth century, especially with Aquinas, another kind of theology, namely, rational theology, was fast gaining momentum. Aquinas created a remarkable philosophical synthesis – the famous Thomist synthesis – out of the numerous streams of ideas flowing in the Latin world of his time. The synthesis was carried out within the Christian theological perspective. Theories that conflicted with Christian teaching were thrown out. Those that appeared to him as logically sound and reconcilable with Christianity were incorporated. Still, as the researches of several leading scholars of medieval thought have clearly demonstrated, the end product of Aquinas' sifting and synthesizing was impregnated with theological, philosophic, and scientific ideas of Muslim thinkers made available in the Latin translations.

Al-Fārābī (*alfarabius*), Ibn Sīnā (*Avicenna*), al-Ghazzālī (Algazel), Ibn Bājjah (*Avempace*) and Ibn Rushd (*Averroes*), to mention only the most famous ones, all exerted a great influence on Aquinas, his teacher, Albertus Magnus, and other medieval Christian thinkers. Robert Hammond has shown that al-Fārābī's influence on Albertus Magnus and Aquinas is clearly visible in ontology, cosmology, psychology, and theology.[27] In the discussion of topics that were of great importance to his natural theology like the principle of causality and the "cosmological proofs" of God, Aquinas merely repeated al-Fārābī's proofs.[28] According to Gilson, Ibn Sīnā's influence on Aquinas in this particular area was even greater.[29]

The Aristotelian doctrine of causality in its enriched Islamized form introduced by al-Fārābī and Ibn Sīnā had a great impact on Aquinas' theological conception of nature as can be seen in his *On the Principles of Nature* and his commentary on the *Metaphysics.* Gilson claims, for example, that, prior to their read-

27. See R. Hammond, *The Philosophy of Al-Farabi and Its influence on Medieval Thought* (New York: The Hobson Book Press, 1947).
28. *Ibid,* p.21.
29. Gilson, *op. cit.*, p. 187.

ing of these Muslim philosophers, the notion of efficient cause was "always more or less confusedly present to the mind of the Christian theologians describing the divine act of creation."[30]

More generally, Gilson has observed the following impact:

> The metaphysical complex resulting from the combination of Avicenna's notion of efficient causality as origin of existences, with the Proclean universe described in the *Book on Causes,* will become very common about the end of the thirteenth century. The upshot will be a universe neoplatonic in structure but permeated throughout with the efficient causality proper to the creating God of the Old Testament . . .[31]

However, Aquinas, like al-Ghazzālī, rejected the Neoplatonic theory of emanation of the world in favour of the biblical doctrine of the "creatio mundi ex nihilo." We will not discuss further this rather wellknown Thomist synthesis. Instead we proceed to discuss another important intellectual current that flowed to the Latin West from Islamic Spain. This was the Latin Averroism.

In the second decade of the thirteenth century, less than twenty years after the death of Averroes, there began a systematic attempt to translate the commentaries of Aristotle into Latin. By the second half of the century, most of his commentaries had become available in Latin. As in the case of Ibn Sīnā, the reception of Averroes by the Christian thinkers was a mixed one. Soon, in the same century, there arose a school by the name of Latin Averroism which identified Averroes with Aristotle and brought to the fore issues of conflict between philosophy and religion and between reason and revelation. These Averroists presented him as the originator of the doctrine of the double truth, the truth of natural reason and the truth of revelation.

30. *Ibid,* p. 210.
31. *Ibid,* p. 211.

However, their claim was false. Averroes believed that reason and revelation lead to the same ultimate truth.In fact, he wrote a work entitled "On the Harmony Between Religion and Philosophy." One should also remember the fact that he was a doctor of law *(Sharī'ah)* and a religious leader of his community. What can certainly be said about him is that he was more rationalistic than other Muslim philosophers. He believed that all religious truths can be rationally demonstrated. It was this "rationalism" which became ever more influential, and which was later pursued in the Latin world independently of revelation.

The theological reaction against the rationalism and philosophism of Averroism, especially those philosophical positions that are directly opposed to the Christian Scripture, faith and wisdom, was intense and even harsh. The name of Averroes soon became a synonym for anti-religious thought. What is of special interest to us here concerns the very nature of this theological reaction. As noted by Gilson and other scholars of medieval thought, the reaction displayed an increasing tendency to employ the same instrument used by the Averroists against the theologians themselves, namely natural reason. This was clearly observable, for example, in the Thomist synthesis. In fact, Aquinas himself was attacked by the more traditional theologians.

This increasingly rationalistic tendency among the theologians, as a pattern of intellectual response to the rationalism of the philosophers, has some implications for the understanding of the scriptural views of nature. A scriptural statement on nature and its phenomena may be accepted either on the basis of faith, its rational demonstration, or the clarity of its symbolical and metaphysical meaning. What the pure rationalism of Averroism helped to bring about was the further eclipse of symbolic interpretations of nature, that intellectual knowledge which is helpful in resolving the conflicting claims of philosophy and theology. In the thirteenth century, the sciences of nature were still cultivated by men of faith and within the framework of Christian intellectuality. But what Averroism also helped bring about in the West was the sowing of seeds of secularization of knowledge and the cosmos and the seeds of confrontation between faith and reason.

Selected Bibliography

1. J. Baltrusaitis, *Cosmographie chretienne dans l'art du moyen-age* (Paris, 1939).
2. G.B. Burch, *Early Medieval Philosophy,* (New York, 1951).
3. ________, "The Christian non-dualism of Scotus Erigena" in *Philosophical Quarterly,* vol. 26 (1954), pp. 209-214.
4. H. Corbin, *Avicenna and the Visionary Recital* (New York, 1960).
5. P. Delhaye, *Medieval Christian Philosophy* (New York, 1960).
6. D.M. Dunlop, *Arabic Science in the West* (Karachi: Pakistan Historical Society, 1958).
7. E. Gilson, *History of Christian Philosophy in the Middle Ages* (New York, 1955).
8. ________ , "Les sources greco-arabes de l'augustinisme avicennant" in *Archives d'histoire et litteraire du Moyen Age,* vol. IV, 1929, pp. 5-149.
9. ________ , *The Spirit of Medieval Philosophy* (New York, 1936).
10. ________ ,*The Unity of Philosophical Experience* (London, 1938).
11. A. M. Goichon, *La philosphie d'Avicenne et son influence en Europe medievale* (Paris, 1944).
12. D. Knowles, *The Evolution of Medieval Thought* (Baltimore, 1962).
13. A. Miele, *La science arabe et son role dans l'evolution scientifique mondiale* (Leiden, 1966).
14. S. H. Nasr, *Three Muslim Sages* (Cambridge, Mass., 1964).
15. ________ , *Man and Nature: The Spiritual Crisis of Modern Man* (London, 1976).
16. J. Needleman, ed., *The Sword of Gnosis* (Baltimore, 1974).

17. J. Oman, *The Natural and the Supernatural* (Cambridge, 1936).
18. P. Ponsoye, *Islam et le Graal* (Paris, 1957).
19. H. Probst-Biraben, *Les Mysteres des templiers* (Nice, 1947).
20. C.E., Raven, *Natural Religion and Christian Theology* (Cambridge, 1953).
21. G. Sarton, *Introduction to the History of Science* (Baltimore, 1927-48).
22. C. Singer, *Studies in the History and Method of Science* (Oxford, vol. I.
23. J. Sittler, *The Ecology of Faith* (Philadelphia, 1961).
24. A. E. Taylor, *European Civilization* (London, 1935), vol III.
25. W. Temple, *Nature, Man and God* (New York, 1949).
26. H. Z. Ulken, "Influence of Muslim Thought on the West: Philosophical Influence before Descartes" in *A History of Muslim Philosophy*, ed. M.M. Sharif, (Wiesbaden, 1966).
27. von Weizsacker, *The History of Nature* (Chicago, 1949).
28. W. M. Watt, *The Influence of Islam on Medieval Europe* (Edinburgh, 1972).
29. G.M. Wickens, ed., *Avicenna: Philosopher and Scientist* (London, 1952).
30. G. Williams, *Wilderness and Paradise in Christian Thought.*
31. H. A. Wolfson, *Crescas' Critique of Aristotle* (Cambridge, Mass., 1929).
32. ________, "The Twice-revealed Averroes" in *Speculum*, vol. 36 (1961), pp. 373-392.

CHAPTER 8

'Umar Khayyām's Criticism of Euclid's Theory of Parallels

Introduction

The full name of 'Umar Khayyām as it appears in the Arabic sources is Ghiyāth al-Dīn Abu'l-Fatḥ 'Umar ibn Ibrāhīm al-Nīsābūrī al-Khayyāmī. According to the twelfth century historian, al-Bayhaqī, who knew Khayyām personally and whose *Tārīkh ḥukamā' al-islām* provides the earliest account of him, as well as according to most other sources[1], this accomplished Muslim poet and mathematician was born near Naishapur, where he spent the greater part of his life and where he eventually was laid to rest. So little is known of the life of Khayyām that the date of both his birth and death are contested by scholars.

1. Examples of sources which provide a different account of Khayyām's birthplace are the 16th-century *Tārīkh-i alfī* of Aḥmad Tatavī and the *Ṭarab-khāna* of Aḥmad Tabrīzī (15th century). These mention the vicinity of Astarābād at the north-east corner of the Caspian as his birthplace. See R.N. Frye (ed.), *Cambridge History of Iran*, vol. 4 (1975), article on "Umar Khayyām: Astronomer, Mathematician and Poet", p. 658.

The latest discovery of Khayyām's birthdate, 15 May 1048, thanks to the research done by the Indian scholar, Govinda Tirtha, and the Soviet scholars, A. P. Youschkevitch and B.A. Rosenfeld, on the basis of certain evidence furnished by al-Bayhaqī, may now at last resolve once and for all this issue.[2] And from evidence in the *Ṭarab-khāna* of the 9th/15th-century writer Yār Aḥmad Rashīdī Tabrīzī the two above Russian scholars have calculated the exact date of Khayyām's death as 12 Muḥarram 526/4 December 1131[3].

Khayyām was an influential figure in the Islamic world, not as the 'Omar Khayyam' of the *Rubā'iyyāt* of the Western fame, but as a great mathematician and philosopher-scientist. Al-Bayhaqī called him "a successor of Ibn Sīnā in different domains of philosophical sciences"[4]. In fact, Khayyām considered himself as belonging to the school of Ibn Sīnā. But in contrast to Ibn Sīnā, Khayyām apparently wrote little. "He was", says al-Bayhaqī, "niggardly in both composing and teaching, and wrote nothing but a compendium on physics, a treatise on Existence, and another on Being and Obligation, though he had a wide knowledge of philology, jurisprudence and history"[5]. His few works that have survived number about a dozen or so treatises on philosophy and the sciences[6]. The most important of these is his algebraical treatise entitled *Risālah fi'l-barāhīn 'alā masā'il al-jabr wa'l-muqābalah (Treatise on Demonstration of Problems of Algebra and Equation)*

2. See Swami Govinda Tirtha, *The Nectar of Grace, Omar Khayyam's Life and Works* (Allahabad, 1941), pp. 70-71; B.A. Rosenfeld and A.P. Youschkevitch, *Omar Khayyam* (Moscow, 1965).
3. Swami Govinda Tirtha, *op. cit.* and B. A. Rosenfeld and A.P. Youschkevitch, *op. cit.*
4. Govinda, *op. cit.*, pp. 32-33.
5. R. N. Frye, *op. cit.*, p. 661.
6. S.H. Nasr, *Science and Civilization in Islam*, p. 53 and p. 160. For a comprehensive bibliography of Khayyām, see B.A. Rosenfeld and A.P. Youschkevitch, "Al-Khayyāmi" in *Dictionary of Scientific Biography*, ed. C. G. Gillispie, (New York, 1970), pp. 331-334. Hereafter, this larger work is cited as *DSB.*

which deals with equations through the cubic order[7]. The nature of this work, which was the best of its kind in medieval mathematics, clearly demonstrates Khayyām's vision of the link between mathematics and the metaphysical significance inherent in Euclidean geometry[8].

Khayyām's next most important scientific contribution, particularly to the discipline of geometry, is his work entitled *"Fī sharḥ mā ashkala min muṣādarāt kitāb uqlīdus" (Concerning the Difficulties of Euclid's Elements).* This treatise contains Khayyām's criticism of Euclid's theory of parallel lines and theory of ratios. In Book I of this treatise, he re-examines the fifth postulate of Euclid concerning the parallel line theorem and attempts to justify it by proposing and proving altogether eight theorems. The theory of ratios and proportions is dealt with in Books II and III of the treatise. Khayyām made several important contributions to this theory in general[9]. It is here that he develops a new and more generalized concept of number by expanding the definition provided by Eudoxos through the use of continuous fractions as a means of expressing a ratio[10]. Khayyām shows that irrational ratios, those with non-terminating continuous fraction developments, and true numbers (i.e. positive integers) can be placed on the same operational scale and, on that account, almost admits the irrational to the status of a number[11]. In this chapter, however, we shall deal only with Khayyām's criticism of Euclid's theory of parallels and its historical significance as seen from the viewpoint of the development of modern geometry.

---

7. This work has been translated into several languages. See S.H. Nasr, *Islamic Science,* note 30, p.85.
8. S.H. Nasr, *Science and Civilization in Islam,* p. 160.
9. See E.S. Kennedy, *op. cit.,* pp. 663-664; S.H. Nasr, *Islamic Science,* p.81; B.A. Rosenfeld and A.P. Youschkevitch, *op. cit.,* pp. 326-327.
10. E.S. Kennedy, *op. cit.,* pp. 662-663.
11. S. H. Nasr, *op. cit.,* p. 81.

Translations and Commentaries of Khayyām's Geometrical Work

There have been translations of the treatise into several languages from the original Arabic. The earliest was the incomplete English translation by a Persian mathematician, 'Alī R. Amir-Moez, which was published in *Scripta Mathematica,* vol. 24, no. 4 (1959), pp. 275-303. It was based upon a text which was claimed to be copied in the year 616/1218 directly from the original handwriting of Khayyām, the date of which is recorded as 470/1077-78[12]. Besides being incomplete, this translation was without any commentary and no text of the treatise appeared with it. About two years later (1961), a Russian translation and commentary of the work, by the two Russian scholars previously mentioned, was published in *Omar Khayyam, Traktaty* together with a photographic reproduction of the Leiden MS on which it was based[13]. This was followed by Jamāl al-Dīn Homā'ī's 1967 Persian translation and commentary of his own reedited text of the Leiden MS[14]. Both the Russian and Persian commentaries provide an extensive analysis of Khayyām's criticism of Euclid's theory of parallel lines as well as a critical evaluation of Khayyām's influence upon the subsequent development of geometry in the Islamic world and, later, in the West.

However, it was the famous American historian of mathematics, David Eugene Smith, who first brought to the attention of western scholars the historical importance of Khayyām's work on parallel lines. He presented the first critical investigation of Khayyām's theory of parallels in comparison with that of Girolamo Saccheri (1667 - 1733), whose *Euclides ab omni naevo vindicatus* (1733) is generally considered as the first significant step

12. Omar Khayyam, *Discussion of Difficulties in Euclid,* trans. 'Alī R. Amir-Moez, in *Scripta Mathematica,* vol.24, no. 4 (1959), p.303.
13. B.A. Rosenfeld and A.P. Youschkevitch, *Omar Xaiiam, Traktati* (Moscow, 1961).
14. J.D. Homā'ī, *Khayyām-namah,* I (Tehran, 1967).

taken in the direction of non-Euclidean geometry[15]. Smith's historic recognition of the significance of Khayyām's theory was made possible by his discovery in Teheran (1933) of a copy of an Arabic manuscript attributed to another celebrated Persian mathematician and philosopher-scientist, Naṣīr al-Dīn al-Ṭūsī (1201-1274).

This manuscript contains an important part of Khayyām's above geometrical treatise as well as al-Ṭūsī's commentary on it. Smith's comparative study of Khayyām and Saccheri, insofar as their theories of parallels are concerned, clearly demonstrates the influence of the former upon the latter. According to Professor J. Ginsburg, Smith's collaborator in this study, his exhaustive research into the bibliography of the subject clearly shows that Khayyām was the precursor of al-Ṭūsi, Wallis, and Saccheri in laying the foundation of non-Euclidean geometry[16]. We will discuss this question later on in greater detail.

The circumstances which led to Smith's discovery of al-Ṭūsī's manuscript ought to be mentioned here, at least for the reason that these directly concern Khayyām. Smith was both a mathematician and a poet, and was very much interested in discovering an intrinsic relationship which might exist between the poetic genius and the mathematical mind through a study of the intellectual complex of those figures who are possessed with these two qualities[17]. He was attracted to Khayyām precisely because he saw him as a representative *par excellence* of this poet-mathematician intellectual complex. Smith, in fact, published a new version of Khayyām's *Rubā'iyyāt* (New York, 1933). It was in the course of searching for Khayyām the poet that he was also led to discover the mathematical treasures of Khayyām. In pursuing this fascinating theme, Smith was in fact dealing with a very rare intellectual species in the history of human thought. Islamic

15. D.E. Smith, "Euclid, Omar Khayyam and Saccheri" in *Scripta Mathematica,* vol. 3, no. 1 (1935), p.8.
16. *Ibid,* p. 6, note 5.
17. One such other figure is Sir William Rowan Hamilton. See *Scripta Mathematica,* vol 10 (1944), p.9.

civilization itself has produced a few other figures, besides Khayyām, who have been accomplished in both domains, but of this species Professor Nasr wrote: "Khayyām is perhaps the only figure in history who was both a great poet and an outstanding mathematician"[18].

There is no doubt that Smith's discovery of the historical significance of Khayyām's geometrical work must have inspired the earliest works of edition, translation, and commentaries of the treatise. It is enough to point out the fact that not long after the publication of Smith's essay (1935), in which he referred to the existence of a Leiden MS catalogued as *Kommentar zu den Schwierigkeiten in den Postulaten des Euklides* (470/1077-78), there appeared the first edition (1936) of the text. That work was undertaken by a certain T. Erani. And the first but incomplete English translation of Amir-Moez was published in *Scripta Mathematica*, the very mathematical journal with which Smith was so much associated.

Khayyām's Evaluation of Previous Commentaries on Euclid's Theory

Khayyām claims at the beginning of the *Sharḥ* that he was familiar with the numerous commentaries of his predecessors, both among the Greeks and among his fellow Muslims, upon Euclid's fifth postulate which he calls "the greatest doubtful matter in Euclidean geometry that has never been proved"[19]. Among the commentators mentioned were Heron of Alexandria (third century A.D.), Abū Ja'far al-Khāzin (d. between 961 and 971), Abu'l-'Abbās al-Faḍl ibn Ḥātim al-Nayrīzī, the Latin Anaritius (d. about 922) and Abū 'Alī al-Ḥasan ibn al-Haytham (354/965 – 430/1039). Khayyām claimed that in all these commentaries either the postulate was accepted without proof or the proof offered was defective. In saying that none of his predecessors had actually proved the postulate, Khayyām's

18. S.H. Nasr, *Science and Civilization in Islam*, p. 53.
19. Omar Khayyam, *op. cit.*, p. 277.

intention was to let others know that he had something new and different to offer concerning the problem of parallels. He believed he had discovered the true proof. Of course, his attempt at proving the postulate, like all previous attempts, ended in failure for the simple but unobvious reason then that the fifth postulate is independent of Euclid's other postulates and, as such, it cannot be proved in terms of the assumptions of the Euclidean system. Nevertheless, Khayyām's reinvestigation of the postulate did open a new chapter in the study of geometry in that it furnished new materials for later mathematicians to work upon, thus leading to the creation of new non-Euclidean geometries.

In this section, we wish to identify some of the important ideas of his predecessors, which Khayyām criticized as irrelevant to the requirements of a proof, and even as something alien to the field of geometry. We will also mention some of the ideas that he had adopted from them, with or without modifications, and which are deemed essential to the whole scheme of his proof. These are followed by Khayyām's criticism of their shortcomings which, he says, prevent them from proving the postulate and other principles that they had accepted without proof. All these will help us to infer the general philosophical and geometrical perspective of his criticism of the postulate.

The person most criticized by Khayyām was Ibn al-Haytham. The latter, who was Khayyām's most immediate predecessor in the long chain of commentators, had introduced, much in the manner of Thābit ibn Qurrah (836-901), the concept of motion of a straight line segment in his attempt to replace Euclid's definition of parallelism by a 'more evident' postulate, namely one which employs the property of equidistance[20]. Ibn al-Haytham's postulate reads:

> if a straight line so moves that the one end always touches a second straight line, and throughout this

20. A.I. Sabra, "Ibn al-Haytham" in *DSB*, vol. VI, pp. 201-202.

motion remains perpendicular to the second and in the same plane with it, then the other end of the moving line will describe a straight line which is parallel to the second.

Khayyām and, later, al-Ṭūsī objected to the procedure used by Ibn al-Haytham to formulate his definition of parallels because, in their view, to introduce a concept of motion that brings with it the idea of geometric continuity is something foreign to Euclidean geometry. Ibn al-Haytham justified his use of the concept by claiming that it already had a precedent in Euclid's definition of a sphere as "the locus of a semicircle rotated about its diameter". But Khayyām rejected the claim, saying that there was a clear distinction between Ibn al-Haytham's idea of motion of a line segment and Euclid's category of motions. Not only that, he even questioned the possibility of a whole line moving and yet remaining normal to a given line and, thus, the posibility of such an idea of motion serving as a basis for any proof of Euclid's famous postulate[21].

One important fruit of previous efforts, which Khayyām further developed in his proof was the analysis of a quadrilateral inherited from the works of Thābit ibn Qurrah and of Ibn al-Haytham. In pursuing further this analysis Khayyām appears to be aware of the connection between the fifth postulate and the sum of the angles of a quadrilateral. Khayyām also claimed that he had applied a principle borrowed from the philosopher Aristotle. According to this principle, two convergent straight lines intersect and it is impossible that two convergent straight lines should diverge in the direction of convergence[22]. Scholars have noted that nothing similar to this principle is to be found in any of the known writings of Aristotle. One predecessor of Khayyām, in whose writings could be traced the closest resemblance to this principle, was Thābit ibn Qurrah.

21. Omar Khayyam, *op. cit.*, p. 277.
22. B.A. Rosenfeld and A.P. Youschkevitch, *DSB*, vol. VII, p. 329. This was omitted in the translation of Amir-Moez.

In the first of his two attempts to prove the fifth postulate, Thābit assumes that if two straight lines intersected by a third move closer together or farther apart on one side of it, then they must, correspondingly, move farther apart or closer together on the other side[23]. Without doubt, Khayyām's principle appears as more refined and of a more generalized character. His application of the principle as a starting point for his theory of parallels indicates to us his awareness of the logical mistake of *petitio principi* that his predecessors had successively committed in their proofs. That Khayyām did not fall into the same error was one of his achievements.

Khayyām's criticism of his predecessors's shortcomings pertains to both philosophical and purely geometrical aspects. Euclid himself was not spared of criticism. In his philosophical criticism, Khayyām refers to the singular neglect of principles that have been established by philosophers of the past concerning the fundamental properties of straight lines abstracted from the perception of spatial reality. One good example is the previously mentioned principle which Khayyām had attributed to Aristotle. The neglect of this principle, says Khayyām, prevented Euclid from arriving at what came to be known in the history of Western mathematics as Saccheri's "hypothesis of the right angle"[24].

Application-wise, Khayyām himself was criticized by al-Ṭūsī for not correctly using one of these "principles of the ancient," namely, the axiom of Archimedes[25]. Khayyām went on to criticize his immediate predecessors for their uncritical acceptance of Euclid and their tendency to be merely satisfied with a partial proof. A complete proof, says Khayyām, demands that a parti-

23. A.T. Grigorian and B.A. Rosenfeld, "Thabit ibn Qurra" in *DSB*, vol. XIII, p. 290.
24. Omar Khayyam, *op. cit.*, p. 282.
25. A.A. al-Daffa and J. Stroyls, "Naṣīr al-Dīn al-Ṭūsī's Attempt to Prove the Parallel Postulate of Euclid" in *Proceedings of the International Congress of the History and Philosophy of Science*, ed. Hakim Mohammed Said, Hamdard Foundation Press (1979), p. 20.

cular proposition be demonstrated both directly and conversely[26]. In his geometrical criticism, Khayyām mentions particularly the confusion about the true distance between two co-planar lines, but al-Ṭūsī leveled the charge of confusion against Khayyām himself. In Khayyām's view, the true distance between two intersecting lines is measured by that connecting line with respect to which the two interior angles are equal[27]. Based on this definition, the distance between two parallel lines equals the length of the connecting line which is perpendicular to both.

If we were to name some of the earlier works on the theory of parallels that had exerted the greatest influence on Khayyām's investigation into this geometrical problem, then we must mention those of Thābit ibn Qurrah and Ibn al-Haytham. Although Khayyām referred to Thābit as only a minor translator of Euclid[28], several of Thābit's important ideas reappeared in his work, albeit in modified or more refined and developed form. In the case of Ibn al-Haytham, we have already seen that Khayyām had made more than just a passing reference to him. And if we were to describe the spirit and the philosophical perspective of Khayyām's criticism of the fifth postulate, then we would say that it was intimately bound to the philosophical foundation of Euclidean geometry as a coherent and distinct system in which the postulate possesses a special character.

Khayyām's Theory of Parallels

Khayyām accepted the first 28 propositions of Euclid's *Elements* without any change. But he sought to replace Proposition 29 with eight propositions of his own, because it was on the basis of this proposition and the 'doubtful' fifth postulate that Euclid had constructed his 'problematic' theory of parallel lines. Euclid's Proposition 29 states:

> A straight line falling on parallel straight lines makes the alternate angles equal to one another, the exterior

26. Omar Khayyam, *op. cit.*, p. 279.
27. *Ibid*, p. 284.
28. Al-Daffa and Stroyls, *op. cit.*, p. 15.

angle equal to the interior and opposite angle, and the interior angles on the same side equal to two right angles.

Khayyām's point of departure in his task of constructing the eight propositions was the 'Aristotelian' principle mentioned earlier. By using this principle which consisted of two statements, each equivalent to the fifth postulate, Khayyām proved that two perpendiculars to the same straight line neither converge nor diverge, being in fact equidistant from each other[29]. This preliminary result was to have an important application in his whole scheme of proof.

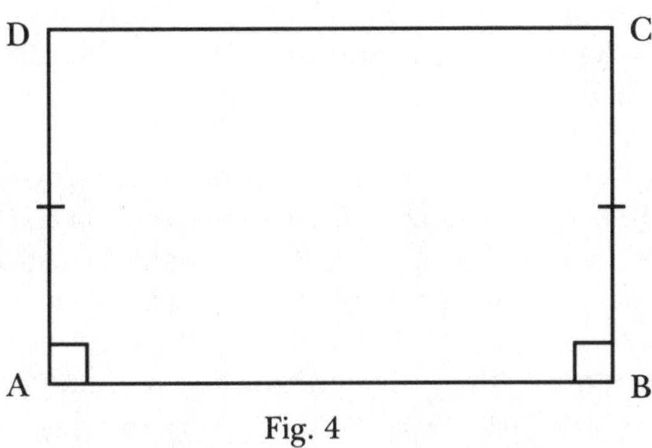

Fig. 4

Khayyām's next step was to construct his Proposition I. This was the proposition with which he began his analysis of what is now known as 'Saccheri's quadrilateral'. He considers an isosceles bi-rectangular quadrilateral ABCD, that is, a quadrilateral in which two sides AD and BC are equal and both are perpendicular to the side AB (see Fig 4). He then shows, without using the fifth postulate, that angles ADC and BCD are equal.

The equality of the two angles implies three possibilities. Both must either be (i) acute, or (ii) obtuse, or (iii) right angles.

29. B.A. Rosenfeld and A.P. Youschkevitch, *op. cit.*, p. 329.

Khayyām demonstrates in Propositions II and III that both angles must necessarily be right angles. The key to his proof is actually Proposition III. Proposition II merely functions as an auxiliary.

In establishing what is called the *hypothesis of the right angle,* which appears again about six centuries later in Saccheri's theory of parallels, Khayyām employs the method of *reductio ad absurdum* (method of contradiction), which is one of the most important logical tools in mathematics. Similar conclusions have been reached concerning the rectangularity of the considered birectangular quadrilateral in the earlier works of Thābit ibn Qurrah and Ibn al-Haytham[30] but their methodological analysis of it is different. It is with Khayyām that we must associate the first clear and systematic application of the method of contradiction in the refutation of the acute and obtuse angle hypothesis.

We will not go into the details here of the proof of Proposition III. It suffices for us to state the gist of his whole argument. Were either the hypothetical acute or obtuse angles to be true, then in each case a contradiction would result. Each supposition would contradict the truth of the preliminary proposition that two perpendiculars to the same straight line are equidistant from each other, established earlier from the 'Aristotelian' principle. Thus, the right angle hypothesis must be accepted as the only possibility. The rest of Khayyām's propositions attempt to show that this hypothesis is equivalent to the fifth postulate.

Khayyām was also aware of certain geometrical consequences, besides the above logical contradiction, which necessarily follow from accepting either of the other two hypotheses. Both he and al-Ṭūsī realized that the acute angle hypothesis would mean the angle sum of any triangle being less than two right angles[31]. Bound as they were to the Euclidean geometrical universe, neither Khayyām nor al-Ṭūsī ventured to investigate the possibility of having another geometrical system in which tri-

30. Al-Daffa and Stroyls, *op. cit.*
31. E.S. Kennedy, *op. cit.*, p. 665.

angles may possess such a property. We were to witness much later on that this is a property enjoyed by the geometry of Lobachevskii (1793 – 1856).

Having established the rectangularity of the quadrilateral, Khayyām further deduces its other properties. In Proposition IV, he shows that the opposite sides of the rectangle are of equal length. And in Proposition V, he demonstrates that it is the property of any two perpendiculars to the same straight line that any perpendicular to one of them is also a perpendicular to the other. This Proposition is used to prove Proposition VII. In Proposition VI, Khayyām proves that any two parallel lines in the Euclidean sense, that is, if they do not intersect, are equidistant. Proposition VII is important because it is none other than Euclid's Proposition 29 of his Book I, which Khayyām has sought to replace. However, he had proved it without appealing to Euclid's fifth postulate.

Proposition VII is the last in the whole series of propositions which he proves in Book I of his *Sharḥ* in order to justify the fifth postulate. It is, in fact, in this Proposition that Khayyām deduces this postulate which states that:

> If a straight line falling on two straight lines make the interior angles on the same side less than two right angles, the two straight lines, if produced indefinitely, meet on that side on which are the angles less than the two right angles[32].

The proof makes use of both the 'Aristotelian' principle and Proposition VI.

Historical Significance of Khayyām's Theory of Parallels

We have remarked earlier that Khayyām's attempt to prove the fifth postulate ended in a failure. Similarly, all attempts of his successors were failures. This is because in each of these proofs the key principle that is utilized is reducible to an equivalent of

32. Thomas L. Heath, *Euclid: The Thirteen Books of the Elements*, vol. 1 (1956), p. 202.

the postulate. But the fact is that this postulate cannot be proved in terms of the other assumptions of Euclidean geometry. Speaking of the realization of the indemonstrability of this postulate, Sir Thomas Heath wrote:

> "When we consider the countless successive attempts made through more than twenty centuries to prove the Postulate, many of them by geometers of ability, we cannot but admire the genius of the man who concluded that such a hypothesis, which he found necessary to the validity of his whole system of geometry, was really indemonstrable"[33].

However, we have also said that Khayyām's attempt did open a new chapter in the history of geometry and possesses a historical significance of its own. It is with this aspect that we will deal in the last section of this chapter.

The most important figure in Islam to have commented upon Khayyām's work is al-Ṭūsī. It is primarily upon the former's work that al-Ṭūsī builds his own theory of parallels[34]. There were several other Muslim mathematicians, such as Ibn 'Umar al-Abharī[35] (d.1265) and Shams al-Dīn al-Samarqandi (fl. 1276)[36], who were both al-Ṭūsī's contemporaries, and his later successors such as the fifteenth-century rector of Ulugh Beg's University in Samarkand, Qāḍizādah al-Rūmī[37], who attempted to prove the fifth postulate. But none of their works is to influence the later development of geometry. Al-Ṭūsī's proof, on the other hand, reached the Latin West and was translated by Edward Pocock. It was, in fact, the only Muslim work on the subject to have enjoyed that privilege. It influenced in various degrees the geometrical studies of Western mathematicians such as Christoph Clavius (1537-1612), Pietro Antonio Cataldi

---

33. Thomas L. Heath, *op. cit.*, p. 202.
34. Al-Daffa and Stroyls, *op. cit.*, p. 20.
35. On this figure, see G. Sarton, *Introduction to the History of Science*, vol. II, part II, p. 867.
36. On his contribution to the theory of parallels, see H. Dilgan, "Al-Samarqandi" in *DSB*, XII, p. 91.
37. See H. Dilgan, "Qadi Zada al-Rumi" in *DSB*, vol. XI, pp. 227-229.

(1552-1626), Johann Heinrich Lambert (1728-1777) and the already mentioned Wallis and Saccheri, particularly the later three.

Both John Wallis (1616- 1703) and Saccheri are known to have written commentaries upon al-Ṭūsī's proof. Herein lies the historical significance of Khayyām's geometrical treatise from the viewpoint of the development of modern geometry. We are told by al-Ṭūsī himself that some of the propositions he had used in his proof were taken from Khayyām. To demonstrate clearly the influence of Khayyām upon Saccheri's work, David E. Smith establishes the fact that the first few of Saccheri's theorems are essentially the same as some of Khayyām's propositions, with not only identical proofs and purpose for which they were put to use but even with the same way of lettering some figures[38].

However, unlike Khayyām, Saccheri carried his research further into the acute and obtuse angles hypotheses. In the course of his investigation, he derives several elementary properties of what was to develop into non-Euclidean geometries. One of these is the existence of asymptotic straight lines deduced from the acute angle hypothesis. He considered these lines to be repugnant to the nature of the straight line and thus set the hypothesis aside. Similarly, he abandoned the obtuse angle hypothesis because to accept it would mean abandoning the idea of the infinitude of the straight line. Saccheri's conclusions suggest to us that he, as much as Khayyām, remains bound to Euclidean geometry.

There are interesting parallels for the historian of scientific thought to reflect upon: the refusal of Khayyām and his Muslim successors to carry their analysis of the acute and obtuse angles hypotheses to its end with all the consequences that these would imply, *and* correspondingly in the domain of astronomy where Islamic astronomers have remained content with a closed and finite cosmos despite having all the technical knowledge neces-

38. D.E. Smith, *op. cit.*, pp. 8-10.

sary to overthrow the Ptolemaic sytem which depicted that cosmos, including knowledge of the heliocentric system[39]. There is the extension of these parallels to the modern West: it is Western mathematicians who liberated geometry from its traditional mould and created purely "artificial" geometries, just as the destruction of the traditional cosmos was carried out by Western astronomers who replaced it with an infinite Universe.

It is a study in contrast of two different philosophies of science. In the words of Professor Nasr, for Khayyām the medieval mathematician, Euclidean geometry corresponds, because of its symbolic nature, to the profoundest aspects of physical reality[40]. For modern mathematicians, the postulates of geometry became mere hypotheses whose physical truth or falsity need not concern them as long as they are consistent with one another[41]. It is with such kind of intellectual activity that Khayyām and medieval minds in general find little sympathy.

39. S.H. Nasr, *Islamic Science*, p. 133.
40. *Ibid*, p.83.
41. Howard Eves, *Introduction to the History of Mathematics*, 1975, p. 386.

CHAPTER 9

Islam and Bioethics

In this chapter, our primary aim is to discuss the nature and the main characteristics of the Islamic response to what is today known in the west as bioethics.[1] We will focus our discussion on the specific issue of the human body in the light of Islamic teachings. This issue has been chosen because many of the highly controversial aspects of contemporary biomedical practices and the ethical issues they have raised concern the treatment of the human body. The views which a particular people hold concerning the human body are clearly reflected in one way or another in almost every facet of their culture and civilization including the arts and sciences, particularly medicine. A discussion of the fundamental Islamic views of the human body will therefore help to throw an important light on the attitude of Islam toward many of the issues that are debated in contemporary bioethical discussion.

---

1 For a bibliography of contempory Muslim writings on the subject and related topics, see M.A. Anees, "A Select Bibliography on Islamic Medicine" in *The Muslim World Book Review,* 5:1 (Autumn 1984).

Nature and Characteristics of the Islamic Response

Thanks to modern means of communication, the worldwide Muslim community is immediately made aware of the latest biomedical innovations in the West. Although from the practical point of view Muslim society is still spared the intrusion of many of these new, controversial technological inventions in the biomedical field, or is not affected by them to the same degree experienced by Western society, it cannot escape from having to deal with their ethical and intellectual or philosophical implications. The very nature and character of Islam as a religion demands that a definite stand be made on these issues. This obliges us to make a few remarks about the character of the Islamic religion itself insofar as this has an important bearing on the question under discussion.

The most fundamental teaching in Islam is the doctrine of Unity (*al-tawḥīd*) which is expressed in the most universal manner possible in the first "testimony" of the Islamic faith, *Lā ilāha illa'Llāh,* usually translated as "there is no god but God." This doctrine conveys the basic attitude and spirit of Islam, which every Muslim seeks to realize in his own being by organizing and integrating all his thoughts and actions into a harmonious whole and a unity. Once this unity is achieved, there is no longer any distinction, be it in the domain of thought or of action, between the spiritual and the temporal or between the religious and the profane.

All thoughts and all actions, including those which are otherwise seen as the most mundane of activities such as carrying out trade or conducting the administrative affairs of the state, then possess a religious character and a spiritual significance. Islam therefore seeks to integrate through its principle of Unity all knowledge and human actions into a single realm of the religious and the sacred so that no true and useful knowledge and no good and beneficial act can possibly be excluded from this realm and be identified instead as secular and profane. By virtue of this fact, no human activity, and that includes the technological, can escape the moral judgment of Islam. Likewise, Islam cannot remain indifferent to any form of science which claims to provide a knowledge of reality or some particular aspect of it. It judges the latter in the light of its own conception of knowledge.

In order to relate in a more concrete manner the character of Islam as the religion of Unity to our discussion of an Islamic response to bioethics, we need to be more precise: how is the principle of Unity specifically applied in Islam, making possible the integration of knowledge and human actions into a harmonious whole? At the level of thought, integration is achieved through the application of the idea of unity and hierarchy of knowledge as well as of existence, an idea which is not unique to Islam, but is common to all traditional civilizations including that of Christianity. However, there is something striking about the Islamic application of this idea that is not found in the same degree in other civilizations.

Firstly, the vast synthesis that Islam had created out of such diverse and historically alien sciences as those of the Greeks, Chaldeans, Persians, Indians, and the Chinese, with which it came into contact, was unprecedented in the history of human civilization.[2] Islam integrated many elements of these sciences into a new body of knowledge, which it further developed, to the extent that these elements were compatible with its own idea and spirit of Unity.

Secondly, Islam produced a large number of universal figures whose names appear in almost every branch of knowledge known to its civilization. The idea of unity and hierarchy of knowledge was a living reality by virtue of the fact that the different levels of knowledge were harmoniously realized within the minds and souls of these figures.

And thirdly, in order to preserve the unity and hierarchy of the sciences, successive generations of Muslim scholars, from al-Kindī in the third/ninth century to Shāh Waliullāh of Delhi in the twelfth/eighteenth century, have devoted a considerable deal of their intellectual talents and genius to the classification of the sciences, for it is through this classification that the

2 See S.H. Nasr, *Science and Civilization in Islam*, pp. 29-40.

scope and position of each science within the total scheme of knowledge is always kept in view. These are some of the striking features of the Islamic concern with the integration of knowledge and ideas.

As we have already emphasized in some of the earlier chapters of this book, in the Islamic perspective, the highest knowledge is the knowledge of *tawḥīd* or Divine Unity. This is the knowledge of the Divine Essence, Names, and Qualities, and the knowledge of the Divine Effects and Acts embracing God's creation. Every other kind of knowledge must be organically related to this knowledge and all ideas, concepts, and theories in every domain of study are to be formulated or evaluated in its light. This supreme knowledge of Unity must serve as a guide in any Muslim attempt to deal with the intellectual and philosophical implications of contemporary biomedical discoveries and their applications, which, in fact, are numerous.[3] It is, however, beyond the scope of this chapter to deal with these implications.

At the level of actions, integration is achieved through the application of the *Sharī'ah*, the Divine Law of Islam, which is the concrete embodiment of the Divine Will. The Divine Law in Islam is concrete and all-embracing in the sense that it includes not only universal moral principles but also details of the way in which man should conduct every facet of his earthly life, both private and social. It is extremely important for us to know the Islamic conception of law if we are to understand fully the nature and characteristics of the Islamic response to bioethics.

The role of the divine law in Islam may be compared in its importance and centrality to that of theology in Christianity. Like the teachings on Divine Unity, the *Sharī'ah* is an integral aspect of the Islamic revelation. It is therefore a religious and a sacred law which serves as guide for Muslims to conduct their life in

3 Many molecular biologists like J. Monod, G. Stent, and R. Sinsheimer have given philosophical and ethical meanings to modern biomedical discoveries that have the gravest implications for traditional religious worldview and ethics.

harmony with the Divine Will. It is the primary source of knowledge of what is right and wrong. In Islam, therefore, its moral injunctions and attitudes are to be found in its Law which, because of its all-embracing nature, sanctifies the whole of human life and leaves no domain outside the sphere of divine legislation.

According to the *Sharīʿah*, there is a hierarchy of values of human acts and objects in the sight of God. Every human act must fall into one of the following five categories: (1) obligatory (*wājib*), (2) meritorious or recommended (*mandūb*), (3) forbidden (*ḥarām*), (4) reprehensible (*makrūh*), and (5) indifferent (*mubāḥ*). It should be remarked here that although in essence all of the *Sharīʿah* is contained in the Quran, the above classification of human acts did not appear until the third century of the Islamic era when Islamic jurisprudence came into existence as an independent science, and Islamic Law became well codified and systematized by men of great genius and religious integrity.[4]

Further, there are several schools of Islamic law which, while agreeing upon the fundamental principles of the law and upon many of the obligatory acts such as the five daily prayers and those that are prohibited such as wine-drinking, may differ in their views when it comes to the question of determining the precise technical legal status of many of the other acts, or with regard to the details of those major obligatory acts and prohibitions. Also, since the teaching of the *Sharīʿah* are meant to be applied in all ages and climes, it is the tasks of doctors of the law (*fuqahāʾ*), especially the experts (*mujtahids*) among them, to interpret and apply those teachings to newly arisen problems and situations in whatever sphere of human activity.

Today, we are confronted with a host of new problems and situations in the biomedical field that never existed before, problems made possible by new discoveries and the applica-

4 For a detailed account of this codification and systematization of Islamic Law, see for example, A. Hasan, *The Early Development of Islamic Jurisprudence* (Islamabad, 1970).

tion of new techniques. Problems like those relating to organ transplantation, artificial insemination, genetic and behavior control are entirely new while such age-old problems as contraception, abortion, and the question of the appropriate treatment of the dying have incorporated new issues into them as a result of the introduction of modern biomedical technology. It is now widely realized that all these problems are multi-dimensional in character. They are at once ethical and legal, medical and scientific, social and philosophical, and thus require a multi-dimensional approach in their solutions.

In the light of the centrality of the *Sharī'ah* in the religious and spiritual life of the Muslims, it is only natural that they would ask this question when confronted with these new developments : Is such and such an innovative act permissible or not from the point of view of the *Sharī'ah*? The first and most important level of Muslim response to contemporary bioethics comes therefore from the deliberations of the jurists (*fuqahā'*) whose legal rulings (*fatwās*) on these matters are immediately sought after by the Muslim community to provide it with the right code of conduct, since they are the authoritative interpreters and guardians of the Divine Law of Islam.

There is, in fact, in Islamic tradition a well-established discipline of biomedical jurisprudence which deals with many of the biomedical issues currently debated in the West, especially those relating to contraception and abortion, the question of dissection of the human body, and the meaning and definition of death with all its implications upon the duties and responsibilities of the living toward the dying and the dead. We may also recall here the fact that some of the Muslim physicians like Ibn al-Nafīs (d. 1288), who is now celebrated as the real discoverer of the minor circulation of the blood, were at the same time eminent figures in the field of jurisprudence (*fiqh*).[5] This

5 Ibn al-Nafīs taught *fiqh* (jurisprudence) at al-Masrūriyyah School in Cairo, and his name was included in the *Ṭabaqāt al-shāfi'iyyīn al-kubrā* (Great Classes of Shāfi'ī Scholars) of al-Subkī (d. 1370). See A.Z. Iskandar, "Ibn al-Nafīs" in *DSB*, p. 603.

traditional biomedical jurisprudence provides the necessary background and guidelines for any Muslim attempt to deal with contemporary bioethics.

In our modern times, many people have spoken of the need for a new value orientation and a reappraisal of the traditional value system in the light of what they term revolutionary scientific and technological progress in the biomedical field. As far as Islam is concerned, although many modernized Muslims have joined this chorus, there can be no question of undertaking a religious reform of the *Sharīʿah* for the sake of conforming to this so-called scientific and technological progress which is the fruit of a totally alien and anti-religious concept of life. Moreover, for millions of Muslims throughout the Islamic world, especially in the Indian subcontinent, modern Western medicine has never proved itself to be indispensable. They have a more well-established medical tradition on which to rely, in the form of the various types of traditional medicine which have survived to this day and which, in contrast to modern medicine, are intimately and harmoniously linked to their religious worldview and ethics.

The traditional Islamic views concerning issues such as contraception, abortion, dissection of the human body, the proper treatment of the dying patients, and the meaning and definition of death, are not going to be affected by new developments in biomedical technology. This is because the Islamic attitudes toward these issues are directly shaped and governed by the immutable teachings of Islam concerning the more fundamental question of the meaning and purpose of human life and death.[6] It is not possible here to go into the detailed Islamic views regarding each of the above-mentioned issues. What we wish to convey here is that in their response to these contemporary issues, present-day Muslim jurists are only reasserting the traditional Islamic views. In other words, new discoveries and new techniques do not provide them with any

6 For a good account of the various views on death and life after death in Islamic tradition, see J.I. Smith and Y.Y. Haddad, *The Islamic Understanding of Death and Resurrection* (Albany, 1981).

logical justification to call into question the ethico-legal basis on which their predecessors have formulated their legal views on the above issues. It must be emphasized, however, that we are only speaking here of cases which have historical precedents in Islam.

Let us illustrate the above point with an example. In traditional sources which contain references to biomedical jurisprudence, we find detailed discussion of the specific conditions and circumstances under which contraception and abortion are permissible in Islam.[7] While Islam generally prohibits abortion at all stages of pregnancy, Muslim jurists, guided by the principle of the *Sharīʿah* that allows necessity to remove restriction and recommends the lesser of two evils given no other choice, agreed that there are exceptional situations which necessitate abortion even when the fetus has been completely formed. This exceptional situation arises when it is reliably established that continued pregnancy will greatly endanger the life of the mother.

As to why the saving of the mother's life is to be given priority over that of the child, a jurist explains: "For the mother is the origin of the fetus; moreover, she is established in life with duties and responsibilities, and she is also a pillar of the family. It would not be possible to sacrifice her life for the life of a fetus which has not acquired a personality and which has no responsibilities or obligations to fulfill".[8]

Now, modern biomedical knowledge and technology have certainly made available new methods of contraception and abortion and introduced new variables into modern man's encounter with these two problems, such as the possibility of having prenatal knowledge of some aspects of the fetus, but in no way do these new scientific and technological developments affect and alter the basic Islamic ethico-legal equations of the problems since the legitimate factors for contraception and abortion in Islam are valid at all times.

---

7 For a modern discussion of these issues but based on traditional sources, see Y. al-Qaradawi, *The Lawful and the Prohibited in Islam* (Indianapolis), pp. 198-202.

8 *Ibid.* p. 202.

Prenatal knowledge of some kind of defects in the child-to-be may have provided many people of our times with a justifiable basis for carrying out abortion because they do not want to have except a perfectly normal and healthy child. But Islamic Law cannot accept these known defects as a legitimate basis for abortion unless they are deemed to endanger the very life of the mother. In the light of clearly spelled out views in Islam as to what are legitimate and illegitimate conditions for contraception and abortion, the question of whether or not to use modern methods and techniques when performing them, once their necessary ethico-legal conditions are fulfilled, becomes essentially a medical issue rather than an ethical one.

Not all the bioethical issues which arise from modern biomedical discoveries and techniques, and which are currently debated in the West have been taken up by Muslim religious scholars. As far as issues that have been debated in the Muslim community are concerned some remain to be resolved in a conclusive manner. But, in most cases, Muslim jurists have achieved quite a remarkable degree of consensus in their legal views, enough to put the controversies to rest. Such was the case with the issue of artificial insemination. When insemination is restricted to the semen of legally married couples, it is permissible from the point of view of *Sharī'ah.* The question of organ transplantation, however, generated lengthy and controversial debates in many parts of the Islamic world. Whatever the technical legal status of each of the still disputed issues may finally turn out to be, one thing is clear. In the encounter between Islam and contemporary bioethics, the nature and pattern of its responses is essentially determined by the teachings contained in its sacred law which is at once ethical and legal.

Islamic Conception of the Human Body

The present section offers a discussion of the human body according to the teachings of Islam. Through this discussion, we hope to throw further light on the attitude of Islam toward contemporary bioethics. In traditional Islamic literature, we find an extensive treatment of the subject by different intellectual schools. However, we can only bring out here those elements that are considered central to the Islamic teachings.

According to Islam, man is God's most noble creation. This fact is symbolized in the Quran by the prostration of angels before Adam upon the divine command.[9] There are numerous verses in the Quran and also sayings of the Prophet, which praise the perfect mould and proportions in which man has been created as well as the beauty of the human form.[10] The Prophet, while gazing at his own reflection in a mirror, prayed to God for his soul to be adorned with perfect moral and spiritual beauty just as his body had been made beautiful.

Man is a creature of many levels and facets. He is body, soul, and spirit. But Islam, faithful to its fundamental doctrine of Unity, views man as a unified whole in which all the parts are interdependent. Islam shares with Judaism and Christianity the view that man is created in the image of God. A consequence of this view is that the human body must also participate in certain respects in this dignity of man as the "image of God". 'Alī, the cousin and son-in-law of the Prophet and the fourth Caliph of Islam, refers in one of his poems to man as the microcosm (*'ālam ṣaghīr*). This idea of man as the microcosm, as we shall see, constitutes one of the most fundamental principles of the sciences cultivated by Islam, particularly the biomedical sciences. These Islamic views of man have important consequences upon the spirit in which Muslims seek to study and treat the human body .

At the level of the law, Islam conceives of the human body mainly in terms of its rights and duties. Islam attaches great importance to the overall health, welfare, and well-being of the body, not for its own sake, but for the sake of the spiritual soul which constitutes the real essence of man. A body that is normal and healthy may serve as a perfect instrument for either virtues

9 *The Quran,* Chapter II (The Cow), Verse 34.

10 "We have indeed created man in the best of moulds," *The Quran* , Chapter XCV (The Fig), Verse 4.

or vices. Islam insists that all activities of the body must be for the sake of the health and felicity of the soul. In other words, in Islam, and this is true in all religions, the idea of having a perfectly healthy body is so that it may act as a perfect instrument of the soul to realize the very purpose for which it has been created.

The relationship between the body and the soul has been described by Muslim scholars by means of various analogies depending on the point of view from which a particular relationship is envisaged. But in all these relationships the body is always subordinated to the soul. Al-Ghazzālī, for example, describes the body as the vehicle or riding-animal of the soul and the latter as a traveler who visits a foreign country, which is this world, for the sake of merchandise and will soon return to his native land.[11] The vehicle should be taken care of and well looked after but not to the point of forgetting or neglecting the final destination of his journey.

Islam enjoins the complete fulfillment of all the legitimate needs of the body. What constitutes the body's legitimate needs are defined and determined by the Divine Law of Islam. In legislating its laws for the human collectivity Islam takes into full account both the strengths and weaknesses inherent in human nature. It is also aware of human tendencies either toward the excessive pursuits of the needs of the body or toward the neglect of its legitimate needs. Both tendencies can have detrimental effects on man's total health.

The general aim of Islamic legislation on such basic needs of the body as food, sex, and dress is to ensure not only man's physical health but also his psychological and spiritual health for these physical needs of man also possess aspects which may affect his psyche and spirit. For Muslims, it is by faithfully observing the religious law that man's physical, psychological, and spiritual needs are harmoniously fulfilled.

In a number of his sayings, the Prophet speaks of the rights

---

11 Al-Ghazzālī, *The Alchemy of Happiness* (Lahore, 1979), pp. 21 and 49.

of the body which every Muslim is required to respect and safeguard. The Prophet was unhappy when he learned that several of his Companions had vowed to fast every day,[12] to pray all night, and to abstain from sexual relations. He reminded them that his own life and practices provide the best examples for Muslims to follow. Those who deviate from his ways are not of his community. Thus Islam is against the denial to the body of its basic rights or needs even in the name of the spirit. We have so far spoken of the basic rights or legitimate needs of the body in rather general terms. Let us now refer to them in a more concrete manner.

The teachings of Islam greatly emphasize the question of personal hygiene and cleanliness. This assertion is likely to be viewed with scepticism by many Westerners, especially those who have traveled to different parts of the Islamic world where they see before their own eyes numerous evidences for unhealthy conditions and unsanitary practices. Whatever are the reasons or causes for the present-day conditions of hygiene and state of cleanliness among Muslim peoples, the fact remains that the *Sharīʿah* contains numerous injunctions concerning hygiene and cleanliness.[13] The teachings of the *Sharīʿah* in this domain became incorporated into the general body of Islamic medicine. In its theory and practice, Islamic medicine views these religious injunctions on matters of hygiene and cleanliness as the best means of preventing illnesses. It also sees certain medical merits in many of the rituals and religious practices of Islam.

Ritual cleanliness requires Muslims to wash themselves regularly. In order to perform their five daily prayers, they must be in a state of ritual purity. To be in this state, they have to perform an act of ablution in which they are required to wash specific parts of the body as prescribed by the Law. Further, Islamic Law requires that after every sexual union both hus-

---

12 The best of fastings, according to one *ḥadīth*, was that of Prophet David who fasted on alternate days.

13 On the importance of the religious element in hygiene in Islam, see S.H. Nasr, *Islamic Science*, pp. 164-66.

band and wife take a ritual bath or the major ablution [14] without which the minor ablutions, as the former ones are called, are deemed invalid before the Law. We may also mention here the traditional Islamic practice of circumcision which is also to be found in Jewish religious tradition and which is not unrelated to the question of hygiene and cleanliness. This practice has come to be widely accepted and recommended by the medical profession of our times.

Another factor of health upon which Islam places great emphasis is diet. The dietary habits of Muslims, as regulated by the *Sharī'ah* have an important effect upon their overall state of health.[15] On the importance of diet from the point of view of Islamic medicine, Nasr writes:

> It plays a much more important role than does diet in modern medicine. The Muslims considered the kind of food and the manner in which it is consumed to be so directly connected to health that the effect of diet was considered by them as being perhaps more powerful than that even of drugs on both health and illness. It is not accidental that the Andalusian physician Abū Marwān ibn Zuhr in the sixth/twelfth century wrote the first scientific work on diet ever composed, the *Kitāb al-aghdhiyah* (Book of Diet), and that food plays such an important therapeutic role to this day in the Islamic world.[16]

From the point of view of the *Sharī'ah,* food in general also falls into the various legal categories previously mentioned. The most important of these, as far as Muslim dietary habits are concerned, is the prohibited category. Included in this category

14 In Arabic, major ablution is called *ghusl.* It necessitates the washing of the whole body. The term for minor ablutions is *wuḍū'*.

15 On the principles of the *Sharī'ah* governing the dietary habits of Muslims, see al-Qaradawi, *op. cit.* , pp.39-78.

16 S.H. Nasr, *op. cit.*, p. 166.

are alcoholic drinks, pork, and meats of certain species of birds and animals. There was no lack of attempts in Islam to provide a kind of philosophical and scientific justification for these dietary prohibitions, some of which also exist in various other religions such as Judaism. For example, the *Ikhwān al-Ṣafā'* (The Brethren of Purity) maintained that plants and flesh of animals that man takes as food have an effect upon both his body and his soul.[17] This is because beautiful and good qualities as well as evil qualities are inherent in each of the three kingdoms of minerals, plants, and animals. It is well to remember that for the *Ikhwān* the three kingdoms come into being as a result of the mixing of the four elements to various degrees by the Universal Soul.

Beautiful and good qualities are manifestations of the good souls, while evil qualities are due to the evil souls. Different sets of qualities are inherent in different plants and in different animals. It is these qualities which affect both the physical body and the soul of man, either in a positive or a negative sense, depending upon the particular plants and animals which he consumes as food. In the context of Islamic spirituality, some religious scholars have also offered spiritual justifications for the dietary prohibitions. According to them, one of the factors which influence one's degree of concentration in prayer, and hence the spiritual efficacy of one's prayer, is the kind of food one eats.

Apart from dietary prohibitions, religious injunctions like fasting, eating less than one's full appetite, and eating slowly also help to regulate Muslim dietary habits. The medical value of these injunctions to the human body is duly recognized and appreciated. But for Muslims the supreme motive in doing all these acts is religious and spiritual, namely obedience to the Divine Will and the salvation of the soul.

While Muslims are enjoined by their religion to strive and pray to God for good health, they are also taught to have the correct attitudes and responsibilities toward illness. Both health and sickness of the body are ordained by God. As for the

---

17 S.H. Nasr, *Islamic Cosmological Doctrines,* p. 70.

believer, he derives benefits from both of them. If he is sick, he views that sickness as a trial from God and bears it with patience, resignation, and thankfulness. When a believer succeeds in responding to his illness in this particular manner, he is then able to derive spiritual benefits from his physical suffering. Diseases, in the traditional Islamic perspective, therefore possess a spiritual dimension and a spiritual significance. In one sacred *ḥadīth* God speaks through the Prophet: "O my worshipper! Good health forms a link between you and yourself but sickness makes a link between you and Me."

Islamic Law does not permit inflictions of bodily pain for the attainment of spiritual well-being. But in sickness or physical afflictions, which is his fate to receive, a believer finds an excellent occasion to derive spiritual benefits from them and to strengthen his relation with God. The following collection of prophetic *ḥadīths* as given by Sūyūṭī, a famous Egyptian scholar of the late fifteenth/early sixteenth century, in his work *Medicine of the Prophet,*[18] further demonstrates the positive value and spiritual significance of illness or physical afflictions in Islamic teachings:

> Verily a believer should not fear sickness; for if he knew what he derives from sickness, he would desire to be sick even to death.
>
> The people who meet with severe pain are the prophets of God, the devout and the very best of men. A man is afflicted in proportion to his love of the Faith. Affliction does not cease for the devout as long as they walk this earth and until they are free from sin.
>
> If God loves a people, he will give them affliction.
>
> There is no sickness or pain which a believer receives that

18 See C. Elgood's English translation of this work as well as that of Chaghmīnī, known by the same title, in *Osiris,* 14 (1962), 33-192.

is not a penance for his sins whether it be a thorn which pricks him or a disaster that overwhelms him.

No Muslim receives any injury without God shedding from him his sins, as a tree sheds its leaves.

As we have said, these sayings of the Prophet seek to stress the positive value of diseases and physical afflictions and to define the correct spiritual attitudes toward them if and when they occur. They do not mean that Muslims ought to prefer sickness to health. Abū Dardā, a Companion of the Prophet, once asked him: "O Prophet of God, if I am cured of my sickness and am thankful for it, is it better than if I were sick and bore it patiently?" The Prophet replied to Abū Dardā: "Verily, the Prophet of God loves sound health just as you do." There are numerous other *ḥadīths* which call on the sick to find medical treatment for their sickness, and on the believers in general to visit the sick and to offer them both physical and spiritual comfort.[19] The Prophet, however, has also advised against excessive use of medicine because "sometimes medicines do leave behind diseases."[20] To appreciate the significance of this prophetic advice, it is perhaps pertinent to refer to the fact that the so-called iatrogenic diseases, namely diseases caused by medical treatment, are today ranked third in importance among all the recognized ailments of contemporary man.[21]

Thus, in both his states of health and of sickness, a Muslim is enjoined by his religion to provide a proper treatment of his body. And when he dies, his body deserves all the respects it should get in accordance with the Islamic Divine Law. Islamic Law requires that burial should take place at the earliest

---

19 For the various *ḥadīths* pertaining to this question see the *Ṣaḥīḥ* of Imām Bukhārī in the two major chapters dealing with sickness and healing, or Elgood's translation mentioned above.

20 See Ibn Qutayba, *'Uyūn al-akhbar*, 3, p. 273, quoted by A. Ali in his "Contribution of Islam to the Development of Medical Science," *Studies in History of Medicine*, 4 (1980), 49.

21 J. Needleman, *Consciousness and Tradition* (New York, 1982), p. 99.

possible time and there should be no unnecessary delays. It is beyond the concern of this chapter to go into the details of the whole set of rites associated with Muslim burial.[22] What we wish to emphasize, however, is that it is the religious duty of the community to make sure that the dead be given their proper and immediate burials. The Islamic respect for the dead also manifests itself in its attitude toward the dissection of the body. Islamic Law does not permit this act although there have been jurists over the ages who question its strict prohibition. Thus, Ibn al-Nafīs, whom we have mentioned earlier, tells us that what prevented him from practicing anatomy was his religion.

In speaking of the total health of the individual, and not just his physical health, it is necessary also to say something, however briefly, about the Islamic view of dress since clothes pertain directly not only to the body but also to the soul. Indeed, a man's clothes are among the things that are nearest to his soul, exercizing upon it a perpetual and immensely powerful influence, although they belong to the outer aspects of his life. The clothes one wears, apart from reflecting the state of one's inner beauty, are also closely related to one's views of the human body.

The fundamental aims of Muslim dress habits, which are again regulated by the *Sharī'ah* are decency, spiritual dignity, and beauty.[23] Decency demands that Muslims wear clothes which cover their bodies. In particular, the dress of the Muslim woman should not be transparent or too tight as to delienate and display the parts of her body. The idea of spiritual dignity includes the question of the preservation of masculinity for men and femininity for women so that the dress of men must clearly be distinct from that of women. The spiritual dignity that one

---

22 For a description of the various processes connected with the preparation of bodies for final burial, see A.A. Tritton, "Muslim Funeral Customs," *Bulletin of the School of Oriental and African Studies*, 9 (1937-39) 653-61.

23 See al-Qaradawi, *op. cit.*, pp. 79-94.

normally associates with the robe and turban of the traditional Muslim male dress and with the veil (*ḥijāb*) of the traditional female dress has the effect of reminding man of his or her spiritual function and responsibilities. Moreover, dress is in conformity with those responsibilities. The spirit of Islamic dress is beautifully summed up by a contemporary scholar:

> His (i,e. a Muslim's) clothes were in keeping with the dignity of man's function as representative of God on earth, and at the same time they made it easy for him to perform the ablution, and they in perfect conformity with the movements of the prayer. Moreover they were an ornament to the prayer, unlike modern European clothes which rob the movements of the prayer of all their beauty and impede them, just as they act as a barrier between the body and ablution.[24]

In Islam, the beauty of the human form is veiled. From the point of view of the Law, the main reason for this veiling is to govern human passions so as to create a healthy religious and spiritual climate in which man is constantly reminded of his duties to God. This veiling is the more necessary in the case of the female body. The esoteric teachings of Islam as embodied in the Sufi tradition have this justification to offer. The female body symbolizes certain esoteric truths concerning the divinity and , in Islam, the inner mysteries are likewise veiled.[25] Therefore, there is also a metaphysical significance in the traditional Islamic dress. In Islam the beauty of the human

---

24 See Abu Bakr Siraj al-Din, "The Spiritual Function of Civilization," J. Needleman ed., *The Sword of Gnosis* (Baltimore, 1974), p. 107.

25 "Woman even in a certain manner incarnates esotericism by reason of certain aspects of her nature and function; "esoteric truth," the *ḥaqīqa* is "felt" as a "feminine" reality, and the same is true of *baraka.* Moreover the veil and the seclusion of woman are connected with the final cyclic phase in which we live – and they present a certain analogy with the forbidding of wine and the veiling of the mysteries." See F. Schuon, *Understanding Islam* (London, 1972), p. 37.

form becomes interiorized and spiritualized and not exteriorized and profanized. Because of the presence of these inner teachings in Islam, which see in the human body a message of the highest spiritual truths, coupled with the strict injunctions of the *Sharī'ah* concerning the display of the human form, including in art, the Islamic appreciation of the beauty of the human form has not led to its profane glorification or the cult of the "body beautiful" viewed as a purely physical and sexual object.

While the beauty of the human form is to be veiled, the dress that veils it should present itself as something beautiful. Once the Prophet said: "Anyone who has an atom of pride in his heart will not enter the Garden." A man then asked him, "What about the one who likes to wear a handsome robe and good shoes?" The Prophet replied: "Surely Allah is beautiful and loves beauty."[26] More important than the beauty of clothes, however, is the beauty of one's outward behavior and bodily movements since it is the latter which reflect in a more direct manner the essence of one's overall beauty. This brings us to the question of the duties of the human body and its various parts.

Beauty of man's general appearance and outward behavior results when movements of the different parts of his body become balanced and harmonized. According to al-Ghazzālī, there is an appropriate pattern of movement for each bodily member based on a general law of balance and harmony willed by God.[27] If man is to achieve a balanced and harmonized relationship between his physical body and his spiritual soul or spiritual heart, which is the center or "nucleus" of his whole being, then his bodily movements must conform to that appropriate pattern. For Muslims, it is in the bodily movements of the Prophet himself that the perfect pattern is to be found. Thus, al-Ghazzālī

26 In another version of this *ḥadīth*, a handsome man came to the Prophet saying: "I love beauty and have been given some of it, as you can see, to the extent that I dislike anyone's having a better pair of sandals than I. Is this pride, O Messenger of Allah?" The Prophet replied: "No. Pride is to reject the truth and to view other people with contempt."

27 Gai Eaton, "Perfecting the Mirror," *Parabola*, 10:3 (August, 1985), 45.

maintains that Muslims, as far as possible, should follow the example of the Prophet even in his bodily movements which, in fact, have been recorded in a detailed manner and preserved to this day as an integral part of the *Sunnah* or prophetic tradition. Millions of Muslims throughout the ages have sought to emulate his manner of walking, eating, sleeping, putting his sandals and so on.

Balanced and harmonized movements of the body are realized by one's acting in harmony with the Divine Law itself. One must abstain from doing those acts which are forbidden and discouraged by the Law since each sinful act, says the Prophet, produces a veil of rust over the heart. At the same time, one must perform acts that are made obligatory and recommended by the law. This is what we mean by the duties of the human body. In his magnum opus, *The Revivification of the Religious Sciences (Iḥyā' 'ulūm al-dīn)*, in a part dealing with the mysteries of fasting, al-Ghazzālī speaks of the necessary conditions for a fasting that is perfect and acceptable to God. Not only in fasting must one abstain from food and sexual pleasures, but one must also restrain his or her bodily members, such as eyes, ears, hands and feet, from doing acts that are sinful before the Law.

The effect of this abstinence is profound, not only on the soul but even on the whole pattern of one's bodily movements. The basic idea of fasting is so that this abstinence becomes a lasting habit resulting from a conscious awareness of its harmony with the Divine Will as embodied in the Law. Moreover, says al-Ghazzālī, by way of this abstinence we remove obstacles, in the form of unchecked carnal desires, to the remembrance of God, that is directed toward the heart. Indeed, according to the Quran, fasting has been prescribed so that man might attain a state of God-consciousness.[28]

Abstinence goes hand in hand with the performance of affirmative or positive acts, the most important of which, from the point of view of the *Sharī'ah*, is the five daily prayers. It has been said in Islam that in the ritual prayer the spiritual, intel-

28 *The Quran*, Chapter II (The Cow), Verse 183.

lectual, psychological, and physical elements of man are all in perfect harmony and equilibrium. At the physical level itself, the whole pattern of bodily movements acted out in the prayer is said to be in perfect balance and harmony and to signify the various possible relationships between Creator and creation. As one scholar has summarized it:

> In the ritual prayer itself the spiritual and intellectual element is represented by the recitation from the Quran and the emotional element by the feeling of fear and of hope with which he is commanded to call upon God, but what might be called the existential element is acted out in physical movements which utilize the body as a vehicle for the spirit. In the first part of each unit of prayer the worshipper stands upright while he recites certain passages from the Quran, and this uprightness, this verticality, is an image of the "straight" (or "vertical") path upon which he asks God to lead him. The body has itself become a symbol of the ray which connects heaven and earth, the divine and the human.
>
> But the Muslim prays not only on his own behalf and on behalf of his fellow men and women but also in the name of creation as a whole; this is an aspect of his function as the "vicegerent of God on earth." The standing is followed by a bowing in which the worshipper is instructed to keep the upper part of his body, from head to hips, parallel with the ground, and it is sometimes said that all the creatures which move upon four legs, their bodies horizontal, are represented by this posture. This bowing is followed by the prostration in which the worshipper places his forehead on the ground, his body folded up as though in the fetal position, and although this is primarily an acknowledgment of the power and glory of the Transcendent it is also, according to certain sages, a representation of the inanimate realm, the mineral order in particular. While bowing he had glorified God as the infinite, the all-

> embracing on the horizontal level. Now in the prostration he is, as it were, reduced to the dimensions of his own innermost "nucleus". In this way the worshipper's physical body has acted out the variety of relationships between Creator and creation.[29]

In Sufism, moreover, there is the "prayer of the heart," the *dhikr* or invocation of the Divine Name, which is the most universal form of prayer. The Sufi technique of *dhikr* is of various forms. This is, however, not the place to go into its detailed discussion. Here, we only wish to mention its connection with the body's natural activity of breathing and with the rhythm of the beating of the heart, in order to emphasize further the role of the body in the spiritual life of Islam. The Prophet is reported to have said: "He who does not vibrate at remembrance of the Friend has no friend."[30] In *dhikr* there is the making use of rhythmical breathing and movements of the body. Such rhythm is the basic characteristic of the Sufi sacred dance which has its basis, among others, in the above *ḥadīth.* Whether the *dhikr* is done silently or in the form of a chant, its aim is to enable man to remember God by invoking his Name at all times so that it becomes ultimately integrated into the very rhythm of the beating of the heart.[31]

It is clear from the foregoing discussion of the human body that Islam attaches great importance to the health of the body, viewed not independently of the rest of the constituents of man, but as an integral element of that state of total health in which the spiritual, intellectual, emotional, and physical elements are all in perfect harmony and equilibrium.

The Human Body as Microcosm

We have earlier asserted that the idea of man as the microcosm

---

29 Eaton, *op. cit.*, pp.47-48.

30. Quoted by Titus Burckhardt in his *Introduction to Sufi Doctrines,* trans. D.M. Matheson (Lahore: M. Ashraf, 1959).

31. See William Stoddart, *Sufism: The Mystical Doctrines and Methods of Islam* (Wellingborough: Thorsons, 1976).

constitutes a fundamental principle of many of the Islamic sciences. The meaning of this idea is that the whole universe is essentially contained in man. In other words, man is a universe in miniature. Here, we will limit our consideration of this idea to its important consequence on the spirit with which Muslim scholars throughout the ages have approached and carried out the study of the human body. There is no doubt that Muslim scholars have viewed its study as a very important one. The body is studied not only for biomedical benefits but also for man's intellectual and spiritual benefits. In their view, the significance of the anatomy and physiology of the human body is not limited to the biomedical sciences but extends to the spiritual domain as well. The spirit of its study is described by al-Ghazzālī in these terms:

> The science of the structure of the body is called anatomy: it is a great science, but most men are heedless of it. If any studies it, it is only for the purpose of acquiring skill in medicine, and not for the sake of becoming acquainted with the perfection of the power of God. The knowledge of the anatomy is the means by which we become acquainted with the animal life; by means of knowledge of animal life, we may acquire a knowledge of the heart and the knowledge of the heart is a key to the knowledge of God.[32]

Since man, being a microcosm, recapitulates within himself the whole of existence, there exists a correspondence between man and the universe. Islamic medicine adopts this correspondence as one of its fundamental principles. As explained in Chapter 6, the human body, like all other animal bodies, is comprised of the four humors (i.e. blood, phlegm, yellow bile, and black bile) mixed according to certain principles[33] just as the

32. Al-Ghazzālī, *Alchemy of Happiness* (Albany, New York, 1873), pp. 38-39.
33 For a more detailed discussion of the humoral constitution of the human body, see S.H. Nasr, *Islamic Science*, pp. 159-62; also his *Science and Civilization in Islam*, pp. 219-25.

world of nature is formed from the mixture of the four elements (fire,air, water and earth). The humors themselves are composed of the elements and the four natures (heat, moisture, cold, and dryness). To be more precise, each humor is related to two elements and two natures so that it possesses qualities at once similar to and different from the other humors. It is this humoral constitution of the human body, which provides the basis for the definitions of health and illness in Islamic medicine. What is called health refers to the state of balance and harmony of the humors. The disruption of this state of equilibrium is called illness. The task of the physician is to restore the balance of the humors.

The correspondence between the microcosm and the universe has important consequences upon diagnosis and treatment of illnesses in the Islamic medical system. The balance of the humoral constitution may be disrupted by both internal and external causes. Muslim physicians pay much attention to the external factors because they are aware that, in consequence of the above correspondence, there exists a constant action and reaction between the total external environment of man and the humors.[34] If Muslim physicians see much medical wisdom in the various injunctions of the *Sharī'ah* that we have previously discussed, it is because they see them as the means which enable man to live in harmony within himself and with his external environment.

It is significant that in our own times a number of individual physicians in the Indian subcontinent have sought to verify the truth of the above correspondence by making use of modern scientific discoveries. They argued, for example, that if the human body is really a microcosm, then it should possess all the elements that are present in the macrocosm. According to the latest study conducted by one of these scholars, eighty-one elements, out of a total of ninety-two that are known to occur

34 According to Muslim physicians, there are six fundamental external factors of health of the individual: breathing, eating, bodily rest and movement, sleep, emotional rest, and excretion and retention (including the effects of sexual intercourse). See Chapter 6 of this book, pp. 107-8.

naturally, are found to be present in the human body.[35]

As we have said, in Islam the human body is not merely studied from biomedical and scientific points of view. The body is far from being only of interest to the physicians since its meanings are not exhausted by man's physical and biomedical understanding of it no matter how far that understanding may reach. Even when the body is studied by Muslim physicians from the biomedical point of view, it is never viewed as a kind of machine which is functioning autonomously. Rather, they see the body of man as an extension of his soul and as being related to both the spirit and the soul. That is why many of them were masters of psychosomatic medicine and psychology. For example, al-Rāzī, the Latin Rhazes, wrote a work entitled *Spiritual Physick*[36] in which he discussed the various moral and psychological illnesses which ruin the mind and the body and ways in which these ailments might be overcome.

If the human body is also of great interest to the philosophers, theologians, and Sufis, that is because it is a great treasure of wisdom and of symbols which point to other levels of reality. Biomedical facts about the body which are of great utility to the physicians, especially anatomy and physiology, are at the same time symbols which demonstrate to us that the wisdom of the Creator pervades the whole of creation. The Quran speaks of the human body as one of the "signs of God." In other words, knowledge of the body necessarily leads man to the knowledge of God. We have already quoted al-Ghazzālī's affirming this view.

According to the Ikhwān al-Ṣafā', man cannot know within his own lifetime the whole universe by going around and studying it, but God, in his Wisdom, has placed everything in the universe in man himself. Thus, by studying himself man can come to the knowledge of all things.[37] The Ikhwān maintained

35 See S.B. Vohora, "Is the Human Body a Microcosm?: A Critical Study," *Studies in History of Medicine*, 5:1 (March, 1981).

36 See Rhazes, *The Spiritual Physick of Rhazes*, trans. A.J. Arberry (London, 1950).

37 S.H. Nasr, *Islamic Cosmological Doctrines*, p. 98.

that the study of human anatomy and physiology is a key to the knowledge of the power and wisdom of the Creator. By making use of numerical symbolism they established a correspondence between the anatomy of the human body and that of the heavens. But they also saw a striking analogy between the body and the terrestrial world. In those physical features of man, which distinguish him from the other animals, the Ikhwān see a spiritual significance. For example, man's vertical position is described as symbolizing an ontological and metaphysical ascent and the yearning of man to reach toward the spiritual world.

Al-Fārābī, generally regarded as the founder of political philosophy in Islam, made use of the symbolism of human anatomy to explain his theory of human society. There is an analogy between the interrelation of the bodily organs and that of the components of the traditional human society. In this context, Muslim scholars generally refer to the body as the kingdom of the heart and speak of it as being analogous to a great city. Famous Sufis like Ibn 'Arabī, al-Jīlī, and Nasafī have dealt with the idea of the body as the "temple" of the spirit. And Rūmī, the great mystical poet of Islam, making such references to the human body as the "whale of Jonah" and as the "shadow of the shadow of the shadow of the heart", and while maintaining that both body and spirit are necessary and good, sees in the contrasting nature and qualities of the body effective illustrations of the true nature of the spirit.[38]

Conclusion

We wish to conclude our discussion of the human body in the Islamic perspective with a few remarks about the symbolism of the male and female bodies. Earlier, when touching on the traditional female dress, we stated that the female body symbolizes certain aspects of the Divine Reality. Now, the profoundest spiritual message of the human body has to do with the fact that

38 See W.C. Chittick, *The Sufi Path of Love: The Spiritual Teachings of Rumi*, (Albany, 1983), pp. 28-31.

the human being is a theomorphic being who reflects God's Names and Qualities. Insofar as the male and female are both human, they symbolize the same truths concerning the divine.[39] But insofar as there is a polarization of the human form into the male and the female, they symbolize different aspects of the divinity. The female is said to symbolize the uncreated aspect of God. It is indeed significant that the Arabic word for Divine Essence (*dhāt*) is in the feminine form. The male, on the other hand, is said to symbolize God as Lord and Creator.

According to Ibn 'Arabī, the contemplation of God in woman constitutes the highest form of contemplation possible. In Islamic spirituality, sexuality is seen mainly in its positive aspects. Its negative aspects are certainly not ignored as clearly indicated by the strict injunctions of the *Sharī'ah* concerning the relationship between the sexes. Sexual union, which is a sacred act when performed within the bounds of the *Sharī'ah*, becomes for the contemplative a symbol of that beatific union originally possessed by the androgynic ancestor of humanity in the paradisal state. These few remarks are intended to highlight the fact that some of the great representatives of Islamic spirituality have attached the profoundest spiritual significance to the sexual aspects of the human body.

Not all Muslim views concerning the human body have been mentioned here. Those that have been mentioned are only treated in a rather scanty manner. However, we hope the above discussion will contribute to a better appreciation of the Islamic views of man in general and of the human body in particular. This will in turn lead to a better appreciation of the nature and characteristics of the Islamic response to contemporary bioethics insofar as that response has been and will continue to be determined by Islam's views of man and of the human body.

---

39 On the spiritual message of the male and female bodies in Islam, see S.H. Nasr, "The Male and Female in the Islamic Perspective," *Studies in Comparative Religion*, pp. 67-75. For a treatment of this subject from the points of view of the various religious traditions, including that of Islam, see F. Schuon, *From the Divine to the Human* (Bloomington, 1982), the chapter entitled " *The Message of the Human Body.* "

CHAPTER 10

Muslim Intellectual Responses to Modern Science

Introduction

The primary aim of this chapter is to present an analytical study of Muslim intellectual responses to modern science, as embodied in the ideas and works of prominent nineteenth and twentieth-century Muslim thinkers. It seeks to investigate how these thinkers perceive the challenge posed by modern science to contemporary Muslim society, and to understand the main ideas which influence their perceptions. Their intellectual responses to the challenge perceived are then analyzed and evaluated in the light of the profound changes taking place during the past two centuries in both the Muslim world and the West, the original home of modern science.

We will also deal briefly with the intellectual response associated with the *Islamization* movement spearheaded by a number of contemporary Muslim intellectuals and which is now gaining momentum in several parts of the Muslim world. We will conclude with an appraisal of the significance of this Islamization effort not only for the revival of Islamic intellectual tradition but also for the future development of modern science itself in the light of the current search by many scientists in the West for new paradigms for the natural sciences .

The First Encounter of the Muslim World with Modern Science

By modern science, we mean that model of studying Nature developed by Western philosophers and scientists since the seventeenth century, including the whole of its practical applications to the technological domain. Significantly, less than four centuries after its birth, modern science appears to be in a profound state of crisis, at least concerning its philosophical foundation. We observe that, of late, numerous works have appeared in the West, harping on the theme of alternative models for natural sciences as well as alternative technological models[1].

The search for new models has been generated by three main factors. First, major advances in the new frontiers of scientific research, such as in subatomic physics, have rendered obsolete the Cartesian and mechanistic worldview which, since the seventeenth century, has provided science with its fundamental assumptions concerning the reality of the physical world. Second, contemporary ecological crisis has brought into sharp focus the question of the whole relationship between man and nature and the issue of appropriate technology . And third, the

1. See, for example, Morris Berman, *The Reenchantment of the World*; Richard L. Thompson, *Mechanistic and Nonmechanistic Science: An Investigation into the Nature of Consciousness and Form* (New York: Bala Books, 1981); and Kurt Hubner, *Critique of Scientific Reason.*

discipline of history of science has enabled Western man to gain a better knowledge of the sciences of nature and technological know-how developed by other civilizations before the modern period, which cannot simply be reduced to being anticipations of modern science.

The Islamization of the natural sciences now widely discussed in the Muslim world is itself only meaningful when viewed in the context of a rising awareness among Muslim intellectuals of this special character of modern science. Islamization is indeed an attempt to provide an alternative model to modern science. This is, however, a new perception and a new response. In the initial encounter of the Muslim world with modern science, the main pattern of intellectual response emanating from the Muslim consciousness was entirely different. It is to this initial encounter that we now turn our attention.

The Beginning of General Western Influence upon the Muslim World

The Muslim world has a long history of encounters with the West. The two civilizations have greatly influenced each other in the process. In speaking of the beginning of general western influence upon the Muslim world, we are actually referring to that particular moment in the history of the Muslim world when it no longer possesses the inner strength and dynamism to withstand the external challenges posed by Western civilization. Unlike in the past when the vitality and creative genius of the Muslim world enabled it to integrate all that is positive from other civilizations into its own worldview and inner constitution, this time, due to its internal weaknesses as well as the highly superior material power of the West, it proves itself impotent to stem the speedy flow of Western culture into its territory, though not without violent opposition. This is what has happened to the Muslim world from the beginning of the nineteenth century onwards.

It is true that prior to this period western ideas and influences alien to Islamic culture had penetrated the Ottoman Empire[2] and a few important parts of Islamic territory had fallen into the hands of Western powers. Egypt was occupied by Napolean in 1798. Malacca, which so soon after its conversion to Islam at the beginning of the fifteenth century had become a major trading center of the Islamic world as well as a center for the propagation of Islam in the Malay world, had been ruled successively since 1511 by the Portuguese, the Dutch, and the British until the second half of the twentieth century. But in terms of both its intensity and scope as well as its discernable devastative effects upon the life of the Muslim peoples, the beginning of western influence upon the Muslim world must be identified with the beginning of the nineteenth century.

The challenge posed by the West to the Muslim world during this period was on all levels of existence – military, political, economic, social, cultural and intellectual. Initially, however, western domination of the Muslim world was military, political and economic. The Muslims were militarily vanquished, politically subjugated, directly or indirectly, and economically exploited. This domination brought about immense changes to the political structure of the Muslim world, its administrative and judicial machinery, educational system, its army and the whole fabric of its socio-economic organization. This was soon followed by religious and intellectual forms of impingement through various channels, some more direct and intensified than others[3].

The most serious threat at the religious level came from the Christian missionaries, particularly through the vast network of schools they had established throughout the Muslim world. There was the intellectual assault on Islam and Muslim societies carried out by the scholarship of the Orientalists. And then there was the invasion of modern thought itself. The invasion has

2. On this question, see H.A.R. Gibb and Harold Bowen, (eds.), *Islamic Society and the West: A Study of the Impact of Western Civilization on Moslem Culture in the Near East* (Oxford University Press, 1957), vol. I, pt. I.
3. Fazlur Rahman, *Islam* (University of Chicago Press, 1966), p. 212.

been greatly facilitated by the establishment of Muslim schools on a European model and the teaching of European subjects, even though the original intention of these schools was to enable Muslims to compete with their European invaders in the field of education and to check the influence of Christian missionary schools. In fact, it was mainly through education that secularism and other Western influences effectively pervaded the whole of Muslim society.

Of all the western products which have flowed unabated into the Muslim world since the beginning of the nineteenth century, it is modern science and technology which must have left the greatest impression and impact upon the Muslim people, and which provided the external stimulus for a critical appraisal of their predicaments. They associated this science and technology mainly with military power and economic progress for they have seen with their own eyes the display of this power on their territory. They realized that it was by virtue of its science and technology that the West became far more superior to themselves. Enlightened Muslims were forced to respond to it in one way or another.

The First Impact of Modern Science upon the Muslim World

The eighteenth century saw the emergence of Europe as the birthplace of many technological innovations and achievements. During the latter part of the same century, European technology has begun to penetrate Ottoman society through two channels – the military and the industrial sector[4]. However the range of innovations introduced in these two fields was not wide enough to stir a consciousness of inferiority complex among the Muslims toward the Europeans. Their impact upon the old military organizations in the Ottoman Empire and the traditional struc-

4. On the beginning of European technological penetration into these two sectors in the Ottoman society, see Gibb & Bowen, *op. cit.*, chaps III & IV.

ture of Muslim economy was nonetheless considerable and highly significant.

But it was the Napoleonic expedition to Egypt in 1798 that brought about the first real impact of modern science upon the Muslim mind. That expedition brought with it a number of Sorbone professors and experts of the *Academie Francaise* and a treasury of French scientific achievements to Egypt[5]. Soon the French invaders were to establish on Egyptian soil a number of libraries, laboratories, workshops, and chemical and military factories. Many religious scholars of Egypt were also able to see for themselves the accomplishments of French science through their visits to France. And with the translation of many French books into Arabic, a larger segment of the Muslim peoples were being exposed to the scientific and technological achievements of Europe[6]. In the meantime, the Egyptian Muslims saw before their own eyes how day by day this science-based power was put to the best use by the West to encroach more and more upon their lands and resources.

This historic encounter between modern Western science and a Muslim world beset by numerous internal weaknesses gave rise to two distinct Muslim attitudes toward that science. The first attitude was one of antagonism and rejection, whereas the second was one of accommodation and approval. However, there were varying degrees of antagonism and approval. Each attitude has been shaped by different sets of motives and grounded on different justifications. For example, the antagonists range from those who see in modern science something characteristically European and fundamentally opposed to the spirit of Muslim science to those who view it as the work of the devil, and from those who attempt to deny its accomplishments to those who

---

5. See I. R. al-Faruqi, "Science and Traditional Values in Islamic Society," in *Zygon, Journal of Religion and Science*, vol. 2, no. 3 (Sept. 1967), p. 23.
6. This information was provided by Shaykh Ḥasan al-'Aṭṭar, an early 19th century Rector of al-Azhar. See 'Alī Mubārak, *Al-Khiṭaṭ al-tawfiqiyyah fī tarjumat al-Shaykh Ḥasan al-'Aṭṭar* (Cairo: Bulaq, 1924), vol. IV, no. 38.

identify the works of science as heralds of the end of the world[7]. Sayyid Jamāl al-Dīn al-Afghānī criticized severely the first group for making a distinction between Muslim science and European science.

The protagonists also exhibited different shades of opinions within their ranks. There was first of all the secular stratum comprising both Muslims and non-Muslims. The latter , who were mostly Christian intellectuals, emerged as the more vocal group. They endorsed the vigorous pursuit of modern science. Judging from their writings, they were initially mainly motived by practical considerations. Science was seen as a source of material power and as the real agent of social change and modernization. Later, however, especially from around the beginning of the twentieth century, with such famous Christian intellectuals as Ya'qūb Ṣarrūf (1852 – 1927), Shiblī al-Shumayyil (1860 – 1916), Jurji Zaydan (1861 – 1914), Faraḥ Antūn (1871 – 1922) and Salāmah Musa (1876 – 1958), the primary motive for totally embracing modern science was philosophical and intellectual. They sought to affirm the status of science as the true source of intellectual enlightenment and to assert the supremacy of the scientific worldview over the traditional religious worldview.

In the case of some of them, the motive was also political. Through science and modern civilization, they hoped to bring down the mental and psychological barriers which shielded the traditionalist and religious reformist position of the Muslims. Speaking of this motive, a contemporary Arab scholar remarks that "in this, one can perhaps detect an unconscious will seeking not so much "the truth" as the political transmutation of the Christian Arab situation in Muslim society. Christian intellectuals, by upholding reason and the scientific approach, were indirectly attacking the sources from which social and political authority derived its legitimacy"[8].

---

7. al-Faruqi, *op. cit.*, p. 238.
8. See Hisham Sharabi, *Arab Intellectuals and the West: The Formative Years 1875-1941* (The Johns Hopkins Press, 1970), p.57.

The impact of modern science upon the Muslim segment of this secular stratum was more visible at the practical level. Its early manifestations could already be seen in the first few decades of the nineteenth century during the rule of Muḥammad 'Alī, very soon after the French conquest of Egypt. It was Muḥammad 'Alī who pursued science and modernization with furious resolution and boldness without any particular regard for religion[9]. He encouraged Napolean to introduce military and industrial techniques into Egypt[10]. He founded schools on the European pattern, where European sciences were taught, at first by European professors whom he had specifically invited, and later by Egyptians trained in the West.

With many students from other Muslim lands coming to study European sciences in these modern Egyptian schools, the spread of the influence of modern science in the Muslim world gained greater momentum.. The scientism and modernism of Muḥammad 'Alī was to have its most eloquent defender in the person of Ṭāha Ḥussein[11]. After Muḥammad 'Alī's death, his pursuit of science and modernization was continued by his descendents. Its intellectual defense and justifications were mainly provided by Arab Christian thinkers. The famous among them have been mentioned earlier. Their ideas were channelled through such periodicals as *al-Hilāl*, *al-Muqtaṭaf*, and *al-Jāmi'ah*. Through the writings of these Christian intellectuals[12], it was no longer just "pure science" and its technological application, which challenged the thinking of Muslim society. What had started to intrude into the Muslim mind in the name of science were the various philosophical currents in modern western thought that have been wedded to science, particularly

9. See H.A.R. Gibb, *Studies on the Civilization of Islam* (Princeton: Princeton University Press, 1982), p. 247.
10. *Ibid*, p. 328.
11. For Ṭāha Ḥussein's defense of Muhammad 'Alī's modernization program, see for example his "Modern Egypt" in Arberry & Landau (eds.), *Islam Today*, London, chapt. 6.
12. H. Sharabi, *op. cit.*, pp. 69-70.

positivism, naturalism, and evolutionism.

For example, Darwinism was introduced into the Arab world by Shiblī Shumayyil who, in his numerous articles, dealt with the social and philosophical meanings of Darwin's scientific discoveries. In 1910, he published a book on Darwin's theory of evolution entitled *The Philosophy of Evolution and Progress.* In his view, only knowledge attainable and verifiable through the methods of the physical sciences can truly be called real knowledge. He is said to have developed the most coherent materialist position in Christian Arab thought.

No less striking influences were to be observed upon the minds of Muslim intellectuals like Muhammad Ḥusayn Haykal, Ṭāha Ḥusayn, and 'Alī 'Abd al-Rāziq, at least during the earlier phase of their intellectual careers. These three highly eloquent and influential secular Muslim thinkers became wholly converted to the modern scientific worldview for which sake they openly expressed their anti-religious sentiments, and degraded and belittled Islam and its heritage even if that meant going against the very scientific spirit that they had espoused. They were so captivated by the methodology of modern science that even after their return to Islam after the twenties they continued to interpret and judge Islam in the light of modern science.

It is itself significant that their return to Islam took place in the light of several intellectual and philosophical developments in the West critical of modern science. Some of these developments indicated a new and genuine interest in Oriental traditions, including that of Islam. Haykal, for example, admitted openly that he was deeply influenced by these developments. His western intellectual mentors like Auguste Comte (d. 1857)and Hippolyte Taine (d. 1893) had themselves abandoned their total reliance on science as a path of enlightenment, courting instead spiritual guidance[13]. Similarly, Henri Bergson, whom Haykal

13. See C.D. Smith, *Islam and the Search for Social Order in Modern Egypt: A Biography of Muhammad Husayn Haykal* (Albany: SUNY Press, 1983), pp. 97-98.

cited as an example of the "spiritualists" of the twenties confessed his doubt on the ability of science to discover a comprehensive truth system through its scientific principles and methods.

The next group which approved of modern science, but which maintained this approval within the framework of Islam was represented by such outstanding figures as Sayyid Jamāl al-Dīn al-Afghānī, Muḥammad 'Abduh and Rashīd Riḍā. In the Indian sub-continent this line of thinking was represented by Sir Sayyid Aḥmad Khān and Muḥammad Iqbāl, and in Turkey by Namik Kemal. Within this group as well we encounter a diversity of views as to how modern science should be intellectually and religiously justified and incorporated into Islam. But in none of these attempts to come to terms with modern science have its fundamental premises and methodology been seriously questioned.

There is no doubt that modern science has left a considerable intellectual influence upon these Muslim thinkers and reformers, and even tempered with some of their religious views. Their attempt to justify modern science on religious grounds was meant to serve a double purpose: first to defend true Islam from the intellectual onslaughts of Orientalism and the highly secularized and westernized Arab Christian thinkers who appealed to modern science as the basis of their rejection of the traditional and religious worldview; and second, to liberate true Islam from the clutches of the religious establishment who, in the name of safeguarding the *Sharī'ah* and the traditional legacy, resisted *ijtihād* and maintained a negative attitude toward modern civilization of which science is one of the major fruits. In their interpretation of true Islam, conformity with modern science was accepted as an important criterion.

We have dealt till now with the impact of modern science upon Muslim society in one particular area only in the Muslim world, namely Egypt. But then Egypt was one of the most important religious and intellectual centers of the Muslim world. Perhaps because of that special position, it became an attractive target of western imperialist designs. Egypt was among the earliest Muslim lands to have been penetrated by secularization and westernization, and also the worst affected.

Another such area is the Indian sub-continent where the impact of modern science was already felt as early as the eighteenth century. As in the Ottoman Empire, it was the military domain that was first exposed to European technology. In the early eighteenth century, on the eve of the building of territorial empire by the British East India Company, when the Mughal Empire was in a state of decline, European technological superiority was duly acknowledged as clearly indicated in the Empire's military policy of appointing Europeans to higher posts[14].

Later, in the second half of the century, a number of Muslims who visited Europe, including I'tiṣām al-Dīn, an emissary of the Mughal Emperor, Shāh 'Alām II, put into writing their first impressions of modern western civilization and its technological superiority. One of the earliest and also the best accounts to be published was provided by Mirzā Abū Ṭālib Khān who visited Europe during 1799 – 1803. Entitled *Masīr-i ṭālibī fī bilādi afranjī*, and written nearly a quarter of a century before the impressions of the Egyptian scholar , al-Ṭahṭāwī, Abū Ṭālib Khān's work was one of the first introductions to modern western civilization written by a Muslim.

At the intellectual level itself, there was some interest shown toward modern science by the rulers of Awadh (Oudh) even before the nineteenth century. For example, Newton's *Principia* was translated into Arabic under the patronage of Āṣaf al-Dawla (1778 – 1792). This was, however, an isolated interest. It was not until the introduction of British educational, cultural, and economic institutions in the early nineteenth century that the impact of the modern sciences began to gain momentum[15].

The modern sciences were first taught in English in 1835. The first engineering college was established at Roorkee in 1847 and the first medical college in Bombay in 1845. The intellectual

14. Aziz Ahmad, *Islamic Modernism in India and Pakistan 1857-1964* (Oxford University Press, 1967), p. 5.
15. *Ibid*, p. 23.

figure who more than any other paved the way for a favourable response to modern science and these institutions was Karāmat 'Alī Jawnpūrī (d. 1873), a disciple of the great theologian, Shāh 'Abd al-'Azīz (the son of Shāh Walīallāh). In the early twenties of the century, in the course of supporting Sayyid Aḥmad Barelwī's reform movement in Bengal, he developed a trend favouring the assimilation of western sciences. He urged Indian Muslims to learn European languages so that western scientific works can be translated into Arabic, Persian, and Urdu. Although his views on modern science were already known around this time, these were not put into writing until after the 1865-'Mutiny' when he published them in his work, *Ma'ākhiẓ al-'ulūm.* He was therefore the founder of that intellectual school of Indian Muslims, called by Professor al-Faruqi the "One-Book school", which identifies the Quranic worldview with the scientific worldview.

The two greatest representatives of this school were Amīr 'Alī, Karāmat 'Alī's own pupil, and Sayyid Aḥmad Khān. Through their numerous writings, modern science left a great impact upon the Muslim minds of the sub-continent. Sayyid Aḥmad Khān (1817 – 1898) devoted his intellectual energy to the cultivation of modern science among Muslims. In 1864, he founded a scientific society for the purpose of popularizing western science, primarily among Muslims. The Society translated European works on physical and social sciences into Urdu, and published a bilingual journal[16]. As in Egypt, what gradually filtered into the minds of Muslims of the sub-continent was not just the knowledge of pure science and its technological applications but also its underlying philosophies and worldview. In order to accommodate and justify the latter, Sayyid Aḥmad Khān had to reinterpret Islam. In fact, he did call for the construction of a new *'ilm al-kalām* (theology) that would establish a clear and sound relationship between Islam and modern science.

At the institutional level he established in 1874 the Anglo-Muhammadan Oriental College at Aligarh, modelled on Cam-

16. *Ibid,* p. 37.

bridge University, which aimed among others at the liberalization of ideas and the promotion of a broad humanism and a scientific worldview. As a propagandist, he undertook the publication of a journal, *Tahdhīb al-akhlāq*, named after the famous ethical treatise of Ibn Miskawayh, but apparently modelled on Addison and Steele's *Spectator* and *Tatler*. One of the primary aims of the journal was to bridge the chasm between the premises of modern science and the data of revealed religion. This was an influential mouthpiece of modernism, which significantly shaped the development of Islam in the subcontinent.

The westernism of Sayyid Aḥmad Khān and his school was opposed at the popular level by figures like the poet, Akbar Allahābādī (d. 1921), and at a more intellectual level by Shiblī Nu'mānī (d. 1914), and Abu'l-Kalām Āzād (d. 1959). In his response to modern science, and more generally modern civilization, Shiblī Nu'mānī adopted an attitude quite similar to that of Rashīd Riḍā and Muḥammad Farīd Wajdī of Egypt, with whom he in fact maintained a close contact. Though fascinated by modern learning, his programme was not to reform Islam according to some alien criteria, but to revive it from within. His vision envisaged the rehabilitation of Islamic learning in its entirety, along the lines of its flowering under the 'Abbāsids in Baghdad[17].

In general, we can say that the overall impact of modern science upon nineteenth-century Muslim world has been quite profound. Economically, militarily, intellectually, and even theologically, its influence has been extensive. Many who were at the forefront of the movement defending Islam from the encroachment of westernism were themselves significantly affected in their ways of thinking and their intellectual attitudes by that science. The encounter of the Muslim world with modern science was to produce a wide spectrum of intellectual responses from the Muslim intelligentsia. The response pattern is now analyzed in the following section.

17. *Ibid*, pp. 77-86.

Modern Science as a Challenge: Views of 19th and 20th-Centuries Muslim Thinkers.

Muslim thinkers of the nineteenth and the first half of the twentieth centuries, whether religious or secular, saw modern science as a major challenge to the Muslim world. With respect to their perception of this challenge, we may divide them into two main groups. The first group defined the challenge in positive terms: Muslims must strive to learn and acquire the modern sciences. The second group advocated confrontation and rejection. We describe this particular view of the challenge as negative. Let us now look more closely at some of the arguments presented by each group in justifying its own position.

The Positive Challenge of Learning and Acquisition

The first major Muslim intellectual figure of the nineteenth century to respond positively to the challenge of modern science was Ḥasan al-'Aṭṭār al-Khalwatī[18]. Born in Cairo around 1766, he was a contemporary of the famous Eygptian historian, 'Abd al-Raḥmān al-Jabartī, and a teacher of the more famous Rifā'a al-Ṭahṭāwī. His intellectual response was perhaps more significant than that of many of his contemporaries. He was not only an important religious figure, being *Shaykh al-Azhar* from 1831 until his death in 1835, but also a scientist of great ability. He wrote many works, among others, on metaphysics, astronomy, mathematics and medicine.

Al-'Aṭṭār obtained his scientific education in Turkey where he had the opportunity of meeting several European scientists, particularly in the field of medicine. It was through this acquaintance that he came to know of advances made by contemporary western science. He was certainly in favour of Muslims learning western science. But bound as much as he was to the scientific worldview of the Islamic tradition in which he was brought

18. On the life and works of this figure, see Peter Gran, *Islamic Roots of Capitalism: Egypt 1760-1840* (Austin & London: University of Texas Press, 1979), chaps. 4-8.

up, his whole approach to European science was primarily guided by the desire to integrate its accomplishments into that worldview. This was best illustrated by his attitude to western medicine. While he was perceptive and bold enough to make use of western medical advances to criticize Ibn Sīnā's medical works, he remained faithful to the traditional philosophical framework of Islamic medicine perfected by the "Prince of the Physicians" himself. Because of much infighting among the *'ulamā'* at al-Azhar, al-'Aṭṭār never had the opportunity to translate his progressive intellectual views on modern science into concrete educational programmes during his rectorship at that prestigious institution.

Al-'Aṭṭār's intellectual perspective very much resembles that of present-day Muslim scholars who argue for the Islamization of the sciences. He was well versed with both Islamic philosophy, on which he, in fact, wrote numerous treatises, and the underlying philosophy of western science. The next major figure of the nineteenth century to show a positive attitude toward modern science was Sayyid Jamāl al-Dīn al-Afghānī, who however differs from al-'Aṭṭār in one important respect. Although Afghānī too knew Islamic philosophy, which he had studied in Persia and attempted to revive at al-Azhar, he never received a formal training in any of the modern natural sciences. Perhaps, this was the main reason why we fail to find a concrete application of the principles of Islamic philosophy to his discussion of modern science. His analysis of that science was not critical enough to the point of distinguishing between its universal elements and its "Western" elements insofar as the latter defined and determined the particular worldview of western man. Afghānī conceived of modern science as a universal science which transcends nations, cultures, and religions, although he recognized the role of cultural values in the domain of technological applications. Thus he criticized the religious scholars for their negative attitude toward modern science:

> "The strangest thing of all is that our *'ulamā'* these days have divided science into two parts. One they call Muslim

science, and one European science. Because of this they forbid others to teach some of the useful sciences. *They have not understood that science is that noble thing that has no connection with any nation, and is not distinguished by anything but itself.* Rather, everything that is known is known by science, and every nation that becomes renowned becomes renowned through sciences. . . .

How very strange it is that the Muslims study those sciences that are ascribed to Aristotle with the greatest delight, as if Aristotle were one of the pillars of the Muslims. However, if the discussion relates to Galileo, Newton, and Kepler, they consider them infidels. The father and mother of science is proof, and proof is neither Aristotle nor Galileo. The truth is where there is proof, and those who forbid science and knowledge in the belief that they are safeguarding the Islamic religion are really the enemies of that religion. The Islamic religion is the closest of religions to science and knowledge, and there is no incompatibility between science and knowledge and the foundation of the Islamic faith".[19]

In urging Muslims to study modern science, Afghānī argued that science is neither eastern nor western, neither Islamic nor non-Islamic, but is universal in character and the pride of every civilization. This argument is certainly valid if by modern science he means factual knowledge of natural phenomena empirically established by the modern scientific community, as distinct from their philosophical assumptions concerning physical reality, which constitute the foundation of that knowledge. It is the latter that is mostly opposed to the Islamic view of Reality. Afghānī was, in fact, aware of the main philosophical currents in contemporary West that had entered into the conceptual structures of modern science, including Darwinism or evolutionism and ato-

19. See N.R. Keddie, *An Islamic Response to Imperialism: Political and Religious Writings of Sayyid Jamal al-Din "al-Afghani"* (University of California Press, 1983), p. 107.

mism, which he criticized in his work "Refutation of the Materialists"[20].

He spoke of the indispensability of philosophy for the cultivation of the sciences. But what kind of philosophy did he have in mind? Is there such a thing as universal philosophy? This is not clear to us. We are not quite certain whether or not he accepted the philosophy of modern science as the philosophy for all cultures and civilizations. Nonetheless, he did call on contemporary Muslims to formulate a philosophy that would excell the works of Fārābī, Ibn Sīnā, Ibn Bājjah, Mulla Ṣadrā and all the past Muslim philosophers. In our view, Afghānī failed to provide a convincing refutation of the claim made by many of the religious scholars that there is a basis for distinction between Islamic science and European science.

Afghānī further argued that there is no incompatibility between science and the foundation of the Islamic faith. Thus Muslims should not reject science. On the contrary, Afghānī reminded us, true Islam is favorable to philosophy and science. It is the closest of religions to knowledge. It was the Quran which first taught philosophy to Muslims, and which planted in their souls the roots of the philosophical sciences. This philosophic spirit generated by the Quran enabled the early Muslims to cultivate all the sciences within a relatively short period of their emergence upon the stage of world history. In a lecture on *Teaching and Learning* delivered in Calcutta, India on November 8, 1882, Afghānī reminded his Indian audience:

> "The first Muslims had no science, but, thanks to the Islamic religion, a philosophic spirit arose among them, and owing to the philosophic spirit they began to discuss the general affairs of the world and human necessities. This was why they acquired in a short time all the sciences with particular subjects that they translated from the Syriac, Persian, and Greek into the Arabic language at the time of Manṣūr Davānaqi"[21].

20. *Ibid*, pp. 150-180
21. *Ibid*, p. 105.

In Afghānī's view, acquiring the philosophic spirit is more important than acquiring the sciences themselves since the latter can only be sustained by the former. Therefore, what is of primary importance to the Muslims in their encounter with modern science is the cultivation of the spirit of scientific inquiry itself , which, in fact, is demanded by the Quran. The loss of this spirit in the Muslim world has resulted in its stagnation and deterioration, whereas the West has prospered and become powerful because it has nurtured this spirit inherited from the Muslims. In learning science afresh from the developed West, the Muslims are actually engaged in recovering their past glory and refulfilling the long neglected commandments of the Quran concerning the study of Nature.

Afghānī also dealt at length with the indispensability of science to human civilization and with the numerous benefits that accrue from scientific and technological know-how. His arguments in favour of Muslims studying modern science were basically shared by his contemporaries like Namik Kemal in Turkey, Sayyid Aḥmad Khān in India and Muḥammad 'Abduh in Egypt. Where they differed is in their views on the implications of modern science for the traditional *weltanschauung* and for the realm of faith. But this is an important difference. A central issue in the encounter between Islam and modern science concerns these implications.

These famous modern Muslim reformers have taken great pains to spell out the positive aspects and the great benefits of modern science. Their untiring efforts have helped to facilitate the adoption of modern science among the Muslims. But what about its negative aspects or religious implications?Are there not also areas of conflict between Islam and modern science?And if there is such a conflict, what kind of attitude should the Muslim mind adopt?

As far as Afghānī is concerned, his writings and speeches have nothing but praise for modern science. The only instances he ever criticized modern science were when he delivered a critique of some of the scientific theories. Perhaps he did not wish to dwell on areas of conflicts and controversies because that would have discouraged the Muslims from studying modern science. Not to study modern science would result in a greater evil for the Muslims for then they would be condemned to live in stagnation and slumber in the face of western technological superiority and imperialistic encroachments on their lands. To highlight on the negative elements of modern science at that particular moment would not be helpful to his main task of awakening the Muslims from their intellectual slumber and of exposing them to the immense benefits promised by modern science.

Afghānī's disciple, Muḥammad 'Abduh, was of the view that there could not be any conflict between religion and science. The possibility of conflict is between science and the Quran's interpreters. Consequently, he maintains that, the medieval Muslim cosmology and worldview can indeed be challenged by science, but Islamic faith as such cannot be opposed to science[22]. On the contrary, in his view, faith and science are interdependent. This was the case of the early Muslims. The more they knew in religion the more they excelled in the sciences of nature. In other words, the domains of reason and heart, which in other religious traditions are considered mutually exclusive or even opposed to each other, constitute an organic unity as far as Islam is concerned. 'Abduh's view was shared by Iqbāl in the Indian sub-continent.

Quite a different perception of the implications of modern science for the realm of faith came from Sayyid Aḥmad Khān. In his view, it is modern science itself with all its principles and discoveries, which must serve as the criteria for judging the acceptability of a certain faith[23]. The principles of Islam must be reinterpreted in conformity with the laws of nature discovered by modern science, and hence the need for a new theology. The response of the Muslim majority to such a radical view was

22. Fazlur Rahman, *Islam and Modernity: Transformation of an Intellectual Tradition* (University of Chicago Press, 1982), p. 51.
23. *Ibid*, pp. 51-52.

predictable. Sayyid Aḥmad Khān failed to gain support for his "theological program" even in his own Aligarh Muslim College which he had created for the express purpose of integrating religious beliefs into the modern scientific outlook on account of a strong opposition from the religious teachers.

A more "orthodox" response to modern science came from Namik Kemal. He would not admit the claims of modern science save those that are empirically verified. Furthermore, he insisted on subordinating the claims of science to the data of revelation.

The Negative Challenge of Opposition and Rejection

Muslims critical or antagonistic toward modern science constitute the majority group. Included in this category are those identified by the modernists as the adherents of the worldview of *taqlīd.* Many religious conservatives and traditionalists oppose the study of modern science because they see great incompatibility between its worldview and their traditional conceptions of Nature. Their attachment to the traditional worldview is all the more intense with a desire to conserve and preserve the popular religious rites and practices which are only meaningful within the framework of that worldview. In attempting to preserve their particular worldview by shunning and rejecting modern science instead of intellectually challenging its "evils", and rebutting its philosophical standpoints in the light of their own belief system, these religious scholars lend themselves to a just criticism by the modernists .

Also included among the antagonists are those Muslims who, while acknowledging the material benefits of modern science and technology, would not sanction their study because they are the products of western people whose religious beliefs and cultural values are opposed to Islam. There is the fear that Muslims studying modern science from the West would end up appropriating its cultural values and habits. This attitude may be identified mainly with the Muslim masses. Regardless of

---

23. *Ibid*, pp. 51-52.

whether this fear is justified or not, it could hardly be considered an intellectual response. Rather, it is the intuitive response of a people who have lost their self confidence to face the challenge of alien cultures. It is left to the present-day scholars, Muslims as well as non-Muslims, to demonstrate intellectually the naivety of the idea that "useful" modern technology can be introduced into a society without adversely affecting its cultural identity and its social fabric.

Contemporary Intellectual Response – Islamization of the Sciences

The main task of the late 19th-century and early 20th-century Muslim thinkers was to awaken the Muslim people from their intellectual slumber and to encourage them to adopt a positive attitude toward learning the modern sciences. It is understandable therefore that their arguments tend mainly to highlight on the harmony between Islam and modern science and on how this science can benefit the Muslim *ummah.* They were little concerned with the negative impact this science could have on Muslim cultural environment when it is appropriated without due adaptation or adjustment.

Nearly a century later, we could see tremendous progress in the cultivation and appropriation of modern science and technology in the Muslim world, at least in some member countries. But this has been achieved at the expense of the secularization of Muslim minds. How to stem this tide of secularization and yet at the same time achieve unhampered scientific and technological progress becomes a major present-day concern of Muslim intellectuals. This intellectual concern, which must be viewed as a continuation of all previous attempts at resolving the problem of the encounter between Islam and modern sciences, now presents itself as part of a more comprehensive program to deal with the "Islamicity" of all branches of modern knowledge. This program is called the *Islamization* of knowledge.

The theme "Islamization of knowledge" is now a popular one

in many parts of the Islamic world. This theme will be fully dealt with in one of our works under preparation. We have decided to include this brief discussion on "Islamization" in the present chapter in order to show that the Muslim response to modern thought in general, and modern science in particular, is still an ongoing process.

An important event which greatly contributed to that popularity was the First World Conference on Muslim Education held at Mecca in April 1977. With regard to the Islamization of the natural sciences, several conferences have been organized, and a number of academic institutions and organizations established with the expressed view of realizing its very aims. Still, writings of a serious nature on the subject are very few. We have in mind here the writings of such scholars as al-'Attas, al-Faruqi and S. Hossein Nasr[24]. Nevertheless, even from these few writings that we have, we are able to draw an important picture of what Islamization is all about, what it has achieved, and what is yet to be done.

The primary aim of Islamization of the natural sciences is to formulate an all-embracing study of the natural world, together with its technological applications, based upon the principles of Islam. That such an aim is indeed a legitimate and valid one for the Muslims has been convincingly shown by the above writings. The arguments involve both a profound criticism of modern science, showing its limitations and shortcomings as a model of studying Nature, and an exposition of the principles of Islam which are relevant to natural sciences and in which, in fact, are already embodied all that is positive in modern science. The next main task of Islamization is to make a concrete application of these principles to the various branches of the natural sciences.

---

24. See for example, S.M.N. al-'Attas, *Islam and Secularism*; *The Positive Aspects of Tasawwuf: Preliminary Thoughts on an Islamic Philosophy of Science*; I.R. al-Faruqi, *Islamization of Knowledge: General Principles and Work Plan* (Virginia: International Institute of Islamic Thought, 1982); *Tawhid: Its Implication for Thought and Life* (Virginia: Int. Institute of Islamic Thought, 1982); S.H. Nasr, *Man and Nature*; *Science and Civilization in Islam*; and *Islamic Cosmological Doctrines.*

This is yet to be realized in the form of text books and methods of instruction appropriate for each level of education. Similarly, there is the urgent need to define and identify the appropriate technological needs of the Muslim *ummah* in its various phases of social and economic development.

Conclusion

We believe that Islamization of modern science understood in the above sense is the most apt intellectual response for Muslims to adopt toward that science. Only through Islamization can Muslims achieve scientific and technological progress and at the same time retain and even fortify their Islamic intellectual, moral, and spiritual outlook. Its success will have a great significance not only for the revival of Islamic intellectual tradition but also for the future development of modern science itself. Today, many modern scientists are earnestly searching for new paradigms for the natural sciences. Islam can once again play its providential universal role of providing the essential ingredients for these new paradigms and solving the numerous problems that now confront modern science but which the secular West has proved impotent to solve. However, the success of Islamization depends a great deal on the concerted and coordinated efforts of all Muslim intellectuals.

References

1. Charles C. Adams, *Islam and Modernism in Egypt* (London, 1933).
2. Aziz Ahmad, *Islamic Modernism in India and Pakistan 1857-1964* (Oxford University Press, 1967).
3. Bashir Ahmad Dar, *Religious Thought of Sayyid Ahmad Khan* (Lahore: Institute of Islamic Culture, 1957).
4. Osman Amin, *Muhammad 'Abduh* (Washington D.C: American Council of Learned Societies, 1953). Translated from Arabic by Charles Wendell.

5. A.J. Arberry, and Rom Landau, (eds.), *Islam Today* (London: Faber and Faber Ltd.).
6. Niyazi Berkes, *The Development of Secularism in Turkey* (Montreal: McGill University Press, 1964).
7. Werner Caskel, "Western Impact and Islamic Civilization" in *Unity and Variety in Muslim Civilization*, Gustave E. von Grunebaum (ed.), (University of Chicago Press, 1955), pp. 335-360.
8. R. Ismail al-Faruqi and O. Naseef, (eds.), *Social and Natural Sciences: The Islamic Perspective* (Jeddah: Hodder and Stoughton & King Abdul Aziz University, 1981).
9. R. Ismail al-Faruqi, *Islamization of Knowledge: General Principles and Work Plan* (Virginia: International Institute of Islamic Thought, 1982).
10. ——————— "Science and Traditional Values in Islamic Society" in *Zygon, Journal of Religion and Science*, vol. 2, no. 3 (Sept. 1967), pp. 231-246.
11. N. Richard Frye, (ed.), *Islam and the West: Proceedings of the Harvard Summer School Conference on the Middle East, July 25-27, 1955* (The Hague, 1957).
12. H. A. R. Gibb, *Modern Trends in Islam* (New York: Octagon Books, 1978).
13. ——————— (ed.), *Whither Islam?: A Survey of Modern Movements in the Moslem World* (New York: AMS Press Inc., 1973).
14. ——————— , *Studies on the Civilization of Islam*, edited by Stanford J. Shaw and William R. Polk (Toronto: S.J. Reginald Saunders & Co. Ltd., 1962).
15. H.A. R. Gibb and Harold Bowen, (eds.), *Islamic Society and the West: A Study of the Impact of Western Civilization on Moslem Culture in the Near East* (Oxford University Press, 1957), vol. I, parts I & II.
16. Peter Gran, *Islamic Roots of Capitalism: Egypt (1760-1840)* (Austin: University of Texas Press, 1979).
17. Yvonne Yazbeck Haddad, *Contemporary Islam and the Challenge of History* (Albany: SUNY Press, 1982).

18. Muhammad Iqbal, *The Reconstruction of Religious Thought in Islam* (Lahore: Iqbal Academy & Institute of Islamic Culture, 1989).
19. Nikki R. Keddie, *Sayyid Jamal al-Din al-Afghani: A Political Biography* (University of California Press, 1972).
20. ____________, *An Islamic Response to Imperialism: Political and Religious Writings of Sayyid Jamal al-Din al-Afghani* (University of California Press, 1968).
21. Elie Kedourie, *Afghani and 'Abduh: An Essay on Religious Unbelief and Political Activism in Modern Islam* (Frank Cass & Co. Ltd., 1966).
22. ____________, *England and the Middle East: The Destruction of the Ottoman Empire 1914-1921* (London: Bowes & Bowes, 1956).
23. George Makdisi, (ed.), *Arabic and Islamic Studies in Honor of Hamilton A.R. Gibb* (Dept. of Near Eastern Languages and Literatures, Harvard University, 1965).
24. S.H. Nasr, *Islamic Life and Thought* (Albany: SUNY Press, 1981).
25. ____________, *Islam and the Plight of Modern Man* (London, 1976).
26. ____________, *Man and Nature* (London: Allen & Unwin Ltd., 1976).
27. Fazlur Rahman, *Islam* (University of Chicago Press. 1966).
28. ____________, *Islam and Modernity: Transformation of an Intellectual Tradition* (University of Chicago Press, 1982).
29. Ernest Renan, *L'Islamisme et la Science* (Paris, 1883).
30. Mordin Serif, *The Genesis of Young Ottoman Thought* (Princeton, 1962).
31. Hisham Sharabi, *Arab Intellectuals and the West: The Formative Years 1875-1914* (The Johns Hopkins Press, 1970).
32. Charles D. Smith, *Islam and the Search for Social Order in Modern Egypt: A Biography of Muhammad Husayn Haykal* (Albany: SUNY Press, 1983).
33. Wilfred C. Smith, *Modern Islam in India: A Social Analysis*, (Albany: Lahore, 1963).

34. ———, *Islam in Modern History* (Princeton University Press, 1957).
35. A. A. Thanwi, *Answer to Modernism* (New Delhi: Adam Publishers & Distributors, 1981).
36. Murray Titus, *Indian Islam* (Oxford University Press, 1930).
37. ———, *Islam in India and Pakistan* (Calcutta: Y.M.C.A. Publishing House, 1959).
38. Christian W. Troll, *Sayyid Ahmad Khan: A Reinterpretation of Muslim Theology* (New Delhi, 1978).

CHAPTER 11

Islam, Science and Technology: Past Glory, Present Predicaments and The Shaping of the Future

Introduction

Muslims today live in very difficult and challenging times. Demographically speaking, they are a major force to be reckoned with. Nearly a billion souls or one-fifth of today's mankind are Muslims. Their economic potentials are enormous. Their countries which constitute a sizable chunk of the inhabited parts of the globe are blessed with rich natural resources. And yet their influence on the world's economic and political affairs as well as on scientific and technological progress is marginal. Militarily, they are also weak. As it is now, they are certainly not playing a significant role in shaping world history.

Ever since Muslims were conscious of the decline and stagnation of their own civilization, especially following their military defeat and their political, economic, and cultural subjugation at the hands of Western colonial powers, they have sought to identify its root causes, analyze outstanding problems, and prescribe effective cures to their malaise. Debates and discussions on this question are still going on today, both at popular and academic levels.

However, far from reaching a general consensus, Muslims are even divided on basic issues. Past attempts at finding solutions to the problem of Muslim backwardness and stagnancy, initiated by both traditionalists and modernists, have only been partially successful. We can benefit from both their successes and their failures. While we should emulate and further consolidate the good works and successful programs they have pioneered, be these theoretical (conceptual) or practical in nature, we need to avoid repeating their mistakes and failures through identifying their causes and overcoming them.

In formulating their responses to modern Western civilization and its imperialist designs, many of our predecessors were greatly influenced not only by the prevailing situations in the Muslim world of their times but even more so by situations existing in the West. As we have seen in the last chapter, one of the important issues which they then sought to address was the problem of Muslim backwardness in the field of science and technology and the question of Muslim attitudes toward modern science. But many radical changes have taken place in both the Islamic and Western worlds since figures like 'Abd al-Qādir al-Jazā'irī, Jamāl al-Dīn al-Afghānī (Astrabadi), Muḥamad 'Abduh, Rashīd Riḍā and Zia Gokalp made their intellectual and political responses to western thought and culture, or even since as recently as the times of Iqbāl.

One of these changes is the presence of large Muslim minorities in western countries, including a sizable number of highly educated Muslims. This development promises far-reaching consequences on the future intellectual and cultural transformation of the West. In Spain, once a glorious and envious part of Islamic civilization and a focal point of transmission of Islamic intellectual culture into the Latin West, an interesting debate is going on between the old intellectual establishment and a group of young intellectuals on the place of Islamic civilization in Spanish cultural and intellectual history.

Another significant development in the West is the emergence of many intellectual and socio-cultural groups and movements highly critical of western rationality and western faith in science and technology as the panacea to all the ills of mankind.

In our present attempt to rebuild Islamic civilization it is only appropriate that we undertake a critical evaluation of past failures and successes in both the Muslim world and the West besides taking account of contemporary situations, particularly at the level of ideas. In this chapter, we will focus our attention on the problem of revival of Islamic civilization in the particular domain of science and technology.

Contemporary Challenges and Present Predicaments

Even prior to modern times, achievements and progress in science and technology have generally been accepted as a major indicator of the greatness, brilliance or advancement of a human civilization. But it is in modern times alone – in the past two centuries or so – that science and technology have become an obsession to the point of being made the sole indicator of human progress and development.

In the case of many people, science has taken the place of established traditional religion as the main, if not the sole, source of worldview, epistemology, and ethics and morality. Science is made the decisive arbiter of conflicting truth-claims, that is, in the case of those people for whom the word "truth" still possesses some meaning. And technology is still widely believed to be the practical solution to all problems and the cure to all ills facing mankind.

The obsession with science and technology at the expense of time-honored spiritual and moral values is in itself one of the great misfortunes of our time. It is an even greater misfortune when the obsession is with material power alone. Although especially during the last half a century there has been a gradual weakening of faith in the miraculous power of science and technology to solve the staggering problems of humanity, let alone to create paradise on earth, as more and more of the destructive effects of man's scientific and technological inventions become clearly visible, the development of science and technology continues to be shaped by those who profess or succumb to the above line of thinking.

The secular and profane view of science and technology we have just described is totally alien to the Islamic worldview and the Quranic teachings on human civilization, progress, and development. It is clearly stated in the Quran:

> You are the best nation *(ummah)* produced for mankind,
> Enjoining what is right, forbidding what is wrong, and
> Believing in Allah.[1]

The above verse is one of the numerous verses in the Quran, which provide Muslims with an explicit formula for the successful creation of a great and glorious civilization upon a spiritual and moral foundation, and which set forth the general criteria for judging the quality of a human civilization. The formula and the criteria in question are embodied in the three fundamental universal principles, namely (1) the promotion, cultivation and enforcement of what is good, right and virtuous, and everything that is denoted and implied by the Quranic term *ma'rūf*, (2) the censure and prohibition of evils and vices and everything that is termed *munkar*, and (3) faith *(īmān)* in the One God.

The above verse also implies that Muslims are called upon to be the "model nation" which is described elsewhere in the Quran as "people of the middle way" *(ummatan wasaṭan)*.[2] This divinely ordained sosio-political ideal would be within the grasp of Muslims only if they were to remain faithful in words and deeds to the mentioned principles.

The first two principles, which are essentially ethical and moral in nature, find their detailed expositions and applications in the *Sharī'ah*, the most modern of divine laws. The Islamic *Sharī'ah* is superior to all others laws, both divine and human, in the sense that it is at once more comprehensive and detailed and

---

1 *The Quran*, Chapter III (The Family of 'Imrān), Verse 110.
2 *The Quran*, Chapter II (The Cow), Verse 143.

also more holistic and integrated in nature compared to the moral systems in all other religions, which are of a rather general nature. Consequently, the Islamic *Sharī'ah* is the law most suited to deal in an effective manner with the problems of modern society on the ethical and moral plane.

As for the last principle, that is, faith in the One God, it is essentially intellectual and spiritual in nature. The nature of the Islamic faith is such that the distinction between knowing and believing is rather blurred.[3] This principle finds its detailed articulation in the six fundamental articles of faith, which taken together constitute the spiritual or metaphysical foundation of the Islamic worldview. A systematic and rational exposition of these articles of faith by Muslim scholars led to the birth, development, and flowering of many religious and philosophical sciences in Islamic culture.

The first article, namely, the principle of the Unity of God, becomes the subject of religious and philosophical study in that science called *'ilm al-tawḥīd*, the science of Divine Unity. Out of the second article, that is, belief in angels, is produced a vast literature on what is called angelology, the science or study of angels. The third and fourth articles, namely, belief in revealed scriptures and belief in divine messengers respectively, have given birth to various sciences of divine revelation and prophecy, including faculty psychology and comparative religion. These sciences are of great importance to Islamic philosophy of science. The fifth article, belief in the Hereafter, leads to the formulation and systematization of that science called eschatology, the science of man's return to God. The sixth article, belief in the divine measure of all things, constitutes an essential element of Islamic cosmology and is important for the understanding of the relationship between God and the universe.

In general, we would say that, in Islamic civilization, the different sciences such as cosmology, psychology, and the

3 *Īmān* (belief) not only presupposes a certain level of knowledge, but is also a particular mode of knowing.

natural and mathematical sciences are all ultimately based on principles embodied in the six articles of faith.

The science of *tawḥīd* has always been regarded as the highest science in the hierarchy of knowledge, since it is the origin and the end of all other sciences. It is the science that gives meaning, direction and purpose to the other sciences. It is also the source of their unity. Every science that claims itself to be Islamic must be organically related in one way or another to the principle of *tawḥīd*.

As the science of *tawḥīd* is concerned with the unity of the Divine Names and Qualities, the different particular sciences may be seen as so many commentaries upon the "Beautiful Names" *(al-asmāʾ al-ḥusnā)* of God. In our view, the mathematical, physical, and biological sciences cultivated and developed by Muslim scientists over the centuries when Islam held sway over much of the civilized world may be legitimately called by the collective name of *Islamic Science*, because these sciences were directly based upon and conceptually in harmony with the belief system of Islam to which we have just referred.

But what about the present situation? There is no doubt that Muslims are confronted with a serious problem which they must overcome, the sooner the better. Those of us who are sufficiently acquainted with modern science and its philosophies will readily admit that, at least as far as its mainstream philosophy is concerned, it is hardly in conformity with the religious and spiritual worldview of Islam. The spirit of modern science is not simply indifferent or neutral with respect to the Islamic "picture of the universe". In many respects and on many points, the presuppositions of modern science concerning man, the universe, and reality can very well undermine the Islamic belief system. If one really understands the meaning of each of the six articles of faith and all of their philosophical and scientific implications, then one cannot at the same time be a defender of the philosophy of modern science without falling into philosophical and logical contradictions or without sacrificing one's intellectual honesty.

Modern science has no need of "God as a hypothesis". It seeks to explain natural phenomena without recourse to spiritual or metaphysical causes but rather in terms of natural or material causes alone. As individuals, many modern scientists may believe in a personal God or the Great Ultimate Reality, but as members of the "official" scientific community they must follow the intellectual norm of banishing God and other spiritual elements from the Universe. They are required to study the physical universe as an independent realm of reality completely cut off from non-spiritual worlds.

From the Islamic point of view, however, bringing God and other spiritual entities into science is neither superfluous nor contradictory to the dictates of scientific inquiry and explanation. The quest for material causes is not in the least bit compromised by bringing in the idea of the Divine Principle into the natural domain. This "fact" has been established in history by classical Muslim philosophers and scientists.

For a complete and true understanding of natural phenomena, the knowledge of both physical and metaphysical causes is necessary. There would be no empirical sciences if the study of nature is restricted to metaphysical causes alone. Anyhow, it is hardly possible to grasp the idea of metaphysical causes without referring to physical causes. Conversely, to deny or to set aside metaphysical causes and to rely solely on physical causes would leave many questions forever unanswered. In reality, of course, physical causes are dependent on metaphysical causes. Without metaphysical causes, which may be called "vertical causes", there would be no physical causes which we may call "horizontal causes". These two sets of causes find their legitimate, rightful, and harmonious relationship in Islamic science thanks to the formulation of a holistic and comprehensive theory of causality in accordance with the doctrine of *tawḥīd.*

Modern science, theoretically speaking, has also banished the idea of purpose from nature. But from the Quranic point of view, nature is purposive. An important idea which appears again and again in the Quran is the idea of purpose in God's creation. Says the Quran:

We created not the heavens, the earth,
and all between them but for just ends.[4]

Not for (idle) sport did We create the heavens
and the earth and all that is between![5]

The Quranic word which conveys this important idea of divine purpose in creation is *bi'l-ḥaqq*. This word connotes the idea of a true, just, and righteous purpose. The real purpose of human existence and the creation of the universe of which he is an integral part is so that man might know and serve God. According to one *ḥadīth qudsī*:

Before creation I was alone. I desire to be known. So I create the universe.

Thus, man can know God through his knowledge of the universe. This possibility is a consequence of the fact that the universe, by virtue of being God's creation, manifests His Names and Qualities, the most frequently mentioned in the Quran being Knowledge, Wisdom, Power, and Justice. Appropriately, the Quran calls natural phenomena the "signs of God" *(āyātul-lah)*, since these phenomena point to God's Attributes and Qualities.

The universe is also a manifestation of Divine Unity. The interrelatedness of all things in the universe and the order and harmony that pervade the entire universe point to God's Unity. The Quran itself advances the following argument:

If there were, in the heavens and the earth, other divinities besides God, there would have been confusion in both.[6]

---

4 *The Quran*, Chapter XV (The Rocky Tract), Verse 85.

5 *The Quran*, Chapter XXI (The Prophets), Verse 16.

6 *The Quran*, Chapter XXI (The Prophets), Verse 22.

The Greek word *cosmos* connotes the idea of order, harmony, and justice as opposed to chaos. Following the above Quranic argument, Muslims have taken the unicity of the universe as a legitimate cosmological proof of Divine Unity. In fact, the fundamental goal of Islamic science is to demonstrate the unicity of creation, as reflected in the unity of its laws, with the expressed view of affirming the truth of the principle of *tawḥīd.*

Science thus possesses an intellectual role and function, namely, to help man fulfill his intellectual and spiritual needs, the most important of which is to gain certainty in his knowledge of God. But, by virtue of being an earthly creature, man has also physical and material needs to fulfill. So the second role and function of science is to help man meet these needs at the individual, family, and societal levels. Now, this role too is very much emphasized by the religion of Islam. If Muslims choose to neglect this second role of science, then they are in fact going against the spirit and the general teachings of their religion. The Quran emphasizes again and again that the universe has been created to serve mankind. In the words of the Quran, God's favours to man in His creation are innumerable and inaccountable. In the creative phase of the history of Islamic civilization, the idea and concept of *farḍ kifāyah* as applied to knowledge, that is, the kind of knowledge a society as a whole must acquire and possess for the sake of its well-being, reached a sophisticated level of formulation and systematization so as to embrace this second role of science.

But man has the tendency to abuse the favours of God. For this reason, God warns man to use nature wisely, justly, and with a moral sense of purpose:

> O mankind! Eat of what is on earth, lawful and good; and do not follow the footsteps of the Evil One for he is to you an avowed enemy.[7]

---

7 *The Quran,* Chapter II (The Cow), Verse 168.

> O you who believe! Eat of the good things that We have provided for you and be grateful to God if it is Him you worship.[8]

> Do you not see that God has subjected to your (use) all things in the heavens and on earth and has made His bounties flow to you in exceeding measure (both) seen and unseen? Yet there are among men those who dispute about God without knowledge and without guidance and without a Book to enlighten them.[9]

It should be pointed out, however, that, while Islam does not neglect the role of science in helping to deliver material goods to man, it also insists that this role be realized within the ethical framework of the *Sharī'ah.* Otherwise, science and technology will be misused for immoral and evil purposes as it is being done today on an alarming scale. In the final analysis, science and technology should be viewed as excellent instruments to serve the spiritual and moral goals of man. Unfortunately, in the modern world, they have been used to buttress false ideologies and pseudo-religions, such as atheism and other forms of materialism, and to prop up racism. In the economic sphere, they are turned into instruments of greed, leading to the destruction of the environment. They have also been used as instruments of economic exploitation by the rich against the poor, thus helping to widen the gulf between them.

Science and technology in themselves cannot solve the problem of unequitable distribution of wealth among nations. Similarly, science and technology cannot solve the problem of their misuse by man. The intervention of spirituality and ethics and morality is needed. All the different kinds of misuse of science and technology have to be combated at various levels. The use of science to justify racial superiority and bigotry and

---

8 *The Quran,* Chapter II (The Cow), Verse 168.
9 *The Quran,* XXXI (Luqman), Verse 20.

false philosophies should be combated at the intellectual level with the help of a philosophy of science that is capable of harmonizing the intellectual and material (technological) roles of science as is the case with Islamic philosophy of science. In contemporary philosophy of science, these two roles are no longer in harmony and equilibrium.

The use of science and technology as instruments of economic exploitation should be combated ethically and morally at the political and economic levels especially by the poor and oppressed nations acting as an organized and cohesive group. Mankind today is in real need of an effective ethical and moral system to deal with the misuse of technology that is posing a real threat to its own survival.

The banishment of the idea of divine purpose from the universe has deprived modern science of certain invaluable principles derived from that idea, such as the principle of the hierarchy of beings, which traditionally provide the most intellectually satisfying answers to questions that are at once scientific, philosophical, and religious (or metaphysical). One of the questions of this kind, which fascinates the human mind, is the problem of the origin of things.

Modern science seeks to solve the mystery of the origin of the universe, the origin of species, the origin of man, the origin of language and writing, and the origin of the arts and the sciences without recourse to divine role and intervention. What modern science has furnished us with are theories of origin that are philosophical in nature and yet philosophically unsound, and which are presented as scientific yet lacking in empirical evidence and ridden with logical inconsistencies. Notwithstanding all these, these theories, largely conjectural in nature, have been passionately defended by their exponents and sympathizers as if they are religious dogmas. This situation perhaps has a lot to do with the fact that these theories have been conceived as substitutes to the traditional religious answers to questions that cannot but involve the transcendent. Consequently, these theories must somehow partake of the nature of religious dogmas since man's need for the transcendent has to be manifested also at the intellectual level.

The most wellknown of such theories is the biological theory of evolution.[10] It is interesting to note that the immediate philosophical background to Darwin's *The Origin of Species* is the wide spread of Deism in 19-th century Europe, a philosophy of nature which views the natural world as being an independent realm totally cut off from the hands of the Creator. This theory as well as other theories of origins serve as the philosophical framework for the study of many sciences. These theories fill the pages of many textbooks used by Muslim students in schools as well as in institutions of higher learning. Their nature is such that they have the undesirable effect of weakening the faith of Muslims in their belief system.

There are Muslims today who think that Muslim society should pay less attention to theoretical and conceptual problems and the question of philosophy of science than to challenges in the field of technology. We do not wish to deny the importance of technological challenges for Muslims. However, in our view, theoretical and conceptual problems pertaining to the relationship between faith and science are no less important. For to the extent that we are committed to preserving and defending the Islamic worldview and belief system, on which our vision, spirit, idealism, and personality so much depend, we must be duly concerned with the conceptual problems which modern philosophies of science have posed to that worldview and belief system.

Whatever the shortcomings and dangers of modern science and technology may be, especially as seen from the Islamic point of view, there is no question of Muslims not learning and mastering them. Muslims must acquire scientific knowledge and technological know-how to the point of being

10. For a comprehensive critique of this theory, see O. Bakar, *Critique of Evolutionary Theory: A Collection of Essays* (The Islamic Academy of Science: Kuala Lumpur, 1987).

self-reliant and highly competitive and even to the point of again assuming world leadership. Islam must serve as the main motivating force for the realization of this goal. What this means is that the Muslim quest for scientific and technological progress should be carried out within the framework of an Islamic philosophy of science and technology that is founded upon the Islamic belief system as well as the ethical and moral system embodied in the *Sharī'ah.*

Past Glory: A Source of Inspiration

For many centuries – from the 9th century till the 15th century – Muslims were intellectual leaders in the field of science and technology. As Muslims, we naturally take pride in that glorious chapter in the history of Islamic civilization. Now, to look back on the past glory of one's culture or civilization could either be a good thing or a bad thing depending on one's intentions. If the idea of glorifying past achievements is merely for the sake of self-glorification or to indulge in a kind of escapism from the reality of present-day Muslim problems, then it would be of no use to the development of contemporary Muslim society. But if the idea is to inspire Muslims to again attain greatness by following the positive footsteps of their predecessors in their march to progress, then it is a useful exercise.

In our view, we should study both the "golden period" and the period of decline and stagnation of Islamic science and technology with the view of deriving useful lessons from that history. In studying the golden period, we are mainly interested in knowing the positive factors which helped to bring about progress and advancement in science and technology and the flourishing of creative and original scientific minds. Once these positive factors have been identified, we should re-apply them to the present situation. We should take every measure which would help to ensure that these same factors, supported by new ones arising from contemporary socio-economic conditions, will once again be present and operative in Muslim society.

Similarly, we need to know the factors of decline and stagnation of Islamic science and technology. This question is still hotly debated today. In our view, the cause of decline is a combination of the disappearance of positive factors and the emergence of negative factors. Again, these negative factors need to be identified following which we should take steps to eliminate them if these are present in contemporary Muslim society or prevent them from taking roots if they are presently non-existent. It is amazing that most scholars who have offered explanations for the decline of Islamic science hardly ever refer to its creative phase and its contributory factors. Consequently, if one were to accept their theory of decline as true, then Islamic science simply existed without any creative phase or "golden period" in its entire history.[11]

Although until now there has been no comprehensive and definitive work on the subject of the rise and decline of Islamic science and technology, enough historical material is available to enable us to identify the following as the major factors which account for the rise and brilliance of Islamic science during the golden period:

(1) the role of religious consciousness as a motivating force for the quest of science and technology. From a correct understanding of the tawhidic spirit there flows a general respect for knowledge. In other words, there was a wide dissemination of those teachings of the religion that are concerned with knowledge in all its aspects.

(2) faithfulness to the *Sharī'ah* inspires the study of various sciences.

(3) the birth and rise of great translation movements that lasted for several centuries. The translation movement in classical Islam was the grandest in the history of transmission of knowledge from one culture into another.

---

11 See, for example, our critique of Fazlur Rahman's theory of decline in *Classification of Knowledge in Islam*, pp. 219-220.

(4) the flowering of philosophy that is dedicated to scientific learning, progress, and advancement.

(5) widespread patronization of scientific and technological activities by rulers and wazirs.

(6) the existence of a healthy intellectual climate as illustrated by the fact that scholars of different schools of thought (legal, theological, philosophical, and spiritual) carried out intellectual debates in a frank and rational manner but in a spirit of mutual respect. The scientific debate between Ibn Sīnā and al-Bīrūnī in the 10th century stands out as one of the most extraordinary in the intellectual history of Islam.

(7) the important role played by educational and scientific institutions, especially with the rise of universities.

(8) the equilibrium attained between the major intellectual perspectives of Islam.

In our view, the major factors which account for the decline of Islamic science and technology may be identified with those internal and external forces which resulted in the gradual disappearance of the positive factors enumerated above. Examples of these internal and external factors are political corruption, internal strife, the rise of religious legalism and sectarianism, the neglect of the inner dimension of knowledge in the religion, and untold destruction at the hands of the Mongols.

The Shaping of the Future

Muslims today must be committed to the idea of making Islam the primary motivating force for their scientific and technological development. People may be inspired to study and acquire science and technology for numerous reasons, including religious, ideological, economic, and political. In our view, the best and most lasting motive is the religious motive. Our idea of the "religious" includes the spiritual, ethical, and philosophical.

Materialistic and worldly motives, if the history of science and technology can be of any guide to us, have proved to be less lasting. In this context, let us take note of the fact that modern science is less than four centuries old. And the period during which the materialistic motive stands out as the most dominant is even much shorter!

If it is agreed that the eight factors we have just enumerated are among the most important factors which brought about past outstanding Muslim achievements in the field of science and technology, then we should work toward their realization in contemporary Muslim society. To be sure, they are not easy programs to be implemented considering the prevailing pitiful conditions in many parts of the Muslim world. For how can we talk about Muslims achieving progress in science and technology when in many Muslim countries even the problem of literacy or general education has not yet been overcome. All the eight factors presuppose a high level of general education, a respect for knowledge and men of learning, a sincere attitude toward the general well-being of Muslims, and a strong commitment on the part of Muslim religious, intellectual, and political leaders to the dissemination of Islamic teachings in all their dimensions.

The key to a better future is education. Education is the best form of investment. Accordingly, each Muslim country must allocate the greatest portion of its national income to educational programs. A major goal of this educational drive is to enable "knowledge culture" to take firm roots in contemporary Muslim society. Once the philosophical and social foundation of this knowledge culture has been firmly established, the task of achieving progress in science and technology becomes easier. By achievements, we mean Muslims actually creating and inventing new science and technology, and not simply in possession of them through buying from other people.

APPENDIX

Designing a Sound Syllabus for Courses on Philosophy of Applied and/ or Engineering Sciences in a 21st Century Islamic University

Introduction

One of the greatest challenges of the twenty-first century, which the Muslim world is very likely going to face, would be the economic imperialism, in one form or another, of the world's economic superpowers. This imperialism would mean yet another act of enslavement of the Muslim body, mind and soul. All forms of imperialism imposed by foreign powers, including the military and political kinds we have already seen in our own life time, cannot but have grave implications for the religious and spiritual, political and economic, cultural and social life of the Muslim *ummah.* In short, Muslims will be forcibly prevented from being masters of their own destiny in their own lands!

The most appropriate response to this challenge of economic imperialism would be for the Muslim world to attain economic independence and self-sufficiency, at least in those areas and sectors considered to be of vital or strategic interests to their overall well-being. But this is only possible if all the necessary and important tools of economic development and progress are at their disposal, which is far from being the case at this very moment. One of these tools is sound scientific knowledge and technological know-how which, however, must be clearly rooted in the very social structure and cultural milieu of Muslim society, as well as in the really legitimate and basic needs of contemporary Muslims.

This means that an Islamic university of the coming century should give priority to courses which would help to produce scientists, technologists and engineers, as well as other professional groups, whose role and contribution is recognized to be of utmost importance to economic progress. But it also means that an Islamic university worthy of the name is not simply interested in producing just any kind of scientists, technologists and engineers, who are, qualitatively speaking, no different from those produced by most universities nowadays. Rather, it should be interested in educating a "new breed" of scientists, engineers and technologists, in whom wisdom and knowledge, spiritual faith and rational mind, creativity and moral insights, innovative power and ethical virtues, and ecological sensitivity are fully developed in a harmonious fashion without in any way undermining the possibility of they achieving excellence and eminence in their respective fields of specialization.

This is what we would call scientific and technological education of a balanced and holistic kind for which we should all be striving. It would mean for us abandoning the lopsided and reductionistic kind of scientific and technological education which today constitutes the norm. For in such a kind of scientific and technological education and development, progress and excellence in one field or aspect is often emphasized and pursued at the expense of other equally or perhaps even more important fields or aspects. Even in the West, many intelligent minds are now fully aware of the acute nature of the problem, although its solution is not yet in sight.

The solution demands from us the capacity for designing a correspondingly balanced and holistic kind of syllabus for university courses on applied and engineering sciences. And we are of the opinion that the religious, spiritual, intellectual, moral, scientific and artistic heritage of the Muslims is fully capable of providing us the materials needed to design such a syllabus. An essential ingredient of the syllabus, which also constitutes its philosophical foundation, is a course on the philosophy of applied and engineering sciences.

Aims and Objectives of the Course

The introduction of a course on the philosophy of applied and engineering sciences within the faculty of the same name is directed toward achieving the following goals and objectives:

(1) To produce scientists, engineers and technologists who are not only professionally qualified and competent but are also spiritually, intellectually, and morally and ethically sound human persons on the basis of an integral and harmonious relationship with their Creator, fellow human beings and with the natural environment;

(2) To create a new model of scientific and technological development and progress which is balanced and holistic in nature so that we may achieve development and progress without being burdened with destructive effects on human life and the environment;

(3) To uphold the universal teaching so strongly emphasized in Islam that all knowledge, including of the scientific and technological kinds, is sacred and moral in character implying that the kind of scientists, engineers and technologists we intend to produce should be enlightened enough to be able to anticipate the religious, ethical, and social implications of some of their scientific discoveries and technological innovations;

(4) To produce specialists in the different branches of applied and engineering sciences, who are at the same time well grounded in the knowledge of the fundamental and immutable principles of their religion and of the moral and ethical basis of their culture;

(5) To produce scientists, engineers and technologists with creative, objective, and independent minds and with a way of thinking characterized by rationality and logical clarity;

(6) To produce scientists, engineers and technologists who, while being sensitive to the need to assimilate foreign ideas

and techniques, harbor the conviction that the real key to the scientific and technological progress of the Muslim *ummah* lies in the wise utilization of natural and human resources which Allah has made available for them within their own geographical boundaries.

Some Salient Features of the Syllabus

The materials which constitute the syllabus of the proposed course presented here have been chosen and organized with the view of realizing the above aims and objectives. These cover a wide range of major topics embracing fundamental knowledge of God, man, the universe, the social structure of Muslim society, and the *Sharī'ah* of which ethics and morality is a major component, as befitting the students of an Islamic university. However, the organization of the materials pertaining to this fundamental knowledge has been specifically tailored to the needs of students whose intellectual interest, inclination, and ability is primarily oriented towards applied and engineering sciences.

Relevant metaphysical (spiritual), cosmological, psychological, sociological, ethical, and scientific knowledge is incorporated into the syllabus. But all this knowledge has been conceived and, accordingly, will be treated in lectures and other teaching sessions as a unified whole within the unitary *(tawhidic)* perspective of Islam. Through this syllabus, the student will have the opportunity to approach the study of *al-tawḥīd* (the Unity of God) and the *Sharī'ah* (Divine Law) not as "abstract" concepts, ideas, or general injunctions divorced from their theoretical and practical applications to the domain of applied and engineering sciences with which he is directly intellectually concerned, but rather in terms of the basic concepts and ideas drawn from those sciences and with which he is generally quite familiar. In other words, the customary practice in many universities of teaching *al-tawḥīd* or the *Sharī'ah* on the one hand and science on the other as two conceptually unrelated or mutually exclusive domains of thought is being discarded here.

The syllabus is organized around two fundamental issues,

namely (1) epistemology, and (2) ethics. The topics covered under epistemology deal primarily with the epistemological status of applied and engineering sciences, their conceptual relationship with the *tawhidic* principles (that is, metaphysical and cosmological knowledge) governing the physical (natural) world, with scientific methodology and creative thinking (including mathematical inspiration) and with the epistemological implications of certain aspects of human creativity in contemporary applied and engineering sciences, especially in genetic engineering.

As for the topics covered under ethics, these deal primarily with the ethical nature and status of scientific and technological knowledge, the specific implications of the Islamic doctrine of man's *khilafāh* (vicegerency) on earth for scientists, engineers, and technologists in particular, their social responsibility, the geographical-climatic and socio-cultural context of scientific and technological development, and the ethics of research, biotechnology, and environmental engineering, including contemporary ethical issues in these fields.

In summary, we may say that the first part of the syllabus is basically concerned with the foundation and the methodological tools of the production of scientific and technological knowledge, whereas the second part is concerned with its ethical foundation, its usefulness, its broad and diverse applications, and its significance and practical consequences for human life and the environment.

The Course Content

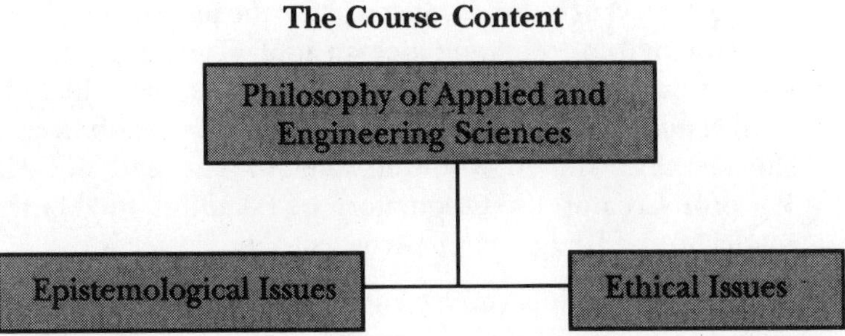

EPISTEMOLOGICAL ISSUES

Epistemological status of applied and engineering sciences

definition of its domain of study

conception of applied and engineering sciences in Islamic and modern western epistemologies (a comparative treatment)

place of applied and engineering sciences in Islamic classification of knowledge.

brief historical background of their development in Islamic civilization.

Tawhidic principles of applied and engineering sciences

the mathematical, biological, and physico-chemical structure of the cosmos according to the Quran and *ḥadīths*, Muslim philosophers and scientists, and modern science.

identifying scientific, engineering, and technological principles from the above structure.

the Quranic concept of "signs of God" *(āyātullah)* as a textual basis of the *tawhidic* principle of the cosmos as a reflection or manifestation of Divine Names and Qualities.

study of selected Divine Names and Qualities which have the greatest relevance and significance for the understanding of fundamental concepts and ideas in applied and engineering sciences, and of their unique characteristics; these include such Names and Qualities of God as the Compassionate and the Merciful, the All-Knowing, the All-Wise and the All-Powerful Creator, the Originator, the Beautiful, the Mathematician, the Designer, the Artist, and the Perfectionist.

applied and engineering sciences as a human imitation of divine knowledge, wisdom, power, and creativity as manifested in the cosmos and more specifically in nature.

Scientific methodology and creative thinking

the structure of human cognitive consciousness; discussion covers the four key Quranic terms, namely '*aql* (intellect-reason), *qalb* (heart), *rūḥ* (spirit), and *nafs* (soul).

the division of '*aql* into its different parts with their respective roles and functions in the thinking process.

the role of the five (external) senses and the imaginative faculty (internal senses) in relation to the thinking process.

Logic as a tool of scientific thinking; understanding fundamental elements of logic and the principles of logical thinking.

elements and principles of scientific methodology, covering such questions as classification of data and the different ways and methods of deriving new information and knowledge from them, including mathematical methods, leading to various levels of theory construction.

Islamic and modern western concepts of scientific and technological creativity; intellectual, spiritual, mental, and even socio-cultural conditions of scientific creativity.

Aspects of Islamic art and design, which are particularly relevant to engineering sciences.

Critique of contemporary applied and engineering sciences in the light of Islamic philosophy of science.

identification of "controversial problematic" concepts, ideas, and theories in such fields as artificial intelligence, information theory, genetic engineering, and environmental sciences.

discussion of epistemological implications of these "controversial or problematic" concepts, ideas, and theories.

ETHICAL ISSUES

Ethical status of applied and engineering sciences.

ethical principles in the Quran and *Ḥadīth* governing the production, acquisition, teaching and dissemination of knowledge.

ethical basis of classification of knowledge into the *farḍ 'ayn* and the *farḍ kifāyah* types, the praiseworthy and the blameworthy, or into the useful and the useless kinds.

ethical status of applied and engineering sciences in the light of the above principles and classification, and its implications for the religious, academic, and socio-economic status of scientists, engineers and technologists in Islamic society.

Principles of the *Sharī'ah* governing the process of scientific and technological development.

the five categories of human acts, namely the obligatory *(wājib)*, the forbidden *(ḥarām)*, the recommended *(mandūb)*, the reprehensible *(makrūh)*, and the permissible *(mubāḥ)*.

man's position as God's *khalīfah* (vicegerent) on earth and its implication for the ethical and moral and social responsibility of scientists and technologists over their discoveries and inventions, as well as its implications for their guardianship over nature and their management of its resources.

geographical-climatic and socio-cultural context of scientific and technological development:

(a) the importance of intimate knowledge of local geographical-climatic conditions so that these (including the "hostile and disadvantageous") may be transformed into assets in the way the Israelis transform barren deserts into fertile, agricultural lands;

(b) geographical-climatic conditions as an important factor in scientific research and development planning;

(c) science and technology, not as instrument of economic exploitation and political domination of one group over another, but as instrument of social justice and economic welfare of all mankind;

(d) socio-cultural values derived from the *Sharī'ah* in shaping scientific and technological development.

Research ethics

aims and objectives of research

concept and criteria of priority in research

the ethics of research funding

concept of secrecy in research

characteristics of healthy research

Contemporary ethical issues in applied and engineering sciences

identification of major ethical issues in such branches of contemporary applied and engineering sciences as agricultural sciences, biotechnology, genetic engineering, and chemical engineering.

resolution of the above ethical issues in the light of Islamic ethical philosophy.

Conclusion

The above course should be made compulsory to all students of the Faculties of Applied Sciences and of Engineering Sciences. The teaching of the course may be spread over the whole duration of the student's Bachelor degree program at the university. At the level of details, we can expect some differences to occur between the philosophy of applied sciences and the philosophy of engineering sciences. However, the above topics are more or less applicable and indeed necessary to both students of applied sciences and students of engineering sciences.

Index

B

J

K

L

O

P

T